d
design travel

中信出版集团 · 北京

序

我们认为，人们今后在和他人交流时，"设计的眼光"会变得越来越重要。

领会了"设计的眼光"，

用这一视角去寻找具有"长效设计"（long life design）特质的物品，

将会更容易理解其中的匠心。

"个性"不仅存在和兴起于大城市的潮流中，它也蕴藏在哪怕最原始的土地上。

现如今，大多数人习惯于一种时间长了就轻易丢弃物品的生活方式，这一现状令人十分担忧。

不过，如果我们是在物的诞生地，被当地的文化和美食吸引，从而买下一件物品，

在很久之后还能讲出属于它的故事，说出是在哪家店铺、通过怎么样的优待而入手，

那么这件东西可能就不会被轻易丢弃了。

消费者需要从根本上改变物的入手方式。

我们创办这一"d 设计之旅"（d design travel）系列，正是希望改变这一现状。

以此为线索，我们将以"设计的眼光"探寻每一片土地。

日本的 47 个都道府县，一地一册，

以同样的方式实地取材、编辑制作，以同样的页数出版，呈于众人眼前。

d 设计之旅

发行人 长冈贤明（Kenmei Nagaoka）

A Few Thoughts Regarding the Publication of This Series
I believe that a "design perspective" will become extremely important for future generations, and indeed people of all generations, to interact with all areas of Japan. By "design perspective," I mean an imagination, which discerns what has substance and will endure, and allows users to easily understand and enjoy innovations. I feel that now, more than ever, a new kind of guidebook with a "design perspective" is needed. Therefore, we will publish a guide to each of Japan's 47 prefectures. The guidebooks will be composed, researched, and edited identically and be similar in volume.

Our editorial concept
- Any business or product we recommend will first have been purchased or used at the researchers' own expense. That is to say, the writers have all actually spent the night at the inns, eaten at the restaurants, and purchased the products they recommend.
- We will not recommend something unless it touches us. The recommendations will be written sincerely and in our own words.
- If something or some service is wonderful, but not without

采编的考量

· 一定要亲自在当地住宿、就餐和购物，一一确认。

· 不写无法让自己感动的东西，只说自己想说的话。

· 推荐给大家的东西，一定会如实地做出评价。
  如果东西足够好但有一些瑕疵，也会指出它的问题。

· 请受访对象核实文章时，只请对方确认那些客观信息。

· 以"长效设计"的视角，只取材能够长久存在的事物。

· 不用特殊的镜头夸张拍摄对象，只拍摄其最真实的状态。

· 采访过的人物和去过的地点，即便是图书出版后，
  也要保持联络，时常回访。

如何选择采访对象

· 符合当地的特色   · 价格适中

· 传递当地的重要信息   · 蕴含设计匠心

· 是当地人正在做的事

SIGHTS
了解这片土地
To know the region

CAFES
在当地，喝茶饮酒
To have tea
To have a drink

RESTAURANTS
在当地，享用美食
To eat

HOTELS
在当地，住上一晚
To stay

SHOPS
在当地，淘到好物
To buy regional goods

PEOPLE
在当地，遇见些人
To meet key persons

problems, we will point out the problems while recommending it.

- The businesses we recommend will not have editorial influence.
  Their only role in the publications will be fact checking.

- We will only pick up things deemed enduring from the "long
  life design" perspective.

- We will not enhance photographs by using special lenses. We
  will capture things as they are.

- We will maintain a relationship with the places and people we
  pick up after the publication of the guidebook in which they
  are featured.

Our selection criteria

- The business or product is uniquely local.

- The business or product communicates an important local
  message.

- The business or product is operated or produced by local people.

- The product or services are reasonably priced.

- The business or product is innovatively designed.

Kenmei Nagaoka
Founder, d design travel

shika no fune

＊1 "d设计之旅"编辑部2016年7月调查结果。 ＊2 数据采集自日本国土地理院网站。
＊3 数据采集自日本总务省统计局网站（截至2016年7月数据）。
＊4 数据采集自社团法人日本观光协会编著的《从数字看观光》（2015年版）。 ※ 括号内数字为全国平均值。

*1 Figures compiled by d design travel. Date as of July 2016.   *2 Extracts from the website of Geographical Survey Institute, Ministry of Land, Infrastructure,Transport and Tourism.   *3 According to the website of the Statistics Bureau, Ministry of Internal Affairs and Communications. Date as of July 2016.
*4 From Suuji de miru kanko, by Japan Travel and Tourism Association (2015 Edition)
※ The value between the parentheses is the national average.

奈良县的数字
Numbers of NARA

美术馆和博物馆的数量[1] (122)
Number of institutions registered under the Kyoto Prefecture Association of Museums
Museums

星巴克咖啡店的数量[1] (25)
Starbucks Coffee Stores

历届日本 G-Mark 设计奖获奖数量[1] (851)
Winners of the Good Design Award

54   10   179

经济产业大臣指定传统工艺品[1] (4)
Traditional crafts designated by the Minister of Economy, Trade and Industry

入选日本品牌培养支持事业的项目数[1] (10)
Projects selected under the JAPAN BRAND program

日本建筑家协会奈良县的注册会员人数[1] (85)
Registered members of the Japan Institute of Architects

日本平面设计协会奈良县注册会员人数[1] (64)
Registered members of the Japan Graphic Designers Association Inc.

高山茶筅
奈良笔
Takayama Chasen (Tea Whisk),
Nara Brushes

2   7   25   10

奈良府办公厅所在地
Capital

市町村[4]的数量[1] (36)
Municipalities

人口[3] (2,724,624)
Population

人

奈良市
NARA City

39   1,400,728

面积[2] (8,041)
Area

km²

年度观光人数[4] (30,230,212)
Annual number of tourists

人

3,690   20,940,000

当地料理
Local specialties

国家指定重要文化遗产的建筑数量[1] （51）
Nationally Designated Important Cultural Property (Buildings)

幢

柿叶寿司
茶粥
奈良酱菜
蕨饼
目张寿司[1]

116

Kakinoha sushi (Pressed sushi wrapped in a persimmon leaf)
Chagayu (Green tea porridge)
Narazuke (White melon pickled in sake lees)
Warabimochi (Bracken-starch dumplings)
Mehari sushi (Rice ball wrapped in pickled takana mustard leaves)

生于奈良的名人（含现在的市名与已故者）
Famous people from Nara

田中一光（平面设计师·奈良市），井简和幸（电影导演·大和郡山市），井上武吉（雕刻家·宇陀市），楳图和夫（漫画家·五条市），尾野真千子（演员·五条市），河濑直美（电影导演·奈良市），驹田德广（职业棒球选手·矶城郡），圣德太子（政治家·高市郡），富本宪吉（陶艺家·生驹郡），廘赤儿（舞蹈家·樱井市），福井谦一（化学家·奈良市），等等。

Ikko Tanaka (Graphic designer, Nara City), Kazuyuki Izutsu (Film director, Yamatokoriyama City), Bukichi Inoue (Sculptor, Uda City), Kazuo Umezu (Manga artist, Gojo City), Machiko Ono (Actress, Gojo City), Naomi Kawase (Film director, Nara City), Norihiro Komada (Baseball player, Siki-gun), Shotoku Taishi (Politician, Takaichi-gun), Kenkichi Tomimoto (Ceramist, Ikoma-gun), Akaji Maro (Butoh dancer, Sakurai City), Kenichi Fukui (Chemist, Nara City), etc.

奈良县的十二个月

12 Months of Nara

全国捞金鱼大赛（大和郡山市） 大赛期间各路捞金鱼高手都会聚集到大和郡山市内的"金鱼广场"，每人手持一把大会指定的"捞子"，比赛在3分钟之内谁捞起的金鱼最多。外地的游客除了参观，也可以参加比赛。你想不想去挑战一下3分钟捞起87尾金鱼的大赛纪录呢？

泼沙节（北葛城郡 河合町） 为了祈求五谷丰登，广濑大社在每年的2月11日都会举行泼沙节。沙粒象征着雨滴，人们猛烈地泼洒沙子，祈求在耕种的时节里能有充沛的降雨，进而带来一年的丰收。节庆期间当地细沙横飞，护目镜和雨衣是出行必备品。（图片来自：奈良县旅游局基金会）

修二会²（汲水节）（奈良市） 修二会是信众向东大寺二月堂的主佛"十一面观音"祈福的重要法事。这一传统自公元752年延续至今，从未中断过。在长达半个月的汲水节期间，最不容错过的要数3月12日深夜的仪式——11根长达6米的竹子前端被绑上大松明火把，僧侣们挥舞着巨大的火把在回廊内奔跑。如果在正下方观礼，可得做好会被烫伤的准备。（摄影：木村昭彦 图片来自：奈良市观光协会）

1 2 3 4 5 6

JANUARY   FEBRUARY   MARCH   APRIL   MAY   JUNE

若草山烧山节（奈良市） 烧山节是奈良为防止灾害与祈祷世界和平而举办的传统仪式，届时整座若草山（又名"三笠山"）都要被点燃。仪式中先要燃放礼花，然后随着法螺号、小号和发令枪齐声令下，若草山被熊熊大火点燃，映出美丽的夜空。鹿群多会被发令枪声吓得四下逃窜，但偶尔也会意外地出现几只处乱不惊的小鹿，若无其事地行走在烈焰当中。

（摄影：WIZ）

吉野山赏樱花（吉野郡 吉野町） 吉野山上共有200种、3万多株樱花，其中大多数都是最具代表性的白山樱。如此密集的樱花胜景，自古以来就有"一目千株"的说法。如果能一边吃着表太郎柿叶寿司一边欣赏樱花，那真是人生一大幸事。

奈良灯花会（奈良市） 奈良公园一带，每年8月上旬都会被两万来支的蜡烛照亮，持续10天左右的奈良灯花会是奈良夏天的一道风景线。蜡烛的灯芯被打结成花朵的形状，"灯花会"的名字便是由此而来。我们住在奈良d标总览介绍的料理旅馆"江户三"时正遇上灯花会，有幸见识到了梦幻般的寺院风景。

十津川盆踊大会 （吉野郡十津川村）盆踊大会每年8月13日开始，分三天在十津川村的小原、武藏、西川三个地区巡回举行。我们参加了在原武藏小学举办的武藏分场，大家都被当时热闹的场面所震撼。若是遇到雨天，活动则会改在古色古香的木结构校舍里举行。十津川的盆踊大会是日本国家级重要非物质文化遗产。

摇摆太鼓 （吉野郡十津川村）横跨在十津川村的溪谷上的古濑吊桥全长297米，高54米，是当地居民日常活动的必经之路，也是日本最长的吊桥。每逢8月4日的吊桥日，桥面上会举行太鼓表演，鼓声在山谷中回荡，声势浩大。20名表演者在桥上击打跳跃，将吊桥震得摇来荡去，紧张惊险，把人吓得身体缩成一团。

切鹿角祭典 （奈良市）每年秋天，切鹿角祭典在春日大社举行，这是从江户初期延续至今的传统仪式。被称作"势子"的专业狩猎助手合力抓住奔跑的公鹿，再由神职人员将鹿角锯下，放到神宫供奉。我们在刚开始本期内容的采访时看到鹿儿们的角还很软很小，但其实这些角很快就会长大变硬。成年公鹿的角是很危险的，所以为了安全起见，即使觉得鹿儿们很可怜，这个仪式也还得继续下去。（图片来自：奈良市观光协会）

主厨嘉年华 （奈良县各地）这是为了促进奈良本地的食材供应商和厨师们之间的交流而诞生的，是奈良县内规模最大的美食庆典。2016年8月在明日香村国营飞鸟历史公园、10月在马见丘陵公园、10月和11月在奈良公园分别举办了各种食材与烹饪相结合的嘉年华活动。石村由起子女士（→ p068）作为组委会一员，也将自己的店铺KURUMINOKI作为分会场参与活动。

7 8 9 10 11 12

JULY　AUGUST　SEPTEMBER　OCTOBER　NOVEMBER　DECEMBER

奈良国际电影节 （奈良市）奈良本地的电影导演河濑直美女士（→ p070）发起的奈良国际电影节是每两年举办一次的国际电影盛典。组委会主席一职由中野圣子女士（→ p066）出任。中野女士管理的SunRoute酒店曾经是当地著名的剧场。电影节上也设有类似戛纳电影节的红毯环节。

东大寺拭佛仪式 （奈良市）每年8月7日早上7点，僧侣和信众都会准时为东大寺大佛举行拭佛仪式。为了从头到脚仔细地擦拭15米高的佛像，仪式中还要使用吊车。曾拍摄过《加美拉》《进击的巨人》的特技电影导演樋口真嗣先生也曾参加拭佛仪式，不知是不是因为他偏好巨型物体呢？

正仓院展 （奈良市）这是奈良最具代表性的展览活动，每年10月下旬开始到11月上旬，在吉村顺三先生以正仓院为原型设计的奈良国立博物馆新馆（→ p032）内举行。博物馆每年都会从9000余件正仓院宝物中精选约70件进行展出。2014年还展出了37款正仓院展的海报。

奈良町屋艺术节 （奈良县各地）艺术节以充满历史感的城镇街道及町屋为舞台，每年选择县内不同的地区举办，而且会邀请当地居民参与。艺术节也成了充分利用闲置旧屋的纽带，连接本地屋主和潜在租户。在废弃的加油站旧址里开设的K咖啡（→ p054）就是其中的一个实例。

春日若宫节 （奈良市）每年12月15至18日都会在春日大社内的若宫神社如期举行。这个例行庆典是持续了870年以上的日本国家级重要非物质民俗文化遗产。其中，17日正午开始的"朝代巡游"最有看点。代表各个时代特色的巡游队伍从奈良县政府门口出发，绕市中心一周再回到春日大社。游行人群穿着不同时代的服饰，还有马匹穿行在队伍中，给人一种时空穿梭的感觉。

Normal for NARA
奈良县的日常

"d 设计之旅"编辑部发现的，
奈良县的日常。

插画·KIFUMI
撰文·神藤秀人

深受奈良人喜爱的灵丹妙药："陀罗尼助丸" 有一天，我坐在车里，一边揉着肚子，一边跟主编抱怨："哎哟，昨晚在竹之馆吃得太多了呀！"主编一听，马上对我说，车门后边的储物箱里有"陀罗尼助丸"然后把装在黄色纸袋里的肠胃药递给了我。我端详了一下这个古怪的名字，将信将疑地用袋子里附带的小勺吞下了 30 粒黑色微苦的小药丸（一勺刚好 10 粒）。传说大约 1300 年前疾病流行，于是修验道的开山鼻祖"役行者"就用关黄柏的木头煮水，让人喝了治病，据说这就是"陀罗尼助丸"的由来。这个药大多数奈良人小时候都吃过，算是家中药箱的常备药。也有人把它带在包里作为应急药，就好像奈良人的护身符一般。在天川村"洞川温泉"的旅馆一条街上，前前后后就有 13 家铺子在卖这个药丸，而且每一家都有自己的包装设计。要是在温泉街一开心喝到了天亮，或是去吉野山赏花之后经过这里，都可以买上几包，带回去送人。

奈良人的"日常生活"中不可或缺的角色——鹿 奈良公园里挤满了各地的观光客，其中当然少不了毕业旅行的学生们。我们也都还记得中学时到东大寺前用鹿饼干喂鹿的情形。真没想到，鹿的数量一下子增加了这么多。最早的时候，鹿被认为是春日神的使者在这里安家，后来鹿儿不断繁殖，现在公园附近估计有一千头了。所以在开车时，即使是绿灯，也要时刻小心，说不定树林里会突然蹿出一只小鹿来。

清早，我们赶在东大寺开门时进殿

Ordinary Sights in Nara Found by d design travel

Text by Hideto Shindo
Illustration by Kifumi

Nara's extremely difficult to read place names
Driving through Nara Prefecture, one finds numerous signs for places written in characters that are impossible to read. This makes navigation difficult, since new signs, still more difficult to read, appear before one has deciphered the first set of signs. Of course, Nara Prefecture residents can read these without any problem.

What's "normal for Nara" can't be discussed without mentioning deer
Nara Park is full of tourists, including students on graduation trips. Of course, the *d design travel* editors also remember visiting Todaiji Temple and feeding "deer crackers" to the deer on their graduation trip when they were in junior high school. The deer were originally considered divine messengers of the Kasuga Grand Shrine. Now they've given birth to Bambis and there are approximately 1,000 deer in Nara Park. One thus has to watch out for deer that appear suddenly from the woods while driving, even

能见到鹿的形象，就连土特产的小酥饼也都做成鹿的形状。与鹿共舞，就是奈良的日常。

生僻的汉字地名，难倒日本人 开车环游奈良，路上会遇到许多日本人都不太会念的汉字，比如"御所"（gose），又或是"生驹"（ikoma），常常让人搞不懂这路牌上的地名该怎么念，这究竟是哪里，究竟该走哪边。好不容易破解了这一批生字，没过多久又出现了一批更难懂的，例如"矶城"（shiki）、"斑鸠"（ikaruga）等等。其实这些地名中的汉字都和这个地方的由来息息相关，比如"忍辱山町"（ninnikusenshyou）就是取自佛教中的用语，"京终"（kyoubate）指的就是平城京的尽头，又如"芝生"（shibou）就是有植物生长的地方。

当然，对于奈良本地居民来说，这些都是小菜一碟啦。

参观大佛。走到回廊外面时，只见两头高大的鹿仿佛天界的门神一般站在那儿，还呦呦地发出可爱的叫声。但当我们环顾四周，才发现到处都是它们的粪便，不仔细看就跟散落在地上的松果似的。我们慌张地询问当地人这可如何是好，当地人淡定地回答道："唔，就算踩到也没关系吧。"……
酒店的标志上、酒庄的酒标上，都

when the light is green. Early in the morning, we visited the Grand Buddha Hall in Todaiji as soon as its gates opened. Out in the corridor were two large deer, standing like Nio guardians. Deer appear in hotel logos, local sake labels, and souvenir cookies. Everyday life in Nara is lived with deer.

"Daranisukegan" a folk medicine loved by Nara Prefecture citizens

When I commented to the editor-in-chief, "Well, we sure ate a lot at 'Take no yakata' last night," as I rubbed my stomach, he told me that there were some "Daranisukegan" in the door pocket, and handed me a yellow paper bag of stomach medicine. I took 30 of the bitter-smelling black pellets with the small spoon that was inside the bag. Nara locals take this medicine since childhood. It's a staple in medicine cabinets, and many locals carry it with them at all times. It's almost like an amulet for them. In the lodging area of "Dorogawa hot springs" in Tenkawa Village, there are 13 stores that sell "Daranisukegan" and they all use different packaging. I recommend getting "Daranisukegan" as a souvenir, especially after drinking in the hot spring area or taking in the cherry blossoms on Mount Yoshino.

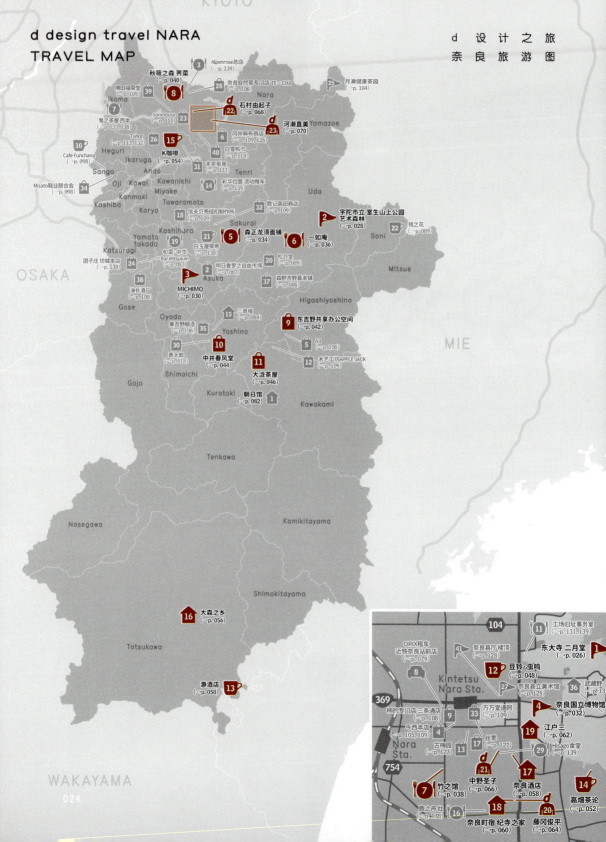

d MARK REVIEW
NARA

奈 良 d 标 总 览

SIGHTS

RESTAURANTS

SHOPS

CAFES

HOTELS

PEOPLE

东大寺 二月堂

奈良县奈良市杂司町 406-1

Tel.0742-22-5511

24 小时 全年无休

从奈良站搭乘巴士，15 分钟后在大佛殿春日大社前站下车步行约 10 分钟即可到达

奈良公园 Nara Park
近铁奈良站 Kintetsu-Nara Sta.
奈良国立博物馆 Nara National Museum
大佛殿春日大社前巴士站 Daibutsuden Kasugataisha-mae Bus Stop

1. 站在东大寺内，奈良美景一览无遗

进入庄严的南大门，经大佛殿向山坡深处而行，
便可到达这一幽静之所。

2. 这里是奈良具有代表性的重要典仪
"修二会"（汲水节）的举办地

修二会，自公元 752 年开始举办，至今从未中断。
仪式结束后，人们将"御松明"（仪式上用的竹质大火把）
燃烧后的残枝带回家当作护身符。

3. 随时可以前来参拜，
是奈良人祈祷和休憩的圣地

二月堂，24 小时对公众开放，灯笼彻夜通明，光影交错，美景令人窒息。
远眺生驹山的日落，同样美不胜收。

这里能见到奈良之光 到奈良旅游，若是和本地人交谈起来，一定会被问道："东大寺去了吗？"如果回答说当然去过了，则会被接着问："那二月堂去了吗？"要是也去了，对方必会追问："那是几时去的呀？"可能还会顺势补充道，二月堂是历史悠久的"修二会"的举办地，那可是国宝级的活动啊；而且那里 24 小时开放，随时都可以去参观；尤其是早上的风景最美，等等之类。

我住在奈良公园附近，便养成了每天早上到二月堂散步的习惯。在淡淡的晨雾中散步，与睡眼惺忪的鹿儿擦肩而过，从南大门潜入寺中，在通往大佛殿的步道右拐，走进深幽的树林，再从两排石灯间的石梯登上平台广场。在广阔的天空下，依山而建的二月堂便跃然眼前。壮丽威严的建筑却仿佛要融进天空里，这不可思议的魅力像富士山一般，让人觉得越看越美。

二月堂坐东向西而建，默默守望着平城宫遗址。南北两侧各有阶梯，我每次都选择走南边的阶梯走廊，身体像被它吸引，径自往上攀登。回廊屋顶将周围的景色遮蔽得严严实实，当你拾阶而上，景色并不会逐渐显露，而要待你登上顶端，美景才会瞬间跃入眼底。

二月堂自身固然美不胜收，然而，从二月堂所看到的风景，更是赏心悦目：明暗交错的天空、云卷云舒的画卷、峰峦叠翠的远山，还有被这些光景包裹着的奈良的城市和街道，以及市井中万家灯火——这一切都是从奈良时代建城至今，每日每月、每时每刻都不曾停止续写的"奈良的日常"。（撰文：空闲 理）

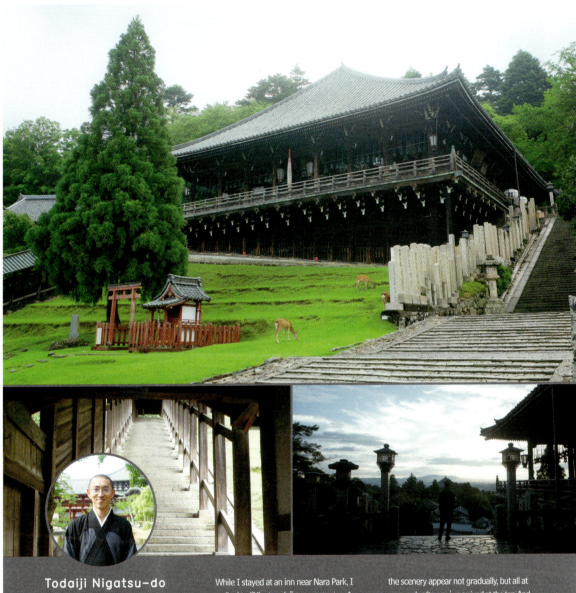

Todaiji Nigatsu-do

1. Located inside Todaiji Temple, Nigatsu-do offers a panoramic view of Nara

2. The stage for "Omizutori" (taking of holy water), a major Nara event

3. An oasis and place for prayer for Nara residents, which can be visited at any time

While I stayed at an inn near Nara Park, I walked to "Nigatsu-do" every morning. I walked through a thin fog, past sleepy-looking deer, through the south entrance, and turned right on the approach to the Great Buddha Hall through a dimly lit forest, up the stairs lined with lanterns to a plaza. In the plaza, under an expansive sky, I arrived at Nigatsu-do built halfway up a mountain. I always walked up the south stairway. When you use the south stairway, the roof of the structure shuts out the surroundings, making

the scenery appear not gradually, but all at once, only after you've arrived at the top. And the view encompasses the brilliant color of the sky, the color of the clouds, the color of the layering mountains, and the city of Nara wrapped in all those colors. It also includes light produced by the lives of Nara residents. All of everyday life in Nara—every second, every minute, and every hour that has passed since the construction of Nigatsu-do during the Nara period—is visible from this special place. (Osamu Kuga)

艺术森林
宇陀市立 室生山上公园

奈良县宇陀市室生181

Tel: 0745-93-4730

4～11月 10:00～17:00（16:30 截止入场）

3月、11月、12月 10:00～16:00（15:30 截止入场）

周二休息，如遇节假日顺延至次日

12月29日～翌年2月休息，

另有不定期休业

www.city.uda.nara.jp/sanzyoukouen

由榛原站驱车约30分钟可达

榛原站 Haibara Sta.

一如庵 Ichinyoan

东吉野共享办公空间 OFFICE CAMP HIGASHIYOSHINO

---

1. 这是一座艺术公园，它将奈良县里山[3]的自然风貌表现得淋漓尽致

公园以"利用自然，创造生态"为理念，再现梯田和森林。
蓄水池的水蜿蜒流淌，形成优美的水道。

2. 利用原本为防治山体滑坡而设计的地势，重新规划，使之兼备美感与多功能

室生村是已故雕刻家井上武吉先生的故里，
艺术森林继承了他生前的构想，
由以色列艺术家达尼·卡拉万（Dani Karavan）先生设计完成。

3. 这里还可以举办各类音乐会和现场活动，非常亲民

舞台上有一个类似纪念碑的建筑，观众席散落在湖面上。

从山体滑坡对策研究中孕育出的灵气宝地 沿着室生川前往有千余年历史的"室生寺"，沿途高耸的悬崖峭壁气势逼人。摄影家土门拳先生也曾迷恋这里的景色，留下了不少作品。照片中的世界空灵幽玄，如今这景象依旧没有改变，令我顿生感动。室生山上公园的艺术森林也像是要与这山麓中的古刹隔空呼应，爬上一条狭窄的陡坡，艺术森林就跃然眼前，像室生寺一样似要与自然融为一体，这不可思议的美景让人不禁惊叹"真的就是这里吗？"

一条大路由南向北纵贯整个森林。沿路有两个湖和一片美丽的吉野杉林，布满苔藓的步道从林中穿过。还有雕刻家达尼·卡拉万的作品点缀其中，包括《螺旋的水路》和《螺旋的竹林》。作品的铁锈红色、混凝土的白色与周围的绿色形成了鲜明对比。第二个湖的旁边耸立着一个兼具日晷功能的作品《太阳之塔》。横跨其上的一组门形作品具象地表现了北纬34°32'的《太阳之路》。在这条延长线上，坐落着奈良县的三轮山、室生寺、长谷寺，还有三重县的伊势神宫等名刹，可见这个地理纬度的不可思议之处。

置身其中，我仿佛感到有一条线，从历史长河的纵深之处跨越千年，向无限宇宙延伸开去。我渴望能在这浩瀚的时空中感受当下自己的存在，感受微拂的风和天上的云，以从容的心情度过稍纵即逝的每一刻。

我去的时候是盛夏时节，想象一下红叶盛开的秋天、白雪皑皑的冬天、樱花盛放的春天，想必任何季节都一样美不胜收。（撰文：空闲 理）

Murou Art Forest

1. An art park that perfectly expresses the natural environment of Nara Prefecture's *satoyama* (mountains bordering arable, rural residential areas)

2. A beautiful and functional place designed to repurpose the site to prevent landslides

3. It hosts concerts and other events that are frequented by local citizens

A single road runs south to north through a forest. Along the road is a moss-covered pedestrian path that runs by two lakes and through a forest of Yoshino cedar. Along the path are also multiple sculptures by Dani Karavan, including Spiral Canal and Spiral Forest. The reddish brown color of rusted steel and whitish concrete create a brilliant contrast against the surrounding trees and green lawn. The *Sun Tower* in the lake also functions as a sun dial. The gate-like piece that intersects it is a representation of the 34° 32' north latitude sun path. Along that same extended line are Mount Miwa and Muroji and Hasedera temples. I visited at the height of summer, but in the fall, one would see foliage, in the winter, white snow, and in the spring, cherry blossoms. I'm sure that it's beautiful in any season.（Osamu Kuga)

甘樫丘
Amakashino-oka Hill

155

209

飞鸟站
Asuka Sta.

飞鸟历史公园
Asuka Historical
National Government
Park

MICHIMO

从飞鸟站步行 1 分钟即可到达

michimo.jp

年末年初休息

09:00～18:00（不同季节可能有变动）

Tel：0744-33-9090

奈良县高市郡明日香村越 13-1（MICHIMO 中心）

1. 超小型租赁电动车，改变了传统的历史古迹参观方式

出地铁站就能租车，它在狭窄的道路也畅行无阻，体积小停车也方便，是环保、零排放的创新电动车。租用时需要普通驾照。

2. 所到之处不但历史悠久而且风景优美，例如"甘樫丘""高松冢古坟"等等

通行范围不限于明日香村，橿原市、高取町的一部分也可到达。
行驶在路上到处都能见到梯田、瓦房等具有飞鸟地方特色的景致。

3. 自带导航导览系统，操作简单，乐趣无穷

车内自带的 iPad 存有多条推荐路线，
就算事先没做攻略，依然可以享受内容充实的行程。

沿着先驱的足迹出发 奈良县的飞鸟地区，1300 多年前就建起了日本历史上最早的正统都城"藤原京"。现在日本人生活中的方方面面——计时与历法、户籍和地址制度、货币等等——都是在那时被制定的。无论是设计还是文化，抑或艺术，都能在这里找到其源头。

MICHIMO 是为了方便人们巡游这些历史名胜而开发的迷你电动车租赁服务。在飞鸟站前的服务中心内办妥租赁手续之后，使用者（必须持有驾照）要参加一个 20 分钟的安全操作讲解。之后你可以在兼备导航和导览功能的 iPad 上搜索心仪的路线。一切准备就绪，关上鸥翼式的车门，踏上历史探索之旅。

推荐的线路中有不少都很吸引人，例如"探索改变时代的事件""飞鸟人最爱的美景"等等，让人跃跃欲试。所到之处的各种资讯也会随时显示在导览界面上。租用时间从 3 个小时到一天，可自由选择。当然你也可以不选择任何推荐路线，随性地开车兜兜风。去"石舞台古坟""入鹿的首冢"等遗迹参观，然后在当地餐馆品尝"古代米"做的午餐。

我选择先到飞鸟寺参拜日本最古老的大佛，走马观花地浏览一下明日香有机蔬菜集市，把终点站设在甘樫丘。时值初秋，日照时间开始变短，幸好我赶在日落前汗流浃背地爬上了坡顶。从瞭望台眺望四周，飞鸟人建造的"飞鸟之都"在我的眼前展开了它美丽的画卷。这画卷至今仍被大家所珍爱。我想 MICHIMO 或许会成为激发人们探索心的动力，促使更多人亲身去体验风土人情，探索日本最古老的文化发源地。（撰文：神藤秀人）

MICHIMO

1. A mini-car rental service that will revolutionize the way you visit historical sites

2. The sites, such as "Amakashi hill" and "Takamatsuzuka tomb" are not only historically important, but also beautiful

3. The service makes navigating the sites of Asuka easy and fun

"Fujiwarakyo", the first capital in Japanese history was built in the Asuka region of Nara Prefecture 1300 years ago. It was there that many aspects of contemporary life, such as the clock, calendar, family registry, addresses, and currency were introduced. Art, culture, and design were all born in Asuka. "MICHIMO" is a service that rents mini-cars for touring Asuka's sights. After registering at the service station in front of Asuka Station, you'll receive a 20-minute lesson on safely driving the mini-car（driver's license required）. You can then choose one of the recommended courses on an iPad, which also serves as a GPS. Close the gullwing doors, and you're ready to start your historical exploration. The multiple courses are organized by exciting themes, such as "events that changed history" and "scenery loved by Asuka locals." At each destination, information about the site will appear on the screen. (Hideto Shindo)

奈良国立博物馆

奈良县奈良市登大路町50
Tel.050-5542-8600
09:30～17:00（16:30截止入馆）
周五、周六（09:30～20:00
（特展期间19:30截止入馆）
周一休息，如遇节假日则顺延至次日
www.narahaku.go.jp
从近铁奈良站搭乘巴士，5分钟可达

1. 始于1946年的"正仓院展"，在此举行

这里展出正仓院宝库里具有千年历史、受到高规格保护的珍宝。
近年来，每年都有超过20万人前来参观，是奈良县的秋日一景。

2. "西新馆"是已故设计师吉村顺三先生模仿"正仓院宝库"设计的

1977年增设的"东新馆"模仿"西新馆"而建。
原来的本馆，即现在的奈良佛像馆，是奈良第一座西式风格的建筑物，由已故建筑家片山东熊先生设计。

3. 奈良公园内，设有文物保护修复处，作为配套设施

为守护和传承奈良县的历史珍宝而设立，日本著名的东大寺、兴福寺，乃至鼎鼎大名的春日大社中的宝物都曾经在此处进行保护修复。

奈良县特有的秋日佳景 常听到有人说"夏天是奈良旅游的淡季"——虽说盛夏时也有不少观光客到访，但奈良盆地的夏天真的是酷暑难当，相比之下，这里的春秋两季则实在是气候宜人。自古以来日本最好的赏樱地点——吉野山，可谓奈良春天的象征。而到了秋天赏红叶的季节，让大多数奈良人引以为傲的，却要数奈良国立博物馆的"正仓院展"。大家都会骄傲地告诉你，樱花或红叶，日本各地都能观赏，但唯独正仓院展，只在奈良才有。

奈良国立博物馆坐落在奈良公园的一角，位于兴福寺旧址内，1895年以"帝国奈良博物馆"之名开馆，是日本第二古老的国立博物馆。来自奈良乃至全日本的佛教美术名作、资料，都集中于此，

进行保存、研究、公开展出。太平洋战争期间，正仓院宝库中收藏的圣武天皇的珍宝被疏散，其中的一部分被移至本馆的库房内收藏。战争结束后的第二年，民众中期望宝物公开展示的呼声渐高，博物馆便向当时的宫内大臣提出"为日本文化重建做贡献"的申请书。由此，1946年10月19日，"正仓院特展"正式开幕（一般开放日由10月21日开始），这就是第一届的"正仓院展"。

首展大获成功以来，博物馆71年间在奈良举办了68次展览，另外3场在东京举办。参观者亦逐年递增，为了缓解拥挤的参观人潮还两次增设新馆。正仓院展每次展期最长不超过20天，但每年也有超过20万人到访，仅此一项，在博物馆界也算是独一无二了。（撰文：空闲 理）

Nara National Museum

1. The museum has featured its "Annual Exhibition of Shosoin Treasures" since 1946

2. The "New West Wing" designed by Junzo Yoshimura is modeled after the Shosoin treasure house

3. Located inside Nara Park, the museum also includes the Conservation Center for National Treasures and Important Cultural Properties

The museum opened in 1895 in the former premises of Kofukuji Temple inside Nara Park. It is Japan's second oldest museum and it exhibits many masterpieces of Buddhist art. During the Pacific War, a part of Emperor Shomu's effects, archived in the Shosoin Repository, were moved to the museum's repository for protection. In 1946, a year after the end of the war, citizens expressed a desire to see these treasures and in response, the first "Annual Exhibition of Shosoin Treasures" was organized and opened to the public. The exhibition was a great success and it has been shown 68 times in the last 71 years (it was shown three times in Tokyo). The exhibition has received an increasing number of visitors, and two new wings have been constructed to alleviate congestion. The exhibition, which only runs for 20 days maximum, is visited by over 200,000 visitors annually. In this sense also, it's truly a unique museum. (Osamu Kuga)

森正龙须面铺

奈良县樱井市三轮 535

Tel: 0744-43-7411

10:00 ～ 17:00

（周日或公众假期 09:30 ～ 17:00 冬季 10:00 ～ 16:30）

周二休息

（如遇公众假期则营业，每月 1 日营业）

周一不定期休息

从三轮站步行约 5 分钟可达

1. 这家的三轮龙须面，美味绝伦

这个面馆所用的细面条都要在自家的储藏室里经过两年熟成[4]，汤汁也是绝品。夏天有冷面，冬天有热面可供选择。

2. 店内使用脐见窑的食器、松木的餐桌、奈良产的麻布做的门帘

面馆开业初期，请已故陶艺家松井菁人先生制作了所有食器，还指导了桌椅的设计，直到现在仍然备受店家珍爱。

3. 紧靠被誉为龙须面发祥地的"大神神社"的第二鸟居左侧

大神神社奉三轮山为神体，是日本最古老的神社、大和国"一之宫"。关于三轮龙须面，也流传着各种美丽的神话传说。

极尽寂静之美的龙须面馆 大神神社是游览奈良的必到之处。而来到了大神神社，你一定要尝一尝那里的龙须面，味道好吃到令人感动。要我说，你就去森正龙须面铺。阳光透过树枝间的缝隙照到参拜步行道上，步行道一路蜿蜒向前，一直延伸到第二鸟居的附近。面馆古朴大气的门脸是从"三轮茶屋"移建至此的，那里是近松门左卫门大师所写的人形净琉璃[5]《冥途的飞脚》中故事发生的舞台。

掀开用奈良麻布做成的门帘进入店内，芦苇遮阳棚下摆放了几个座席。松木烤过之后做成的桌子显得浑厚敦实，椅子也是用同样的松木打造而成。清水泼过的石板路的一角，砌了地炉，若是冬天，地炉里烧上柴，便可温暖如春。我到访的时候是夏天，取地炉而代之地摆放了大水缸，还有几尾金鱼在水里游动。

现任店主森小枝子女士的父亲曾在大神神社任神职。小枝子女士的母亲靖子女士当初嫁过来的时候，参拜步道旁有不少饮食店，但唯独没有卖三轮龙须面的店铺。于是，为了让更多人能尝到自己家乡的美味，靖子女士在 1978 年开起了这家"森正"龙须面铺。我点的是夏季才有的冷汤长面。大海碗里装着清澄的汤底和散发着光泽的龙须面。上面的配菜也是色彩纷呈：蘘荷的淡紫色、虾子的红色、粟米小麦面筋的明黄色、三叶草和秋葵的绿色，还有香菇的黑色，都与清冷的白色面碗，以及日本纸的颜色浑然一体，相得益彰。一碗面看起来就像一幅画，一口下去，那美味令你感叹不枉此行！整间面馆没有一丝奢华，是一家清爽简朴的顶级名店。（撰文：空闲 理）

Morisho

1. Serves very tasty "Miwa somen" (very thin wheat noodles)

2. Features Hozomi kiln pottery, pine tables and trays, and a beautiful hemp shop curtain

3. Located next to the second torii gate of the Omiwa Shrine, said to be the birthplace of somen

Entering through the hemp shop curtain, customers are led to garden seats shielded from the sun by red blinds. The stone pavement, sprinkled with water, is cut into small squares for use as a fireplace in the winter. The current owner Saeko Mori's father was a Shinto priest at Omiwa Shrine. When her mother Haruko married into her father's family, there were many restaurants along the pilgrimage path, but none served "Miwa somen." Morisho was opened in 1978 to serve truly tasty and authentic local food. I had the "cold long somen," which only offered in the summer. I could see the brilliant Miwa somen in the clear broth served in a bowl with a large diameter. Atop the noodles were light purple Japanese ginger, scarlet shrimp, golden yellow millet starch, green okra and cow parsley, and black shiitake. Against the cool white bowl, it looked like a painting on Japanese paper, but when I ate it, it was extremely delicious. (Osamu Kuga)

一如庵

奈良县宇陀市榛原自明 162

Tel:0745-82-0053

午餐时间 11:00 ~ 12:45、13:00 ~ 14:30
晚餐时间 17:00 ~ 20:00（需要预约）

周一、周二休息

从榛原站驱车 10 分钟可达

1. 荞麦面以及各种精致料理，盛放在由奈良本地手工艺人制作的陶艺作品中，色香味俱佳

店内的餐具包括宇陀陶艺家尾形笃先生的作品、川上村先生的
APPLE JACK 木艺工坊出品的桧木碟子等等。

2. 木桶和寺庙的大门也被用作装饰，使店内充满神秘感

店铺由拥有 150 年历史的古民宅改造而成，
店内使用的器物和日用品可供零售，店内还设有艺廊。

3. 宇陀金牛蒡天妇罗、日本圆茄箱寿司、无花果荞麦粉蛋糕等等，都是一流的美味

另外，一定要试试一套六道的午膳大餐。

坚守"奈良的自然观"的荞麦店"一如庵"开在伊势街道沿街的古民居里。店铺外墙上钉着一个巨大的木桶作为装饰，木桶开口朝向街道，里面贴着店铺的菜单。午餐时间分成两段：11 点开始供应可供单点的料理，13 点之后是需要预约的"午之膳"套餐。我选择了"午之膳"。

穿过精心修葺的庭院进入店内，迎面是由耳成山的寺庙相赠的门板和日本传统的自在钩（可调节高低的炉钩）组合而成的装饰。店内有二十余个席位，我选择坐在玻璃的落地窗边，这里能看到流水和绿色植物。

套餐的头一道是荞麦面团和本地蘑菇煮的汤，还放了切成薄片的酸橘；紧接着是七件精致的素食，放在由店主桶谷一成先生设计、APPLE JACK 木艺工坊制作的吉野桧木平碟上。奈良本地的筒井莲藕，拌上芝麻，盛放在当地陶艺家尾形笃制作的小碗里。还有用豆腐皮包裹的黄瓜箱寿司等等，菜式之精致令我几乎忘记了这是家荞麦店。主食是自制面粉做成的金黄色蒸笼荞麦面，配鲣鱼汤汁。在天妇罗之后，荞麦面再次登场，这次是岛根县的本地荞麦，配鲱鱼汤汁。

店主桶谷先生十九岁离开家乡，在游历日本各大神社与寺庙时接触到了精进料理[6]。他意识到有必要创造一个空间让人们认识到无论是动物鱼禽还是草木蔬菜都是有生命的，于是在 2005 年回到故乡开了这家店。他还向当地人虚心学习，每天精进厨艺。他全身心投入其中，不分日夜地钻研积累。从本地蔬菜到杉木桧木的使用，无不是通过料理传达着对奈良自然的崇敬。

（撰文：神藤秀人）

Ichinyoan

1. Soba served on plates made by Nara potters

2. A mystically designed restaurant decorated with old temple doors and wooden buckets

3. It serves more than soba; I recommend Hiru no Zen, the six-plate lunch course

"Ichinyoan" is a soba noodle restaurant housed in an old traditional home facing Ise Honkaido. Lunch is served in two sections. Single dishes can be ordered from 11:00 am. The course menu (reservation required) is served from 13:00. When I visited, the course started with a bowl of broth with local mushrooms and buckwheat dough ball served with thinly sliced *sudachi*, a Japanese citrus. Next, seven vegetarian plates were served on a platter designed by owner Issei Oketani and made of Yoshino cypress by "Kobo Apple Jack." Local Tsutsui lotus roots with sesame sauce were served in a small bowl made by local potter Atsushi Ogata. There was also a "boxed sushi" of cucumber wrapped in tofu skin. The dishes were so fancy I nearly forgot I was at a soba shop. The homemade, golden soba noodles were served in a bonito broth. After some tempura, a second serving of soba, this time *Inaka soba*, country style noodles from Shimane Prefecture, was served in mackerel broth. (Hideto Shindo)

竹之馆

奈良县奈良市南鱼屋町25
Tel:0742-23-6227
17:00～翌日03:00 全年无休
从近铁奈良站步行约10分钟可达

近铁奈良站
Kintetsu-Nara Sta.
169
奈良站
Nara Sta.
754
80
奈良 SunRoute 酒店
Hotel SunRoute Nara
京终站
Kyobate Sta.
122

1. 深夜的沙龙酒家，奈良离不开它

无论是本地客人还是外地游客，无论是本地作家还是外地艺术家，
大家都好像家人一样，聚集到这里。

2. 用货真价实的竹子建成的店铺，
店内的柱子是用二月堂的大松明竹制作而成

店主的弟弟是木匠，从店铺前身的摊档开始就用竹子来搭建，
整个店铺都散发着古韵。

3. 店内的手捏饭团是奈良的深夜美味，
不是熟客还真不知道

即使肚子里塞满了美味的关东煮、乌冬之后，
它还是每个客人都必定会点的一道手工佳品。
要求打包带回家的熟客也不在少数。

所有奈良人都喜爱这家深夜食堂 奈良市可能是最适合早起散步的城市，但营业到深夜的店铺却不多。虽然夜晚的树林和寺庙也别有一番风情，但少了繁华的街道总让人感到有些寂寞。索性早早回到酒店再加个班吧，工作完再泡一个澡才近深夜。正想着不如来一杯啤酒好入眠，我突然接到一通电话："忙完了？ 出来喝一杯吧！大家都在呢，"电话那头是我在奈良旅行时熟络起来的友人，听声音应该已经喝得兴奋了："再晚也没关系，到竹之馆来找我们吧。"

从我住的奈良 SunRoute 酒店走大约十分钟就来到了竹之馆。掀开麻绳编织的门帘，推开移门，即刻引得店内的客人纷纷探头张望，大家都想看看是不是哪个熟人来了。店内的柱子、天花板、屏风、柜台，目之所及都是竹子制成的。就连各处悬挂的别致的吊灯也是用竹子和和纸做的。就在这柔和的灯光下我找到了朋友那张微醺泛红的脸，朋友"喂！ 这边这边！"地招呼着，我还没坐稳，就被灌进去了一杯酒。

在这里，你可以用实惠的价格买到冰爽的啤酒和温热可口的菜肴，甚是愉悦舒心。无论何时光顾，店内总是宾客盈门，于是大家也渐渐熟悉起来。店里的客人就好像山林里的竹笋，竹子与竹子虽然参差不齐有好有坏，彼此却丝毫没有介意，相安无事。

这里原来是通宵营业的，如今只营业到凌晨3点。大家都可以在这儿把牢骚和抱怨一吐为快，而长夜才刚开始。正是有这样可爱的馆子，人们才会有动力迎接明天，才会觉得拼尽全力生活是一件幸福的事。（撰文：空闲 理）

Take no yakata

1. A bar that is also a late night salon indispensable to Nara

2. It's really made of bamboo

3. Midnight rice balls are a Nara specialty enjoyed by those in the know

When I walked in through the rope shop curtain and opened the sliding door, everyone inside looked up expecting to find another regular. The columns, ceiling, partitions, and counter, are all made of bamboo. The lights are also all made of bamboo and Japanese paper. In the dimply lit bar, I found a familiar face flushed with drink and had a quick drink. You can buy cold beer and warm food for little money here. The ambiance is intimate and comfortable. It's always bustling and

I've gradually become acquainted with the regulars, who are like bamboo shoots in a grove. There's good and bad bamboo, but in the grove no one pays attention to such details. The bar's no longer open all night, but it still stays open until 3am. As a customer, you can unload all your gripes and worries and the night will remain young when you're done. It's a truly great bar that will make you appreciate the daily efforts we all make to continue living. (Osamu Kuga)

秋筱森林 荠菜

从大和西大寺站驱车约15分钟可达

从大和西大寺站驱车约15分钟可达

www.kuruminoki.co.jp/akishinomomori/

周二，及每月第三个周三休息

（仅周末及节假日）

晚餐时间 19:00 ～ 21:00

午餐时间 11:00 ～ 12:30、13:00 ～ 14:30

Tel:0742-52-8560（需提前一天预订）

奈良县奈良市中山町1534

1. 由日常生活设计家石村由起子女士在奈良创办的餐厅

店内随处可见一些实用又美观的物件，不经意地传达着主人的理念。

2. 位于奈良郊区的森林中，由建筑家中村好文先生改建，清静而幽远

原来是自带网球场的旅馆，有缘转到石村女士名下，于2004年开业。

3. 极富魅力的多道菜式料理，大部分使用奈良产的食材

食物的味觉、口感、色泽都十分讲究，如同割烹料理[7]一般唯美。

平城中山巴士站
Heijo-Nakayama Bus Stop

神功皇后陵
Jingu Kogoryo

大和西大寺站
Yamatosaidaiji Sta.

平城宫遗址
Nara Palace Site

奈良的形态与色彩，在这里得到体现 驾车驶过平城宫遗址的边缘，我们来到奈良市郊外的"秋筱森林"内的餐厅——"荠菜"，享受憧憬已久的午餐。"荠菜"的主人石村由起子女士也是"胡桃树"咖啡店的创始人，而"胡桃树"可说是当今生活杂货／咖啡馆集合店的先驱。石村女士的胡桃树一条店开张时可是大排长龙的人气店铺，而眼前的"秋筱森林"却隐匿在一小片树林中，非常安静。

屋顶高挑、墙壁雪白、拼接地板颜色明快，桌椅都是实木制成。窗框上点缀着小饰物，露台上爬着葡萄藤，阳光仍可以透过玻璃照进来。虽然是很难预约到的正餐餐厅，但用餐的氛围却十分放松惬意。座无虚席的店堂内，客人的穿着都很随意，就算穿着衬衫也会想解开一颗扣子，不那么拘谨。客人可以依稀听到厨房里备菜的声音，一边闻着食物的香味，一边愉快地等待上菜。菜式逐一出场，每一款都充满了创意。

我去的时候是八月，当季的菜式有：添加了大和当归（一种芹菜）的山药汤、放了夏柿的沙拉、意大利面风味的葛根乌冬、用日本圆茄和金瓜做成的凉拌馅料、日本甜辣椒天妇罗等等。虽然料理中大量使用了奈良县出产的食材，却丝毫不显得牵强或刻意。菜式的摆盘和精选食器本身固然精彩，但最令人刮目相看的还是食材本身新鲜的口感和可爱的形态。窃以为，这就是奈良的土地所培育出来的颜色和形状吧。这就是"荠菜"：朴实无华，设计宜人。（撰文：空闲 理）

Akishino no Mori Nazuna

1. A restaurant opened by Yukiko Ishimura, who continuous disseminates lifestyle design in Nara Prefecture

2. A clean space in the forest renovated by architect Yoshifumi Nakamura

3. An attractive course menu primarily made of Nara ingredients

Inside the airy high-ceilinged restaurant, the walls are bright white, the floor is covered with light-colored hardwood, and the chairs and tables are also wood. The window frames are decorated with small objects, and outside the window, I could see bunches of shiny grapes growing on the terrace. It is a "course restaurant, where it's hard to get a reservation," but once you do, it has a very relaxed and comfortable ambiance. I visited in August, and the course included a yam soup topped with Japanese parsley, a summer persimmon salad, and kudzu udon noodles served pasta style. Although made with fussily selected local ingredients, the presentation, including the plates the food is served on, is subtle and wonderful. The downplayed presentation allows you to carefully consider the freshness and cuteness of the ingredients themselves. These are colors and forms produced by Nara soil. "Nazuna" is a restaurant featuring lovely, unpretentious design and food. (Osamu Kuga)

东吉野共享办公空间

奈良县吉野郡东吉野村小川 610-2

Tel: 0746-48-9905

officecamp.jp

10:00 ～ 17:00　周二、周三休息

从榛原站搭乘巴士约 30 分钟可达

从东吉野村村公所巴士站步行约 5 分钟可达

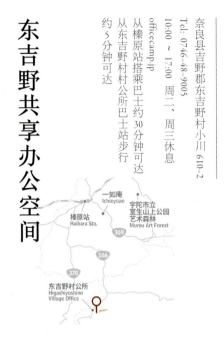

1. 地处东吉野村的大自然环绕之中的共享办公空间，自由自在，使用灵活

500 日元即可使用一天，包括 Wi-Fi 和打印机。
用旧民居改建而成，室内设备完善。咖啡馆也对外开放。

2. 同时出售用本地的杉木和桧木制成的椅子和玩具等产品

店内除了有产品设计师菅野大门先生的原创作品之外，
也有本地木艺工坊 APPLE JACK 出品的器物出售。

3. 定期举办有乡村特色的活动，例如用鱼叉捕鱼，体验劈柴等等

白天可以享受东吉野的自然景色，晚上有丰富的讲座活动。
举办交流会时还可以请宇陀市的 cafe equbo 等餐厅提供上门配餐服务。

健康的营地，孵化健全的人生　从奈良市往南，翻过吉野山，沿着吉野川向东吉野村行驶，就能找到东吉野共享办公空间（OFFICE CAMP HIGASHIYOSHINO）。我抵达时，设计师兼工作人员的坂本大祐先生正在主持一个捕鱼活动后的座谈会。活动聚集了三十多人，有大人有小孩。空间内摆放着同是工作人员的菅野大门先生设计的名为"书凳"的凳子。活动结束后，这些凳子可以叠起来变成组合柜，用来陈列书和商品，使空间的使用灵活便利。

坂本先生 2006 年从大阪移居此处。他在大自然中生活，边工作边探索什么才是更宜居的环境。2013 年菅野先生也从大阪搬到这里。一年后，两人为了让城市和乡村有更紧密的联系、推动县和村的发展，便通过改建旧民居，建起了国内崭新模式的共享办公空间。

如今有很多漫画家、摄影师等创意工作者从全国到访此处，移居这里的人也越来越多。有时村长也会来喝茶，这儿俨然已成了大众休憩的场所。坂本先生还和新锐伐木集团（Lumberjacks）策划了吸引力十足的活动。菅野先生也和奈良的高中生一起，以吉野的杉木和桧木等木材为研究对象，利用间伐所得的木材和做木工剩下的边角料，加上独特的创意和巧思，开发出了"tumi-ishi"等玩具。在我参观的时候，刚好有一群从东京来的公司职员，围坐在屋子中间的榉木桌边开会。我边喝着咖啡边思考，理想的工作究竟是什么样的呢？坂本先生和菅野先生创造出了一个真正舒适的工作环境，并将它介绍给都市中的人们，而他们自身的实践就是"理想工作"的最佳范本。（撰文：神藤秀人）

OFFICE CAMP
HIGASHIYOSHINO

1. A multipurpose shared office set in nature-filled Higashiyoshino Village

2. Sells products such as chairs and toys made of local cedar and cypress

3. Regularly organizes village-specific events such as *ayu* (sweet fish) spearing and wood chopping

When I arrived at "OFFICE CAMP HIGASHIYOSHINO," staff member and designer Daisuke Sakamoto was moderating a talk following a sweet fish spearing event. In the room were "Bookstools" designed by another staff member Daimon Kanno. The Bookstools can be stacked into a tower and used as shelving to display books and other products in the versatile office space. Sakamoto moved to Higashiyoshino from Osaka in 2006. In 2013, Kanno also moved from Osaka. A year later, wanting to foster connections between the local region and the city, they renovated an old traditional home and created a shared office space that's innovative even by national standards. Today, many creative types, including manga artists and photographers from all over Japan, visit OFFICE CAMP HIGASHIYOSHINO and there has also been an increase in transplants. Sakamoto and Kanno have created a truly comfortable workspace, which they've made public to urbanites. They've set a standard by putting theory into practice. (Hideto Shindo)

中井春风堂

奈良县吉野郡吉野町吉野山 545

Tel: 0746-32-3043

10:00 ～ 17:00（16:30 截止点单）

周三休息（冬季仅周六、周日营业）

nakasyun.com

从吉野山站步行约 5 分钟可达

1. 可以在这里学到、吃到、买到吉野的"本葛"

不但能品尝到本葛制成的葛条、葛饼，
还能见识到店主中井孝嘉先生现场制作的样子，
了解关于葛的所有知识。

2. 位于日本数一数二的赏樱胜地——吉野山中

从店铺内的窗户就能望到美丽的树木，
几步路就能走到著名的金峰山寺。

3. 用杉木和桧木修建的店铺，设计中体现着吉野木材的优良材质

由负责吉野町"三奇楼旅馆"的"南工务店"负责建筑施工。
店内还有"极上本葛果子""本葛汤"之类精心制作的土特产。

葛的传播者 我登上了吉野山。这里不仅是日本数一数二的赏樱胜地，而且葛也很有名。Hyotaro、Yakko 等柿叶寿司名店也是鳞次栉比。到了赏花时节，这里一直都是人头攒动。从黑门走向吉野山深处，经过铜鸟居和金峰山寺，前面就是吉野本葛的专卖店"中井春风堂"。在此，推荐大家选择堂食。店里的菜单上只有葛类，点上了葛切、葛饼之后，顾客会被引进开放式的厨房，欢迎大家来学习葛的制作和关于葛的知识，然后就轮到店主中井孝嘉先生登场了。

中井春风堂是代代相传的老字号，以前也卖柿叶寿司和日式点心的馒头等等。潜心学习了传统日本食物和糕点的孝嘉先生在 2009 年决定将店铺改为只卖葛类食物的专门店。店铺也重新装修，一半的空间都使用了桧木和杉木，营造出孝嘉先生理想中的店铺环境。

回到厨房这边，孝嘉先生一边演示制作的过程，一边向大家讲解"葛"是一种什么样的植物、"本葛"和"葛"的区别、本地历史悠久的制粉方法等等。制作葛切和葛饼的材料只有葛粉和水，然后加热，不放砂糖和任何添加剂。完成后的葛切或葛饼一定要在 10 分钟之内吃完，因为葛的特性是，加热后如果又逐渐冷却的话，葛粉和水又会分离。

我在这里学到了关于葛的知识，也品尝到了葛的美味，当然也想把这经验分享给别人，于是买了"本葛粉"和"本葛汤"准备回去送人。孝嘉先生还亲切地补充道："葛根汤你应该知道吧？那个葛也是同样的葛哟。"

真是一家暖胃暖心的特产店。（撰文：神藤秀人）

Nakaisyunpudo

1. A shop where you can learn about, eat, and buy Yoshiko hon-kuzu (kudzu). Factory tours are available

2. Located in Mount Yoshino, one of the best places in Japan to see cherry blossoms

3. The building is designed with cedar and cypress throughout to emphasize the attractiveness of Yoshino lumber

I climbed Mount Yoshino. It's called the best place for viewing cherry blossoms in Japan, but it's also known for kudzu.

"Nakaisyunpudo" is a kudzu specialty shop. I recommend eating in. Kudzu is all it offers. Owner Takayoshi Nakai greeted me. He studied Japanese cuisine and confectionery before deciding to offer kudzu exclusively at his shop in 2009. He renovated half his shop using cedar and cypress to realize his ideal space. He will very meticulously explain what a kudzu plant is, what the difference between kudzu and hon-kudzu is, and which milling method suits the local environment, as he prepares the food. The only ingredients used are kudzu powder and water, which are simply heated. As neither sugar nor other additives are used, the resulting dish has to be eaten within 10 minutes! When it cools down, the kudzu powder and water will separate. Having learned all this about kudzu, I was eager to purchase some souvenirs to share my experience with others. (Hideto Shindo)

大泷茶屋

奈良县吉野郡川上村大泷 420-1

Tel: 0746-53-2350

8:30 左右～17:30 左右　周三休息
12 月至翌年 3 月中旬休息

www.conet.ne.jp/~reform-labo/newpage9.html

从大和上市站驱车约 15 分钟可达

1. 可以在这里买到奈良县的当地美食——柿叶寿司

大台之原的公路通车之后，这里成了旅游途中必经的店铺。
秋季还会选用红色的柿叶包裹寿司，颜色十分鲜艳。

2. 可以在这里了解到关于柿叶寿司的相关知识

店主每天都亲手采摘香气扑鼻的柿叶，然后在店内手工制作寿司，
自产自销。

3. 店铺散发着本地独特的魅力，
一次性筷子和木盒均采用川上村产的吉野杉木做成

为了能让客人在品尝寿司的同时欣赏吉野川的美景，
在岸边建起了"吉野制造"风格的堂食店铺。
店内使用本地的陶艺器物。

大和上市站
Yamato-Kamichi Sta.

金峯山寺
Kinpusen Temple

中井春风堂
Nakai-Shunpudo

262

这里的手工礼物，能让你看到制作者的笑容，感受到当地的风土人情　沿着吉野川驶过伊势的街道，进入东熊野的道路。穿过隧道之后，就能见到对面岸上的铠挂松[8]，以及岩壁上为纪念明治时代的造林王土仓庄三郎先生而凿建的纪念碑。我在开往濑八丁的长途中，在位于大泷水坝附近的大泷茶屋稍作停留。

眼前是吉野川的割泷瀑布在轰鸣声中一泻千里的美景，身后是奈良名产柿叶寿司的专门店。走入店内，三位女性正在手工制作寿司，将备好的鲭鱼薄片放到寿司饭上，再用新鲜的柿叶逐一包裹。我买了鲭鱼和鲑鱼两种寿司的组合装。现场做好的柿叶寿司被整齐地塞到用吉野杉木制成的木盒里。

1961 年大台之原的公路通车时，大泷茶屋的创始人辻井梅野先生希望让路过的人品尝到当地的美食，于是创办了大泷茶屋。茶屋从开业之初，就一直是四位女性围坐在桌子的四角，其乐融融地制作寿司。这个场景到如今也没有改变，店铺被辻井先生的女儿们继承了下来，忙碌起来一天要做两千个。代代相传的桧木箱里装满了柿叶寿司，上面压上重石，摆放一夜之后味道刚刚好。

旅途中我小心翼翼地打开柿叶，迫不及待地塞入口中。米的回甘、鲭鱼的咸鲜、柿叶的清香绝妙地搭配在一起。接着再吃鲑鱼寿司，脑中浮现出几位店主笑着对我说"鲑鱼的也很好吃哟"。虽说如今在车站或商场里都能买到柿叶寿司，但真正的"土特产"，不去到当地是买不到的啊。（撰文：神藤秀人）

Otaki Chaya

1. The place to go for *Kakinoha sushi* (persimmon leaf-wrapped sushi), a Nara delicacy

2. The staff can tell you everything you want to know about persimmon leaf-wrapped sushi.

3. The chopsticks and takeout boxes are made of Yoshino cedar from Kawakami Village to promote local appeal

I visited Otaki Chaya, which is located near the Otaki Dam. Its specialty is persimmon leaf-wrapped sushi, a Nara delicacy. Inside the restaurant, I saw three women in the kitchen place the mackerel, which they'd just prepared and sliced, on top of some sushi rice and promptly wrap the whole thing in a very fresh, green persimmon leaf. The beautiful persimmon leaf-wrapped sushi was prepared in front of me and put inside a Yoshino cedar box. Umeno Tsujii, the first owner of Otaki Chaya opened the restaurant in 1961 in coordination with the opening of the Odaigahara Driveway. The sushi has always been prepared harmoniously by four women sitting around a table in the customers' view and this style is retained today though the restaurant is now run by Tsuji's daughters. Today, you can buy persimmon leaf-wrapped sushi in train stations and department stores. Authentic local souvenirs, however, are things that are exclusively available locally. (Hideto Shindo)

豆铃·虫鸣

奈良县奈良市南半田西町 18-2

Tel:0742-27-3130

12:00 ～ 19:00

周一、周二定休，

其他日期也有不定期休息

www.mamesuzu-sweets.com

从近铁奈良站步行约10分钟可达

近铁奈良站
Kintetsu-Nara Sta.

369

江户三
Edosan

1. 由建造于大正七年（1918年）的奈良町屋改建而成

店主说："自己的家，要尽量自己动手，不断加以修葺，
然后你就跟它心灵相通了。"
所以，他的咖啡馆才会如此让客人备感安心惬意。

2. 店主宇多滋树先生，曾经主演过河濑直美导演的作品《殡之森》

宇多先生精通奈良的文化，也撰写小说，
偶尔还会与你分享在电影外景地或拍摄时的一些趣事。

3. 这个咖啡店在不同的季节会供应各种有趣的奈良特产的点心，一年四季美味不断

秋天来临的时候，在春日山的原始森林里漫步，
把捡到的橡果收集起来，可以用来做美味的饼干。

这个咖啡店就像一场不愿散场的电影 南半田西町的旧町屋前，低调地挂着招牌，乍一看无法判断这是一家什么样的店。我鼓起勇气掀开门帘走进店内，看到榻榻米上熟客们放松的样子，这才顿觉安心。豆铃·虫鸣就是这样一家惬意的日式甜品咖啡店。

两位店主之一，宇多滋树先生原来经营一家旧书店，借着搬到现在这个町屋居住的机会，从2006 年开始经营这家供应饮料、小食的旧书咖啡店虫鸣（CHICHIRO）。又因为机缘巧合，能登山晶子女士的甜品店豆铃（MAMESUZU）的甜点成了店里的主打产品，引得附近的大学生和带着孩子的妈妈们纷纷前来光顾。招牌甜点 KINTSUBA(红豆馅的金锷烧) 甜而不腻，口味淡雅。用晶子女士的故乡北海道产的水果和有机

栽培的食材制作的甜点，也都件件是佳品，常年受到大家的青睐。

宇多先生回忆道，2007 年电影《殡之森》上映后，有一段时间客人突然多了起来。但其实宇多先生平时随和自然，熟客们都喜欢叫他"宇多老爹"，很难想象他就是戛纳电影节红毯上穿着传统和服阔步走来的男演员宇多滋树。

宇多先生还在店里养了不少小动物，有猫、金鱼，还有龟，大家一起悠闲地生活着。宇多先生一年要看超过一百部电影，平时对各种社会问题也有深刻的认识和见解。平日里他总是带着柔和的笑容，有时谈论起战争的话题，眼神也会变得严厉。我想听的故事、该听的故事还有很多。但此刻，就尝一口质朴的甜点，听着店里播放的古典音乐，安静地享受时间流过也不错。（撰文：渊上凉子）

Mamesuzu Chichiro

1. A café housed in a traditional home built in 1918 in Nara

2. Owned by Shigeki Uda, who stars in Naomi Kawase's film *The Mourning Forest*

3. Always serves delicious treats, which are made of interesting local ingredients depending on the season

Shigeki Uda originally ran a used bookshop, but when he moved into his current traditional home in Nara in 2006, he opened the used bookshop/café "Chichiro," which serves beverages and light snacks only. It mainly serves sweets made by Akiko Notoyama, who operates "Mamesuzu." "Chichiro" is now frequented by many locals including college students and moms who bring their children. The café's specialty "Kintsuba" is not refined and not too sweet. Notoyama's bakes desserts, which are made using fruits from Hokkaido, her hometown, and organic ingredients, are exquisite and many fans have patronized the café for the sweets for years. Uda notes that there was a period when the cafe enjoyed increased popularity due to his appearance in the film *The Mourning Forest* (2007). Regulars, however, call him "old man Uda" and he is incredibly and surprisingly down-to-earth for a man who walked down the red carpet at Cannes in a traditional *hakama*. (Ryoko Fuchikami)

瀞酒店

奈良县吉野郡十津川村神下 405

Tel: 0746-69-0003

11:30 开店，售完即止　周三、周四休息

dorohotel.jp

从大和八木站出发，约 2 小时 40 分钟车程

1. 在瀞峡的悬崖峭壁上建起的咖啡馆

位于吉野熊野国立公园内奈良县一侧，

可以眺望横跨三重县、和歌山县以及奈良县的大峡谷的美景。

2. 由建成超过 100 年的酒店重新设计改建而成

招牌和门牌都修复一新，还复刻了明信片和店旗上的图案。

3. 定期举办"瀞峡八景"之类的展览，传播当地的魅力

与三重县的"木花堂"、和歌山县的"selection ROCA"联手，

在店内展示和售卖本地艺术家的手工作品。

大和八木站 Yamato-Yagi Sta.

309

168

大森之乡 Omori no sato

425

169

深山仙境中的咖啡店　我从北边的奈良市内驱车往南，一度进入和歌山县境内，然后再转回到奈良县，经过三个多小时的长途跋涉，跨越奈良县、和歌山县、三重县，最后到达可以俯视熊野川的风景名胜"瀞峡"。瀞酒店几乎就在三县交界的位置上，耸立在离水面大约 20 米的峭壁上。这险峻的位置不禁让人担心：要是有台风来袭，酒店怕是会被吹得片瓦不留。

最初的酒店是 1917 年时为了方便运输木材的伐木工住宿而建的，后来因为游览船停泊在此，作为观光景点的旅馆而繁荣了一阵子。当时酒店的主人觉次先生是现在这里的主人东达也先生的曾祖父。2001 年的时候酒店停止营业。而后，在 2011 年的水灾中，酒店一楼的一部分被大水冲走。回到故乡的达也先生，决定保留这座深受家人和熟客喜爱的酒店。于是 2013 年，这里作为咖啡店再次开始营业。

端坐店内，客人可以一边眺望窗外壮美的景色，一边品尝店家用本地水果自制的糖浆调制的苏打饮料，还有好吃的小林盖饭（日式洋葱猪肉盖饭）。虽然时过境迁，店铺本身不再有以前的繁华，但峡谷和山川的风景依然如故。酒店的木质回廊、隔间、扶手等等都尽可能修复成当时的状态。达也先生说，希望这里有机会可以再一次作为酒店对外开放。

我从游船停泊的岩堤下的河堤向下走，抬头回望瀞酒店。从威风凛凛的酒店向和歌山县那边的吊桥方向望去，还能看到酒店的分馆。我相信，总有一天，这座建筑能被修复一新，重现当时全国旅客纷至沓来的景象。（撰文：神藤秀人）

Doro Hotel

1. A café built on a precipice of crags in Dorokyo

2. It features the original designs of an over-100-year-old hotel

3. It also regularly organizes themed exhibitions such as "Eight Views of Dorokyo" to promote the region

Dorokyo is a scenic spot that looks down on the Kumano River. "Doro Hotel" stands above a sheer cliff soaring 20 meters above sea level. The building began its life as a hotel for raftsmen in 1917 and eventually became an inn catering to tourists who would arrive regularly on pleasure boats during the days of current owner Tatsuya Higashi's great grandfather Katsuji. The hotel went out of business, however, in 2001. Returning to his hometown, Tatsuya Higashi decided that he would preserve the hotel which had been loved by family and regular customers. He reopened the hotel as a cafe in 2013. Much time has passed since the hotel's heyday and its site is no longer a bustling tourist destination. The landscape, however, remains the same. The original exterior hallway that circumscribes the building, ornamental handrails, and transoms have all been restored as faithfully as possible. Eventually, Higashi hopes to reopen the hotel as a lodging facility. (Hideto Shindo)

高畑茶论

奈良县奈良市高畑町1247

Tel.0742-22-2922

13:00～18:00 周二、周三、周四休息

如逢节假日顺延至次日

从近铁奈良站搭乘巴士，

约10分钟后在破石町巴士站下车，

步行约5分钟可达

近铁奈良站 Kintetsu-Nara Sta.
奈良酒店 Nara Hotel
奈良公园 Nara Park

1. 露天咖啡馆，让你感受奈良的天空

坐落在有100年历史的西式庭院里，从1981年营业至今。
令人心情舒畅，同时还可以品尝美味的红茶和蛋糕。

2. 位于奈良的风景区高畑，西洋风格设计，是隐于闹市的好去处

咖啡小屋开在一条狭窄的小路上，屋顶不高，外表并不引人注目，
土墙的一扇小门，就是它的出入口。

3. 靠近春日山原始森林，与志贺直哉故居相邻

店铺就在通往春日大社的小路上，
这条路据说被志贺直哉先生取名为"耳语小径"。
那是个经常有艺术家出没的地方，我也想去那里悠闲地散散步。

艺术家的隐世情怀 白桦派的大文豪志贺直哉先生曾在奈良的高畑建起了自己设计的家，并在这里居住了13年。虽说大家都只记得他说的那句"奈良无美食"（志贺先生在他的随笔《奈良》中写道："美味是区别于果腹之物的存在。"而同一篇文章中也写到了豆腐和其他食物的美味之处），其实志贺先生对奈良有着深厚的爱，他留下的故居也是相当的摩登洋气。

故居边建起的小洋楼，用古色古香的象牙色土墙围着，椿树叶子鲜艳的绿色给院子增添了几分色彩。这里居住的是画家中村一雄先生和夫人纪矩子女士，夫妇俩为了使高畑再次成为文人骚客可以聚集聊天的地方，将庭院建成了露天咖啡馆。

似乎故意要引人注意一般，他们在土墙上挖了一个小门作为出入口，小小的店招上写着"高畑茶论"。雪松参天的庭院深处，有一间外墙漆成白色的小木屋，室内装饰也简洁清爽，挂着两盏满月一般的装饰灯。屋外的院子里松散地摆放着几张白色的桌子，和一些白色的铁艺椅子。从野外采来的可爱的花束被装在玻璃容器里装饰庭院。与志同道合的朋友一起来这里坐坐，恍惚之间会觉得自己仿佛也成了白桦派的一员。

志贺直哉先生曾写道："就算被弓箭追击，被盾牌阻拦，也无法挡住我想要回到奈良的心情，这真是不可思议。"先生的这种心情，似乎从以前画家墨客云集、被称为"高畑沙龙"的故居散发开来，也感染了到访高畑茶论的人们。在这个"凿壁求友"的庭院里，包括我在内，大家都在相同念头的驱使下走到了一起。（撰文：空闲 理）

Takabatake Salon

1. An open air café in Nara

2. Modernly designed, the café feels like a hideaway and is located in Takabatake, a scenic zone in Nara

3. The café is adjacent to the former Naoya Shiga residence and near the virgin forest of Mount Kasuga

Naoya Shiga, one of the best known writers of the "Shirakaba school," designed and built his home, which he lived in for 13 years, in Takabatake, Nara. The Western style house adjacent to Shiga's former home is surrounded by a tusk-colored earthen wall and adorned by rich green camellia leaves. The painter Kazuo Nakamura and his wife Kikuko, who live there, opened this garden café to provide a place in Takabatake where people could gather and talk. Himalayan cedar soar to the sky in the earthen garden that houses the small, white walled wooden café. The interior of the café is made of untreated lumber and features two lamps that shine like full moons. Outside, white tables and wire chairs are placed spaciously and lovely flowers that appear freshly picked from the wild are displayed in various glass vases. Come with a friend and you'll feel like a member of the Shirakaba school. (Osamu Kuga)

K 咖啡

奈良县大和郡山市柳町 4-46

Tel: 090-6986-3255

10:00 ～ 17:00　周四休息

kcoffee.jp

从近铁郡山站步行约 10 分钟可达

1. 店家自己烘焙咖啡豆，店铺创意来自一个艺术项目

最初是一个废弃的加油站，
后来被用作"奈良町屋艺术节"的展览场地，再后来改建为咖啡店。
店铺的视觉设计，由本地出生的插图画家南夏希女士负责。

2. 位于大和郡山的地标性地区"金鱼街"

门口放着一个电话亭造型的金鱼缸，里面有许多金鱼在游来游去。
很多人在营业时间之外也慕名到访。
咖啡店附近还有 Tohon 书店、"纺车"（Tsumugi）咖啡店等店铺。

3. 举办各种活动，活跃当地商店街的气氛

每个月的第四个星期六，都会在一家鞋店的旧址举办"Fukuse 集市"；
另外，大家还会用鱼盆装着自己的商品，参加"鱼盆集市"。

从这个店铺开始，了解城下町·郡山 了解大和郡山的人都会知道"金鱼街"。从 1724 年柳泽吉里成为初代藩主之后，藩士们从事的副业都和金鱼相关。那些金鱼养殖地，现在也多是金鱼的资料馆、金鱼批发店等场所。然而，对于我这个不熟悉那段历史的人来说，K 咖啡或许更有存在感。

那个脑洞大开的电话亭金鱼缸就竖立在柳町商店街的入口处。电话亭的门缝用压胶封死，里面灌满了水，大概有 50 条金鱼在里面欢快地游来游去。更惊奇的是，这地方曾是个废弃的加油站，原来的招牌"GENERAL"仍赫然高挂着。

加油站里面有一栋改建过的小屋，透过窗户，能看到一边冲泡咖啡，一边还在笑脸迎客的店主森和也先生。和也先生原来在大阪从事餐饮工作，后来跟着妻子来到了她的家乡大和郡山。一次偶然的机会，他在奈良町屋艺术节上开起了咖啡店。活动结束时他和大家商议，想利用加油站这个位置继续开咖啡馆。于是 K 咖啡就从 2014 年延续至今。

我点了一杯冰的黑咖啡，感觉就像是趁着给爱车加油时小憩片刻。慕名来看金鱼的游客、从外地骑摩托车环游至此的人，都会在此驻足，和也先生时不时要从他的小窗口里探出头来为他们指路。还有小学生，有盯着金鱼目不转睛的，有扔书包玩的，有从神社到商店街来回瞎跑的，十分热闹。来往的人络绎不绝，一手拿着咖啡，一边发现大和郡山的各种美好。"我希望这里能给小镇上的所有人带来快乐。"和也先生质朴的气质也和这个地方如出一辙。（撰文：神藤秀人）

K Coffee

1. A coffee roaster and café which was born out of an art project using a traditional home

2. A landmark of the "goldfish city" Yamatokoriyama

3. It organizes events to promote its local shopping arcade

Those in the know will know Yamatokoriyama as "goldfish city." The city features numerous goldfish-related facilities including wholesale markets and even a museum. "K Coffee" is located at the entrance of the "Yanagimachi shopping arcade" and is instantly recognizable by the extremely odd telephone booth, the door of which is caulked to seal the water and approximately 50 goldfish inside. The location of "K Coffee," clearly a former gas station still bearing its former signage, is equally surprising. In the renovated shack in the back, Kazuya Mori smilingly brews coffee and serves it through a window. I ordered an iced coffee and sat down where a gas pump used to be. I could see Mori poking his head out of his window and giving directions to tourists drawn in by the telephone booth/fish tank. Customer after customer left with a coffee in hand to explore Yamatokoriyama and Mori's unassuming presence perfectly matched the city. (Hideto Shindo)

大森之乡

奈良县吉野郡十津川村武藏 487

Tel: 080-2543-5552

住宿费：二人同行时，
7 000 日元 / 位 / 晚
www.totsukawa-stay.com

从大和八木站出发，
约 2 小时 20 分钟车程

大和八木站
Yamato-Yagi Sta.

瀞酒店
Doro Hotel

1. 住在奈良的深山中，体验亚历克斯·克尔 (Alex Kerr) 先生设计的民宿

民宿坐落在十津川村温泉街的最深处，一个叫作武藏的小村落里。
民宿旁边是利用小学校舍改建而成的教育资料馆，
住宿的客人也可以随意参观。

2. 业主和管理人都是当地人

办理入住手续和打扫屋子的都是住在武藏的当地人。
这里还有各种地域文化交流活动，尤其一到每年 8 月的舞蹈节，
人们便从日本各地赶来，聚集于此。

3. 十津川的杉树做的椅子和桌子，还有其他完备的生活设施，保证你长期居住也没问题

Wi-Fi、浴室、洗手间、空调、洗衣机和干衣机、冰箱、
厨房用品、调味料等等，一应俱全。

村庄是一个宝藏　十津川村是日本的第一大村庄，面积比东京 23 区加起来还大。从村子中央的温泉区的温泉街出发，往深处去，登上陡峭的山路才能到达武藏村。我驱车悠闲地穿行在农田宁静的风景中，遇到的当地人都面带笑容地往田埂上避让，我也微笑着向他们回礼。

旧武藏小学的木结构校舍里，榉木的隔间非常漂亮。校舍的对面建起了一座颇具现代感的平房，这就是每天只提供两组住宿的民宿"大森之乡"。两间客房分别以围绕村庄的山峰的名字命名，西式的房间叫"行仙"，日式的房间叫"烧峰"。

到了预定入住时间，一位武藏妇女作为负责人出来迎接我，替我办理入住手续。这里由出生于美国、研究东洋文化的克尔先生担当设计。室内摆放着手工和纸做成的灯具。杉木做成的桌子和椅子上，年轮的花纹也非常美丽。冰箱里放着做早餐的大米和蔬菜等，多是本地自产的食材。（早餐需要预约。）

1970 年武藏小学停办以来，有 100 年历史的教职员工宿舍楼也废弃了。武藏的居民先是将校舍作为居民中心保存了下来。如今还能在这个校园里看到日本重要非物质文化遗产的"大踊舞蹈表演"，这里已然成了圈内知名的大踊舞胜地。

2014 年，在众人的翘首盼望中，宿舍作为"大森之乡"重获新生。据说当时克尔先生对这里的一面石墙一见钟情。如今我在这面墙下的露台上可以望到寂静的星空。这风景对于深爱着故乡、坚持保护当地建筑的武藏人来说也是弥足珍贵吧……真是纯朴到令人羡慕的一个地方。

（撰文：神藤秀人）

Omori-no-Sato

1. Lodging facility deep in the mountains of Nara designed by Alex Kerr

2. Locally owned and operated

3. Furniture made of Totsukawa-grown cedar and other features make it perfect for long-term stays

"Omori-no-Sato" is located in the Musashi settlement, which is up a steep hill deeper into the mountains from the village's centrally located hot spring district. Driving slowly in the squiet landscape of farms, locals smilingly moved out of the way into the footpaths, and I bowed smilingly in return. The modern, renovated folk home of Omori-no-Sato is located across from the wooden former Musashi Elementary School building. It hosts a maximum of two parties per night. I arrived on time, was greeted by a local woman who is the superintendent, and checked in. Japanese paper lanterns were placed atop, beautiful cedar tables and chairs showing beautiful growth rings. Inside the refrigerator in my room were rice, vegetables, and other ingredients for breakfast (reservation required). Almost all of the ingredients are locally produced. From the terrace facing the stone wall, which Alex Kerr fell in love with and inspired him to use the site, I could see a quiet sky full of stars. (Hideto Shindo)

奈良酒店

从近铁奈良站步行约15分钟可达

www.narahotel.co.jp

26 017 日元／位／晚（含晚餐和早餐）

住宿费：二人同行时，

Tel.0742-26-3300

奈良县奈良市高畑町 1096

1. 位于奈良公园内，由辰野金吾先生设计的古典酒店

瓦片的屋顶、桧木的玄关、石膏的墙面——
酒店的建筑和谐地融入了奈良的环境。庭院里有时还会跑来野生的鹿。

2. 作为迎宾馆，馆内的装饰和艺术品都向客人们展示着奈良的魅力

装饰品包括陶艺家大盐正人先生做的"赤肤烧"[9]的宝珠形装饰、
模仿传统灯笼设计的水晶吊灯等等。

3. 设有餐厅、酒吧等，还备有"茶粥"一类的本地美食

可以在趣味十足的空间里品尝一杯咖啡，
还能品尝到用日本茶和当地自酿酒调制的鸡尾酒。

穿越历史的老牌迎宾馆，至今长盛不衰 在市内吃过午餐之后，我来到了奈良公园荒池边的奈良酒店。热情的门童替我打开了厚重的桧木大门，穿过楼顶足有 9 米高的中庭，引我走向大堂深处的酒吧"THE BAR"。我被带到面向庭院的座位，俨然像是受到了豪门的款待，往品味不凡的沙发上一坐，顿觉自己也身家非凡。印象里传统的老牌酒店都是拘谨正式的场合，但在这个酒店里本地人很多，气氛也很轻松。

酒店包括两个部分：1909 年开业的本馆，和1984 年加建的新馆。建筑样式融合了西式和日式的风格，尤其是本馆的建筑，非常有趣。前台的壁炉台借鉴了大鸟居的设计，主楼梯的扶手上有用奈良传统工艺赤肤烧制成的宝珠形装饰。酒店有超过 120 间客房，走到最尽头的

房间要穿过一条长约 200 米的昏暗走廊，有时脚踩过木板还会发出吱吱声，也十分有意思。紧急情况下使用的铁镐、消防用的水桶，还有当年因为使用烧煤炭的暖炉而在门上特别设置的换气扇，这些东西都还保留着。1914 年引进的刻有美丽浮雕的蒸汽取暖器，竟然也沿用至今。

在这里，经营者不会为了追求便利而对既有建筑随便进行改造，哪怕非改造不可，也要把修缮控制在最低限度，所以那些历史悠久但依然为大家所喜爱的设计才得以存留。正因为如此，奈良酒店百年以来长盛不衰，从而能让国内外的观光者和名人贵客，以及本地人——甚至还有当地的鹿儿们——都被她的魅力所吸引，时常光顾。（撰文：神藤秀人）

Nara Hotel

1. A classic hotel located in Nara Park and designed by the late Kingo Tatsuno

2. Furnishings and art decorating the interior promotes Nara's attractions in this hotel originally designed as a guest house for foreign VIPs

3. The rstaurant, lounge, and bar serve local items such as *chagayu,* green tea porridge

When I visited the "Nara Hotel," I was greeted by a nice doorman, who opened the heavy cypress doors for me and showed me to a seat in the lounge facing the hotel garden in "THE BAR" past the lobby with the nine meters high ceiling. I felt noble as I sat in the regal couch. The hotel comprises the main building, built in 1909, and the new wing, which was added in 1984. Together, the two buildings offer a combination of Japanese and western styles. The original building is particularly charming. The mantelpiece of the fireplace in front of the lobby desk is modeled after a red tori gate. The main staircase is adorned with locally made *Akahadayaki* pottery ornaments. The building has been renovated, not to improve convenience, but rather to maintain integrity to the original design. The hotel is full of old-world charm and long-loved designs. (Hideto Shindo)

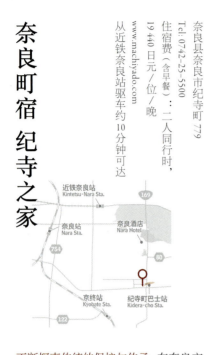

奈良町宿 纪寺之家

奈良县奈良市纪寺町 779
Tel. 0742-25-5500
住宿费（含早餐）：二人同行时，
19 440 日元／位／晚
www.machiyado.com
从近铁奈良站驱车约 10 分钟可达

近铁奈良站
Kintetsu-Nara Sta.

奈良站
Nara Sta.

奈良酒店
Nara Hotel

京终站
Kyobate Sta.

纪寺町巴士站
Kidera-cho Sta.

1. 对于"将奈良的町家保存下来"的活动来说，这里具有划时代的存在意义

2011 年，这间即将拆除的町宿在千钧一发之际，被抢救了下来。
借此契机，"保存町家"的呼声才被唤起，使得五处町家得以保存。

2. 用现代化的便利空间改变了大家对古民宅的刻板印象

老屋中用传统技艺和实木打造的建筑特色被全部保留，
同时屋内被改造成更便于日常生活的宜居空间。

3. 屋内的装饰、工作人员的制服、早餐用的食器和摆盘方式……无不透露着浓浓的创意

坚持学习奈良长久延续下来的传统，并融入当代的风尚和艺术；
开拓新的需求，并不断提高和发展。

不断探索传统的保护与传承 在奈良市中心以南的纪寺町，有一间精致美观的传统町屋经过修缮后被保留了下来，那就是奈良民宿——纪寺之家。进门处精心打扫过的石子路边，点缀着龙芽草可爱的小黄花，显得分外清新秀气。办理入住之后，我拿到了一把小巧的钥匙，瞬间觉得自己成了这个美丽的町屋中的一名居民。这里有"前院的那间"、"旁边的那间"等五间客房。看着屋子现在的样子，你完全想象不出这里原来是等着被拆除的弃屋。多亏有藤冈建筑研究所及时喊停，他们认为，"这么好的老建筑，一旦拆了不可能复制重建，但如果进行修葺却可以成为很好的住宅"。于是他们不但对老宅实施了成功的修缮工程，之后还拿下了租赁权，加入现代化的生活设施，在 2011 年将这里

作为民宿开始对外营业。

我住的那一间房叫作"有走廊的那间"，从玄关开始有一条笔直的走廊贯穿整个结构细长的房间。房内暖气充足，还有设备齐全的厨房。这里既保留了町屋原来的面貌，又大胆加入了当代生活必需的现代化设施，屋内的座椅靠垫、澡盆、淋浴用的小凳子等等，都是奈良手工艺人的原创作品。

工作人员还很用心地将推荐游览的地方和店铺做成地图，并定期更新，服务真可谓细心周到。此外，这里不但对来奈良旅游的人来说是理想的观光住宿选择，对于想在奈良安家、寻找町屋的人，或者想修缮自家町屋的人，这里也提供咨询服务。真是一家十分有趣的民宿。（撰文：空闲 理）

Kidera no ie

1. An innovative inn that is a part of an effort to preserve local traditional homes

2. A modern and comfortable space that transforms the image of an old folk home

3. The guest room furnishings, staff uniform, and the plates that the breakfast is served on all exude attentive originality

"Kidera no ie" is a property south of central Nara featuring beautifully renovated traditional homes. After checking in and receiving a small key to a guest room, guests become "residents" of a traditional home. Astonishingly, the traditional homes constituting "Kidera no ie" were all previously slated for demolition. It was Fujioka Architecture Labo, that halted the destruction, asserting that once demolished the traditional homes could not be rebuilt and that if renovated, they would make wonderful houses. After its impressive renovation of the traditional homes, Fujioka Architecture Labo rented them and used them as model homes. In 2011, it opened the homes to the public as an inn. I stayed in the "room with the long dirt-floored hallway," which is fully heated and equipped with a sophisticated kitchen. It preserves the original charm of a traditional home and also features many amenities necessary for contemporary lifestyles. (Osamu Kuga)

江户三

从近铁奈良站步行约15分钟可达

www.edosan.jp
含晚餐和早餐
19440日元／位／晚，
住宿费：二人同行时，
Tel:0742-26-2662
奈良县奈良市高畑町1167

1. 在奈良公园的森林里过夜

靠近浮见堂和春日大社的一之鸟居，兴福寺原址上，
11栋有历史渊源的茶室风格建筑错落林立。

2. 备受文人墨客推崇的旅店，已故小说家志贺直哉、画家藤田嗣治等都曾下榻此地

从开业以来不断有文化名人光顾，
店内还有志贺直哉先生命名的"若草锅"。

3. 随处可见"赤肤烧"（陶艺）、"奈良一刀雕"（木刻玩偶）之类的奈良珍品

客房里摆放了许多有历史感的装饰品，原兴福寺的三斗
（柱子顶部支撑横梁的部分）也被用作旅馆内的装饰。
奈良本地艺术家创作的泥人也是很值得推荐的纪念品。

奈良国立博物馆
Nara National Museum

369

近铁奈良站
Kintetsu-Nara Sta.

169

奈良酒店
Nara Hotel

80

享受寺庙中的归隐生活 高度超过50米的兴福寺五重塔是世界文化遗产之一。眺望着1300年前修建的春日大社，一路向东而行，穿过大鸟居之后就是一片树林，那里林立着共11栋小屋组成的料理旅馆"江户三"。现在，其中以"铜锣""太鼓""鱼鼓"等乐器命名的五栋可供预订住宿（须整栋预订）。此外还有餐厅"八方亭"，旅馆前台所在的主屋那一栋还设有澡堂。一栋栋小屋错落有致的样子，就像一个可爱的小村落。

我去采访的时候是八月，刚好遇上一年一度的奈良灯花会，旅馆外人头攒动，无数的蜡烛和提灯从春日大社的参拜步道一直延伸到大殿。适逢20年一次的"式年造替"仪式（即神殿的定期翻修）——春日大社内部的一些重要空间只在这时才会向公众开放，气氛也会与平时不同。

位于如此寺院云集的核心地区的江户三，最早由大阪西区的江户堀三丁目的店铺起家，1907年才搬到此地开始经营高级料理店。其间有的房间还被用作啤酒屋，直到战后才转为经营料理旅馆。如今它已不再是高级的料理店，而是为来到奈良公园的男女老幼提供一个轻松舒缓的环境。

第二天清早，我在早餐之前来到了东大寺的大佛殿。清晨的奈良公园里鲜有行人，只有半梦半醒的鹿儿们向我转过头来。我赶在7点30分寺院开门时入内参拜，在杳然无声的寂静中，独自站在壮观的大佛脚下，举头仰视。我想，虽然游客摩肩接踵的奈良也很好，但住在江户三，就要体验一下"素颜的奈良"。（撰文：神藤秀人）

Edosan

1. Stay inside the Nara Park forest

2. An inn historically loved by artists such as the late novelist Naoya Shiga and painter Tsuguharu Fujita (aka Leonard Foujita)

3. The inn is furnished throughout with Nara gems such as Akahada pottery and Itto-bori carved dolls

The over-50-meters-tall five-storied pagoda of Kofukuji Temple is a World Heritage site. Walking east with the over 800-year-old temple complex in view, you'll see the building constituting the dining inn "Edosan" inside the forest adjacent to the Kasuga Shrine's Ichino Tori gate. The five buildings currently open to guests (rented by the building) are named after musical instruments such as "Dora" [gong], "Taiko" [drum], and "Gyoku" [fish-shaped wooden gong]. In addition, there is the restaurant "Happotei" and the main building which houses the bath and reception desk. "Edosan" began as a shop in Osaka and opened as an upscale Japanese restaurant at its current location in 1907. Before breakfast, I visited the Great Buddha Hall in Todaiji Temple. I arrived and prayed as the temple gates opened at 7:30 and looked up at the Great Buddha alone and in near-total silence. Bustling Nara is also nice, but I hope you'll stay at "Edosan" to experience the real Nara. (Hideto Shindo)

藤冈俊平

藤冈建筑研究所·纪寺之家

www.machiyado.com
fujioka-architecture-labo.com

大和八木站
Yamato-Yagi Sta.

309
168
瀞酒店
Doro Hotel
425
169

1. 令古老的民居焕然一新，并亲自经营"纪寺之家"

不仅修理和使用旧民居，还另辟蹊径，
追求比单纯的现代住宅更为舒适和美观的居所。

2. 建筑世家的长子，立足奈良，从事日本传统住宅的设计

泥瓦匠、园林师、木工等等，各种精巧的手艺代代相传。
父亲藤冈龙介先生是藤冈建筑研究所的总负责人。

3. 纪寺之家中的设施和装饰都融入了设计感，体现着现代奈良的风格

与前辈和同辈伙伴同心协力，推动奈良精良的制作工艺的发展，
时而合作，经常探讨，积极传播奈良的文化。

安居，是世代相传的前提，也是祖祖辈辈的心愿
将奈良市的传统町屋改建成"纪寺之家"，这个划时代的改造项目由藤冈建筑研究所担纲。研究所的主要负责人藤冈俊平先生也参与了民宿的运营工作。纪寺之家不只能满足观光游客的住宿，更重要的是，通过尽可能地保留了旧民居的原貌，同时加入现代生活必需的设施，改善了町屋的居住体验。以此为契机，或许还会让更多人认真考虑选择这样的町屋作为安居之所。

当时看上这栋旧町屋时，它是一个什么样的状态，又是怎样将它修缮一新的？买一栋町屋或者租一栋町屋的费用怎么算？——大家或许都对纪寺之家充满了好奇。但是，如果你以客户的身份去敲开藤冈建筑研究所的大门，那

你还真不一定受欢迎；然而，如果作为纪寺之家的房客，即使在离店之后改天来找藤冈先生闲聊，他也会用通俗易懂的语言详细地给你解释，还会拿出施工前拍下的照片给你看。

与藤冈先生一起走在奈良的街上，随处可见需要保护和活用的町屋。他数次停下脚步，仔细观察房屋的各个细节部位，并向我解释这些百余年前匠人们的技术结晶，言语中满溢着热爱之情。藤冈先生现在和家人一起居住的地方就是他出生长大的地方。藤冈先生深爱着的奈良正在一点点消失，但以他的热诚、对奈良的深厚认知，再加上丰富的专业技能和实践经验，要保护奈良的现在和将来，他一定是其中的关键人物。（撰文：空闲 理）

Fujioka Architecture Labo/ Kidera no ie
Shunpei Fujioka

1. Operates "Kidera no ie" which revolutionizes the image of an "old folk home inn"

2. The eldest son of an architect family and based in Nara, he designs traditional Japanese residences

3. The design of the fixtures and furniture in "Kidera no ie" express a contemporary Nara aesthetic

One innovative aspect of "Kidera no ie," an inn housed in a renovated old traditional Japanese house in Nara, is that Shunpei Fujioka of "Fujioka Architecture Labo," who handled the renovation, also operates the inn. Although the hurdle for consulting an architectural firm regarding the cost and methods of its purchase or rental and renovation of the old home and its original condition as a client are rather high, if you stay at "Kidera no ie," you can casually ask Fujioka directly during your stay, or even after you check out at a later date. Fujioka lives with his family in the old traditional home he grew up in. He loves and has thoroughly studied the "disappearing Nara," has ample experience and know-how on how to preserve it, and is thus an invaluable asset to Nara's future. (Osamu Kuga)

中野圣子
奈良SunRoute酒店

从近铁奈良站步行约10分钟可达

二人同行时，11340日元／位／晚

Tel：0742-22-5151
www.sunroute-nara.co.jp

奈良SunRoute酒店

奈良县奈良市高畑町1110

1. 现任奈良SunRoute酒店总经理

酒店的前身是著名的尾花剧场。

酒店工作人员都对奈良了如指掌，酒店图书馆里有不少奈良相关的书籍，已经超越了普通的商务酒店，使人产生常住的冲动。

2. 奈良国际电影节组委会主席

酒店是电影节放映会场之一，也是组委会运作的地点。

每个月在奈良市各处也会举办展映活动。

3. 奈良灯花会的主负责人

她和志愿者们一起，在历史悠久的奈良公园周边探索新的庆典活动，并不断深化、改良，使之深入人心。

她奔走在历史和风土人情之间，是一条连接奈良的本地人和游客的纽带　在魅力无与伦比的奈良公园附近，不仅有像二月堂的修二会（汲水节）、春日若宫大谷节这样历史悠久的庆典活动，近年来，又推出了不少新的活动。其中最出类拔萃的当然要数每年8月的奈良灯花会。举办期间，奈良公园一带会点亮约两万支蜡烛。虽然实际举办的过程中遇到了各种困难，但如今奈良灯花会在本地已深入人心，近年有超过90万人参加。然后到了9月，就是奈良国际电影节了，奈良公园最大的草坪广场春日野园地等地方也会变身为放映会场。这两个活动不仅内容精彩，而且充分利用了奈良公园的场地。奈良浓重宁静的夜色，更为活动平添了几分特别的魅力。

2016年这两个活动的运营负责人都是奈良SunRoute酒店的总经理中野圣子女士。中野女士本身也在许多活动中担任志愿者，经验丰富。她提出，要为奈良创造出新的庆典，就一定要充分了解奈良的历史，于是她参与创办了"奈良名胜知识鉴定考试"，奈良SunRoute酒店前台的所有员工都是持有二级以上合格证的"奈良通"。中野女士还说："参加庆典的经历可能会改变一个人的人生，每个人都应该有这样的权利。"奈良从1300多年前就开始接触各种外国的人和文化，其厚重的历史要通过酒店的员工、参加庆典的志愿者，和众多的奈良民众一起再发掘，使它更活跃，让它以有趣的、符合时代的姿态传承下去。（撰文：空闲 理）

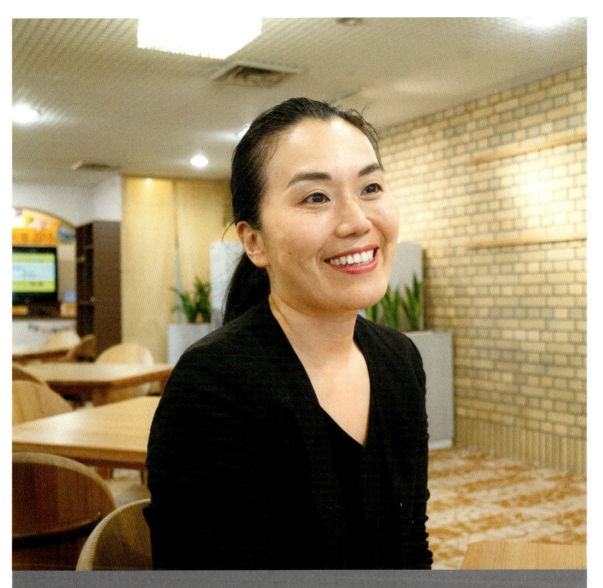

Hotel SunRoute Nara
Satoko Nakano

1. Current president of "Hotel SunRoute Nara," which is housed in a former cinema

2. Chairperson of the "Nara International Film Festival" executive committee

3. Leader of "Nara Tokae," a popular summer event in Nara

Approximately 20,000 candles are lit in Nara Park for the "Nara Tokae" lantern festival held every August. As the park is filled with architectural national treasures, it must have been difficult to get this festival approved. Nevertheless, it has drawn around 900 thousand visitors in recent years. The "Nara International Film Festival" is held annually in September. Masako Nakano ran both events in 2016. Explaining that one, must know Nara's history to organize new festivals in Nara, she also helped create the "Nara Mahoroba Sommelier Certification" and the front-end staff at her hotel all hold level two or higher certification. For 1300 years, Nara has been a place where locals interact with foreigners. Nakano has reexamined and interestingly revitalized Nara's rich history to pass it on to future generations. (Osamu Kuga)

石村由起子

胡桃树

从新大宫站步行约 15 分钟可达

www.kuruminoki.co.jp

周五至周日 11:30 ～ 21:00 全年无休

11:30 ～ 17:30

Tel.0742-23-8286

奈良县奈良市法莲町 567-1

佐保川
Saho River

新大宫站
Shin-Omiya Sta.

近铁奈良站
Kintetsu-Nara Sta.

1. 她精心设计着奈良的衣、食、住，并原原本本地将这些魅力介绍给别人

1984 年创办了精品杂货和咖啡集合店的先驱"胡桃树"。

2. 她是将日本的当代设计介绍给奈良的人

她在奈良举办名为"生活学校"的讲座充满原创性，
还在东京创办了集购物与咖啡屋为一体的"时光森林"。

3. 她是了不起的培育家。她能看出别人无法发现的魅力，推动并开发奈良县那些未经开发的处女地

"胡桃树""秋筱森林""鹿之舟"，
这些现在人气爆棚的地方都是用以前老旧的设施改造成的。

通过"与奈良倾心交谈"来孕育店铺与文化

"我认为有些东西是浑然天成的，或者说'存在即合理'，似乎只有这样的东西才与奈良相称。我从日本乃至全世界为奈良挑选各种东西，再将它们带回奈良，看看究竟是不是真的合适。一旦发现'啊！好合适啊！'我会欣喜若狂地和大家分享我的发现。"——和石村由起子女士有过几次会面之后，我逐渐认识到，她就是这样的一个人。

石村女士在奈良创立的"胡桃树"咖啡馆一条分店，简直是生活方式设计店的圣地，引来日本各地大量追随者的朝拜。如今咖啡馆迎来了第 33 个年头，依然人气不衰。石村女士总是爱把这家店称作"我的孩子"。

石村女士当初因为结婚而辞掉了在建筑商店负责店铺设计的工作，因为要生育，就从大阪搬到了奈良。没想到没多久，她在一条的铁道边，遇到了一间只开了一扇铁门的简朴小屋。石村女士从小就希望长大以后开一家让老爷爷、老奶奶还有小朋友大家都喜欢的店，而不可思议的是，在一条看到的这家店铺和石村女士小时候手绘日记里画的一模一样，简直是命中注定的相逢。手绘日记里还写了店铺的名字，就叫"胡桃树"。石村女士说，回想起决定开店的那一天，感觉从那天到现在就是一眨眼的工夫。"一路走来，我也不是一个人在培育'胡桃树'这个孩子，"石村女士认为，"一直都是奈良和我一起在照顾它，奈良就像是'胡桃树'的父亲。"（撰文：空闲 理）

Kuruminoki Ltd.
Yukiko Ishimura

1. A person who carefully designs the acts of dwelling, wearing, and eating in Nara Prefecture and communicates them attractively

2. A person who identifies the attractions of places that would overlook

3. A person who conveys the latest Japanese design to Nara locals

Yukiko Ishimura selects objects from all over Japan and the world and brings them to Nara to see if they fit here. She relishes the moments when she finds a perfect fit between Nara and her selected objects and she shares her discoveries with others. "Kuruminoki Ichijo Store," which she created, is like a "holy place" for design which people from all over Japan make pilgrimage to. Opened 33 years ago, its popularity refuses to wane. Ishimura calls "Kuruminoki" her child. She also says that in recollection, the time between her initial decision to open the business and now feels like a flash. I thought to myself, however, that she did not raise this child alone. Nara, who was always by her side, was the father of "Kuruminoki." (Osamu Kuga)

河濑直美

www.kawasenaomi.com

1. 出生并居住在奈良的电影人，
通过其作品将奈良的风景永久保存

她执导的电影大多发掘当地人来饰演主角。

无论是电影或宣传片都用"纪录片一般本真的声音"让观众产生共鸣。

2. 代表作《萌之朱雀》（1997年）、
《殡之森》（2007年）等都在奈良县取景

前者在当时的西吉野村拍摄，获得戛纳国际电影节金摄影机奖；

后者在奈良市拍摄，在戛纳得到了评审团大奖。

3. 她在自己的故乡发起了奈良国际电影节

河濑女士认为自己也是受到了电影节的栽培，

所以为操办电影节不遗余力。2016年第四届奈良电影节，

她也作为执行总监四处奔走。

她让世界听到奈良的声音 在奈良常住之后我才开始留意到身边的各种事情：天空的宽广、云朵的形态、树木的绿意、河川的夜色，还有透明感。我还热爱这里的自然，以及在这里生活着的奈良人。看了河濑女士执导的电影，这些自然和生活中的细节就会像走马灯一般生动地出现在脑海里。河濑女士说："有些风景就好像是特意为我们拍电影准备的一般，好几次都是拍摄完之后风景就突然消失了。"

河濑女士认为自己的处女作《拥抱》（1992年）不仅是她创作电影的原点，也是她人生的原点。在这之后，河濑女士创作的作品以纪录片为多，包括《拥抱》的续篇《在世界的沉默中》（2001年）等。甚至在观看剧情片《萌之朱雀》和

《殡之森》的时候，我也会有一种在看纪录片的感觉。可能是因为这两部电影中都有很多"细心聆听人物讲话的场面"，让人印象深刻。

在奈良拍摄电影时，河濑女士会请当地人来扮演主要的角色——祖母、父亲、母亲、姐姐、哥哥、妹妹、单相思者、不解风情的人、想见而见不到的人，或是永远不能再见的人。这些人的声音，还有那些无法用声音表达的"声音"，吸引着观众来到电影院，通过银幕来聆听这些听得到或听不到的声音。其实不只有人能发出"声音"，风也能，云也能，自然界到处都能听到各种声音。河濑女士的作品，会让耳朵在"奈良的声音"中得到净化，令人真想收拾行囊，直奔奈良而去。（撰文：空闲 理）

Naomi Kawase

1. A filmmaker born, raised, and lives in Nara, who immortalizes Nara's landscapes

2. She shot *The Mourning Forest* (2007) and *Moe no suzaku* (1997) in Nara Prefecture

3. She presented the idea of and realized the "Nara International Film Festival" in her hometown

When I watch films directed by Naomi Kawase, I vividly recall the various things, such as the expansiveness of the sky, beauty of the clouds, greenness of the trees, blueness of the river, their transparency, and the people who love nature and live in Nara, which I only became aware of after long stays in Nara. Kawase states that in fact, "There have been many sceneries that disappeared immediately after I filmed them. It was as if they were waiting to be preserved as an image." She casts locals in the key roles of her films, which are set in Nara. They play grandmother, father, mother, sister, brother, someone who has fallen in love, someone who cannot reciprocate love, someone who you cannot see even though you want to, and someone you can no longer see. Viewers confront the screen to pick up their voices and other soundless voices. I aspire to travel through Nara keeping my ears open to something like Nara's voice, as if I were watching a Kawase film. (Osamu Kuga)

Nara Hotel

147

空闲之旅 I

主编的奈良之旅

Osamu Kuga
空闲 理

Kuga Travel 1: Editor's Travel Notes

By Osamu Kuga

在我心中，奈良县就像一条贯穿南北的大道，越往南就越接近保存完好的古代历史，而越向北走，则越接近现代世界。奈良县的最南端有日本最大的村庄十津川村，它与横跨和歌山县及三重县的熊野地区接壤。神话中第一代日本天皇神武天皇就是在熊野遇到了为他指路的八咫乌，将他带到大和国（现在的奈良县）。他们翻越了崇山峻岭，终于到达了吉野山——这里至今仍是赏樱胜地。从现在的地图上看，吉野町位于奈良县最中心的位置。

按照神话的描述，神武天皇继续北上，到达现在橿原市所在的位置，在大和三山[10]之一的亩傍山脚下修建了橿原宫，并在公元前660年左右即位，成为第一代天皇。《日本书纪》中也将橿原记载为日本的建国之地。在今天的橿原市，还能见到在1890年为纪念神武天皇而修建的橿原神宫，以及神武天皇的古皇陵等古迹。古代的神话和真实的历史在这里交会融合，令人着迷。另外，在我看来，橿原和

吉野之间的边界将奈良现在的文化圈分为南北两派，我斗胆认为，此地以南为"山野文化"，以北则是"都城文化"（皇都就在北边）。而位于奈良县正中心位置的吉野地区，在后来的历史进程中，因为室町时代的后醍醐天皇在此建立南朝政权的关系，山野文化和都城文化就在这里相互融合，因此这些地区还夹带着一些有趣的无政府主义元素。

话说回来，日本的历史从熊野发源，经由吉野再到橿原，就是从古坟时代向飞鸟时代的演进。飞鸟京在橿原市以西，也就是现在的明日香村，这里曾是日本历史中的超级巨星圣德太子以及苏我氏家族活跃过的历史舞台。公元694年建成的藤原京，是日本历史上第一座按照条坊制布局的都城，位于现在的橿原市稍稍往南的位置。再后来，公元710年迁都平城京，也就是现在的奈良市，这里就接近现在奈良县的最北端了。到了公元794年，又稍稍往北一些，迁都至平安京，那就是现在的京都了。

(→p. 078)

但令我感到有趣的是，现代人对于"现代奈良"的印象多是大佛、东大寺的鹿、奈良公园等奈良市内的部分，并不会想到平城京以北的地区，而是将视线全部集中在东部。奈良似乎从由南往北再往北的日本历史舞台中飞脱出去了，并没有随着时代的脚步走向未来，而是选择保持原貌，停留在奈良时代，"奈良"这个名字就好像一个封印，把历史封存在这个地方。

借着采访的机会，"空闲之旅"将分上下两部分，逐一为大家介绍我在从南到北探索奈良的过程中去过的名胜和名店。

通向十津川村的奈良南部之旅

从编辑部所在的东京市世田谷区出发到奈良县，需要先搭乘新干线到京都站，然后在京都换乘近铁特快列车。在京都站新干线换乘近铁的闸口，摆放着一个奈良县的吉祥

divided culturally into north and south. To be precise, the south of Yoshino and Kashihara is the mountain culture, and north of these towns is the culture of *miyako* — the emperor's capital. In the year 710, Heijyokyo's capital was changed — when the capital relocated from Kyoto to Nara. Nara City is situated at the northernmost edge of Nara Prefecture. Further north is Kyoto, which became a capital in 794.

I will be dividing this article in two to introduce shops and tourist spots of Nara Prefecture from the south to the north.

Travel through southern Nara: Totsukawa Village

From Tokyo to Nara, we have to take the *Shinkansen* to Kyoto from Tokyo and then transfer to Kintetsu Tokkyu Express at Kyoto, which costs 1130 yen, and only takes 30 minutes between Kyoto Station and Nara Station. Right by the Nara Park, near the station, is where we can find some of the major shops and neighborhoods Nara is known for, but I bypassed this so I could rent a car and drive south.

The drive from Nara city center to the "Doro Hotel" — the former hotel turned café and the *d mark* shop — took nearly

物"迁都君"欢迎到访的客人。近铁特快列车的票价为 1 130 日元，30 分钟左右就能到达奈良站。奈良站靠近奈良公园，这一带有众多奈良标志性的景点。但我们这次的目的地是奈良县的最南端，所以我径直去附近的汽车租赁店租了车，随即出发。

在奈良境内自驾出行很少用到高速路，大家都是不紧不慢地走马观花。路上经常会遇到车多拥挤的情况，通常都会比导航的时间迟一些才能到达目的地，所以在做计划的时候最好多留一些提前量。这里的地名常用到一些生僻的汉字，常常有人因为不会念而无法输入正确的导航地址，因此，出发之前最好做足准备。

从奈良市到奈良 d 标总览最南边的目的地濑酒店，开车需要 3 小时以上。我们沿着清澈见底的河道行驶，遇到可以停车的地方就稍作休息。时值盛夏，我们脱了鞋赤脚走在河里解暑，凉爽的河水舒服极了，但湿了脚没法继续赶路就麻烦了。幸好手边带了一条"白雪布巾"

的手帕，吸水性好，又干得快，十分方便。

越往奈良县的南边走，河流的水量越发丰沛。河流清澈见底，让我情不自禁地连连感叹山川的秀丽，自然的美好。渐渐地，水流变得湍急，能看到巨木和巨石被激流冲走的痕迹，台风吹过后光秃秃的岩壁显得十分醒目。十津川村的附近被称为"奥吉野"（即吉野的深处），属于台风频发、降雨丰沛的地区。

一段漫长的山路戛然而止，眼前豁然开朗，我们又重新回到晴朗的天空下。不知不觉之间，我们已经进入了和歌山县境内。经过了熊野本宫大社，到濑酒店还有大约 30 分钟的路程。当我们再次回到奈良县内，著名景点"濑峡"赫然出现在我们面前。俯瞰濑峡，它比想象中更壮观，河水也清澈得超乎想象。看到了这风景，车上的大家都觉得这个远路绕得值了！我们沿山路下行，驶近河流，河水清澈到可以见到鲇鱼在水里游泳，观光船上坐满了兴奋的游人，个个脸上都洋溢着喜悦的笑容。

three and a half hours. A long winding drive through the mountains ended all too suddenly, and I unexpectedly found myself under the bright blue sky. Before I knew it, I had crossed into Wakayama Prefecture, and once I passed Kumano Hongu Taisha Shrine, I was only thirty minutes away from the "Doro Hotel." I once again entered Nara Prefecture and was in awe of the view — valleys and the sparkling river down below — and once I got down to the riverbank, I could clearly see fish swimming in the water. Everyone on boats and canoes looked content. It is worth the drive to see this view.

Once in Totsukawa Village, you must go see Tanize's Suspended Bridge, which spans 300m across and 50m up in the air. To be honest, it's very scary. The wood looks rather flimsy, and there's no limit to how many people can be on it at the same time. Several times, I seriously feared for my life when the bridge shook so much. The worst was when a group was coming toward me. The only thing I could do was to stand still and wait for them to pass. Once I made it across, the sense of accomplishment was beyond words, but that's before I remembered that I had to go back on the bridge. I was still just as (→p. 080)

向北回到十津川村武藏，我们借宿在 d 标总览中曾经介绍过的民宿大森之乡。这一带虽然地处深山，却可以搭乘奈良交通公司的巴士到达。以一头奔跑的小鹿作为商标的奈良交通公司运营着日本最长的巴士线路，驶经奈良的各个地方。

到了十津川村就一定要去一下著名的古濑吊桥。桥高超过 50 米，单程约 300 米长，说实话挺叫人害怕的。脚下的木板踩着不踏实，桥上也不限制人数，不断有人从桥上经过，桥身就不停地颤动摇摆，让我担心自己真有可能会掉下桥去。每当前面有大队人马接近的时候，我只敢纹丝不动地站在原地，等他们经过我之后再继续向前。终于到达对岸时，我心中不禁腾起一股骄傲的成就感，完全忘记了还要原路返回。回来的路还是和去时一样的可怕，半点也没减少。然而，对于当地人而言，这是他们每天生活的必经之路。吊桥上还贴着"禁止游客在吊桥上骑单车"的警示牌。别以为这是开玩笑，当地人可真的是骑着单车、开着摩托，驾轻就熟地从桥上通过的。

古濑吊桥的脚下有一间风景不错的咖啡馆，实在恐高的朋友不如在这里坐坐，等着你勇敢的朋友们探险归来，那样也不错。（要问我是怎么知道这个去处的，我可不会告诉你是因为我们编辑部的佐佐木小姐半路吓得跑了回来，就在这个咖啡店里喝着咖啡等我们。）

十津川村这个名字，总让人联想起西村京太郎先生 1973 年起开始连载的推理小说"十津川警督"系列。西村先生有一次到访十津川，住在一家旅馆中，每天剪贴报纸寻找灵感。据西村先生说，当时他想为主人公取一个令人记忆深刻、明快又有力的名字，随手摊开地图就看到了"十津川"，于是他的主人公就得到了"十津川省三"这个名字。不过事实上，住在十津川村子一带的人，并没有姓十津川的。

scared going back, unfortunately. Locals use this bridge several times a day to come and go, and there's a warning to tourists not to ride their bicycles. It's not a joke: locals take their bicycles and motorcycles across this flimsy bridge. There's a café by the bridge, so if you are afraid of heights, you can sip coffee as you wait for your friends to come back.

Central Nara: Yoshino Mountains
I drove north toward Kawakami Village to stay at "Asahikan," a 140-year-old hotel. The hotel, constructed during the Taisho Era, is built along the hill. In order to reach the garden, you have to go up to the second floor. Located at the bottom of Mount Omine, the hotel was originally a place for pilgrims and ascetics. Now, it's for hikers and climbers and it serves very good *ayu* fish. It also allows single travelers to stay.

Kawakami Village is also known for Otaki-chaya, which is known for its delicious *Kakinoha* sushi (Persimmon Leaf Sushi). Mackerel is sliced very thinly, just like they did in the past. This restaurant also uses disposable chopsticks made out of Yoshino pine from Kawakami Village. One can't talk about (→p. 082)

前往吉野山的奈良中部之旅

我们一路向北来到川上村，住进了开店已有约 140 年之久的老店朝日馆。大正时代的房子在一个陡坡上依势而建，从一楼走上二楼，二楼的窗外才是庭院，这种少见的设计十分有趣。旅馆建在大峰山的登山入口处，原本就是为方便登山者投宿而建的。现在，这里的登山客仍络绎不绝，还可以尝到旅馆美味的鲇鱼。独自旅行的人也可以在这里住宿，这是个充满欢乐的老店。

说起川上村，就一定要去大泷茶屋品尝最美味的柿叶寿司。薄薄的鲭鱼片从开店到现在从没变样。这是家正统、清爽的名店，店内的一次性筷子都是用川上村产的吉野杉木做的。吉野杉是日本文化中不可缺少的优质木材，是制作各种传统桶类容器的材料（详见 p98 文章介绍）。在"日本视野"（NIPPON VISION）中关于吉野杉的采访中，我们重点介绍了位于吉野

町吉野川沿岸、收集吉野杉木和吉野桧木的吉野储木场。我们去采访时刚好遇上他们在为当月的"原木市集"做准备，大量的杉木和桧木堆在岸边，从对岸就能看见。当时的场景也被详细地记载在当地木材从业者组成的团体"Re: 吉野生活会"发行的《储木书》上。

吉野储木场的历史、日常的运作，甚至这里每一个储木工匠的个性和想法，都被详尽而朴实地记录了在刊物中。如此精心的编撰让人想亲自去储木场看一看，或是先去他们的网站看一看。刊物和网页的内容都是由"吉野町地区共济合作队"的成员渡会奈央女士和野口明日香女士发起的"发条堂"协助编撰的。

我们在吉野做采访时，就住在渡会女士管理的旅馆三奇楼里。这个古建筑原来是一家餐厅，后来用吉野杉木和桧木进行了翻新，现在作为旅馆，可以让住客体验在本地定居的感觉，同时也是吉野木材的展示空间。你可以下到吉野川的河岸和朋友们一起野炊烧烤。附近也有

Japanese crafts without mentioning Yoshino pine. For more details, please read "Nippon Vision" on page 98.

We featured Yoshino Choboku, the lumber storage area, when we visited the Yoshino pines along Yoshino River in Yoshino Town for the "Nippon Vision" article. At the time we visited, they were preparing for the lumber festival so there were many pines and Japanese cypresses lying about. Do read this month's issue of *Choboku Book*, published by "Re: Yoshino to Kurasu Kai." There are many interesting articles about the history of Yoshino Choboku, the daily life, and the people working there. Once you

read these articles, you will want to visit, and if that's the case, do go visit their website, *Yoshino Choboku: Ki no Machi no Kurashi* (*Yoshino Choboku: Life Amongst the Trees*). The website, as well as the book, is produced by "Nejimaki-do," the duo composed of Nao Watarai and Asuka Noguchi, who moved to Yoshino Town and joined *Yoshinocho: Chiiki Okoshi Kyoryokutai* (Yoshino Regional Revitalization Volunteer Group).

The very same Nao Watarai manages "Sankirou," a guesthouse, and that's where we stayed while we were researching Yoshino. A former high-end restaurant,　(→p. 084)

酒厂，我在那儿买到了当地出产的酒，还用吉野杉木做的枡（方形的日本酒盛器）品尝了本地佳酿。三奇楼旅馆的客房都是独立的房间，住在属于自己的私密空间里，轻松自在，一晚住宿 4 000 日元起。第二天吃早餐之前，我在小巷错综复杂的街区里穿行，看到了很多残存的古旧建筑，心潮澎湃。小镇的最高处是一片墓地，在那里可以俯瞰整个小镇。横跨吉野川的铁桥上的近铁列车正平稳前行，行驶的前方正是吉野山。在下一辆列车通过之前，我可以惬意地欣赏这让人安静的风景。清晨的河堤上有人在捡垃圾，有人在钓鲇鱼，还能望见吉野储木场的屋顶。忽然吹来一阵清风，我心中不禁赞叹：这样的小镇还真是不错呢。

橿原市和明日香村——日本历史的第一现场

在明日香村的住宿就选在橿原市橿原神

they renovated it using Yoshino pine and Japanese cypress. It is a guesthouse where you can try out what it would feel like to move here, and it serves as a showroom for Yoshino lumber as well. You can go down to the riverbank and barbecue with a view of the river. I went to the nearby sake brewery, bought a local sake, and drank it out of a wooden cup made of Yoshino pine. The rooms are all private, not shared, and the cost is 4,000 yen per night (without dinner or breakfast). The next morning, when I went searching for breakfast in the neighborhood, I kept coming across these

宫前站附近。不用说，清早在橿原神宫散步是再惬意不过的事了。神宫周围还有巨大的公园、体育馆、博物馆等等，气氛跟东京的明治神宫外苑地区颇为相似。

夜晚的时候，我和住处附近一个酒吧的老板约好了去喝酒。酒吧里精选了各地，包括本地的好酒，店主还把行走四方的好酒之徒才会知道的下酒小菜盛得满满地拿出来招待客人。洗手间的墙壁上贴满了店主去各地旅行时从当地的知名餐馆、酒吧带回来的杯垫，我还在其中找到了我们在《d设计之旅：东京》中采访过的新宿三丁目的Donzoko酒吧的杯垫。听店主说他是40年前去的，而现在那家店还在使用同样的杯垫，这样的巧合真是让人莫名地欣喜。

第二天，我驾驶着d标总览中介绍的MICHIMO超小型租赁电动车在明日香村享受了愉快的旅程。我在一天时间里参观了许多景点，包括公元596年建成的日本最古老

的飞鸟寺，同样是日本最古老的、开光已有1400年以上的释迦牟尼像，在圣德太子出生地建造的橘寺，在大化改新前夜被暗杀的苏我入鹿[11]的首冢，以五彩壁画闻名的高松冢古坟，等等。

走过这些遗迹，我重新认识到，虽然通过博物馆或资料馆中的展览也可以了解关于历史的点滴，但是亲身到访"第一现场"，用自己的双眼去发现，还是意义非凡。

明日香村的行程结束之后，我无论如何都想在日落前赶到甘樫丘展望台。那里的山脚下据说曾是苏我家族的宅邸。登上丘顶，看着夕阳落进远处的大和三山（橿原市内三座山的总称，包括香具山、亩傍山、耳成山），回想整整一天见识的飞鸟的历史，有一种融入其中的感觉。

如果你在周五到访明日香村，可以去每周都在明日香梦之自由市场举办的明日香有机市场逛逛。一大早新鲜采摘的本地有机蔬

amazing old buildings that made my heart beat faster from excitement. There is a graveyard at the highest part of the village — from there, I saw a Kintetsu train crossing the bridge slowly heading toward Mount Yoshino. I could have sat there all day long. Beginning in the early morning, people were picking up garbage on the riverbank and fishing for *ayu*. Beyond them were the roofs of the Yoshino Choboku lumber mills. The breeze passed above all this. It was a beautiful morning.

The Historical Place: Kashihara City and Asuka Village
I stayed near the Kashiharajingu-mae Station in Kashihara City to go to Asuka Village. Needless to say, an early morning walk through Kashihara Shrine was a treat. I drove a "MICHIMO" (a d mark car) to Asuka Village to visit Asuka Temple, the oldest temple in Japan, built in 596, and the Buddha statue that was made more than 1400 years ago and housed in the temple. There are many more. It's not a bad idea to learn all this through exhibitions in museums and archives, but it takes a while to sort out all the information in our heads; maybe it is better to go (→p. 086)

菜整齐地摆放在帐篷下的摊档上。光顾的客人多是本地餐厅的主厨或店主。从这里采购的蔬菜，会变成这个周末的特别菜式端上餐桌，出现在食客面前。真是完美的流水线！所以说，每周五晚上，在明日香、橿原周边地区比较有本地意识的餐厅尝到新鲜本地蔬菜的可能性特别大！我在明日香有机市场遇到了田村光史先生，于是去了他掌勺的时令菜中餐馆"旬菜·中华 Bar Mitsukan"吃饭。田村先生的店在八木站附近，店里还有丰富的藏酒。店里的当日精选蔬菜沙拉、特制麻婆豆腐都是必点的美味。这家店在当地颇有人气，想去的话最好提早预约。

樱井市——去山边小径漫步

到了樱井市，就会想把汽车抛在一边，用双脚丈量一下土地。这附近有许多适合徒步的山边小径。所谓"山边小径"其实是堪称日本最古老的一条山间步道，从日本最古老的神社之一大神神社所供奉的三轮山山脚下出发，一路从南到北延伸到奈良市春日山的山麓。

沿途并没有整修妥善的步道，多半是自然形成的土路和砂石路。有些路段还有被草木覆盖的部分，一不留神就容易走岔了。尽管如此，在从樱井站到大神神社的数公里路上漫步，周围有花儿的芬芳、小草的清香，还有小鸟和动物出没。阳光灿烂也好，细雨蒙蒙也好，你能真切地感受到，自己完全置身于大自然中，这感觉简直无与伦比！放眼望去，无垠的天空下，云朵似乎正往三轮山飘去，美丽的景色同样令人着迷。

去往曾尔高原的路

虽然本期的"空闲之旅"的宗旨是"从南到北追寻奈良历史的足印"，但是我无论如何

there yourself and see with your own eyes. At least that's what I was reminded of when I was there.

Don't forget to visit "Amakashi no Oka" at the sunset. When I saw the sun setting behind the Yamato Mountains, all the history of Asuka I had learned in one day seemed to become part of me.

If you visit Asuka Village on Fridays, do visit "Asuka Bio Marche," an outdoor market held every Friday at "Asuka Yume no Rakuichi." Organic vegetables grown in the area are on sale here, and many of the shoppers who come here own restaurants and cafes, serving dishes made out of the vegetables bought here over the weekend. This means that you can eat delicious Yamato vegetables at slow-food restaurants in the area on Friday nights. I myself went to the Chinese Bar, "Mitsukan," near Yamato Yagi Station, owned by Koji Tamura, whom I had met at the market that day. Their salad-of-the-day and renowned Mapo Tofu is worth the trip, but be sure to make reservations, for it's a very popular restaurant.

Sakurai City: A Hiking Trip
When you visit Sakurai City, be sure to leave your car (→p. 088)

也想给大家介绍一下由樱井市一路向东的曾尔高原。

我先是开车前往宇陀市，经过 30 分钟左右的车程，来到了被幽深的溪谷包围着的室生寺。走进森林的深处，来到奈良时代末期（也存在其他说法）始建、平安时代初期建成的室生寺的秘境。内院中的一处，长满了热带蕨类植物。这景象让人联想起奈良县安堵出身的陶艺家富本宪吉先生具有代表性的羊齿草花纹。富本先生擅长将故乡的景色转化成原创的设计纹样。也许他创作羊齿草花纹的时候也到访过室生寺吧。

回到宇陀松山城的旧城市中心，我穿过大宇陀一排排的老街区，商店门前挂着的麻制门帘在风中轻轻摇曳，让人感到一阵清凉。这里有超过 450 年历史的传统老店"森野吉野葛本铺"，后山上还有种植着 250 种草药的草药园。我在店里买了包装精美的葛汤。说到大宇陀的美味土特产，一定要提一提松月堂的甜点

Kimigo-romo——用蛋清打泡后加琼脂定型，外层包裹蛋黄，然后烤制成酥皮的点心，淡雅的甜味包裹着柔软的口感。

在快要到达曾尔高原的地方有一家当地的啤酒厂。把啤酒厂建在这里，可能是因为曾尔村水质清甜的关系吧。穿过啤酒厂就能看到一个名叫"钱之花"的摊档，一定要尝一尝那里卖的草饼，简直是无比的美味。店主每天都用新鲜采摘的艾草和馅料制成草饼，颜色鲜艳，香糯软黏，好吃到上瘾。这个铺子开业至今已有 25 年，真希望这美味可以一直保持下去。

我们终于来到了曾尔高原。如果是秋季，能在这里看到一片金黄色的芒草，尤其夕阳西下时的壮丽景象，是出了名的人气景点。我去的时候是夏天，游人稀少，但我很庆幸看到了不一样的曾尔高原。芒草还是鲜亮的绿色，反射着仲夏猛烈的日光，一阵风吹过，好像银色的波涛泛起。在那中间有一条白色

in the parking lot and walk around. There are enough hiking trails to explore, and one of the oldest paths connects Omiwa Shrine atop Mount Miwa to Mount Asuka in Nara City, connecting north and south. It is not a paved path, but is a trail that disappears in some places if you are not paying attention. However, you can feel the breeze and the rain and the sun and feel the presence of animals and birds, as if you are getting closer to nature.

The Road to Soni Plateau

This issue's concept for "Kuga Travel" is "Nara, from South to

North, and to further North, " but there is a place that I would like to introduce, even though it's situated to the east of Sakurai City. So, I headed toward Soni Plateau.

I passed through the old neighborhood of the Udamatsuyama Castle, where shop entrances were adorned with hemp curtains. "Morino Yoshino Kuzu Honpo," a herbal shop, has been here for nearly 450 years, and the hill behind it is a herbal garden with nearly 250 herbs growing there. I bought a stomach medicine wrapped in a beautiful wrapper as a gift to take home. The iconic gifts from Ouda are *Kimigoromo* from "Shogetsudo." Made out

的路，我感觉自己是走在光和风的混沌中，却又好像是漫步在大海上，或在云端一般飘飘欲仙。这般美景，也是奈良"南北通途"之外一定要介绍给大家的。

of yolk, it is not just beautiful to see but also sweet and soft.

There is a beer brewery right before arriving at the Soni Plateau. Maybe Soni Village has good water. Right across from the brewery is "Zeni no Hana," a stall that sells *kusamochi*, a must for everyone. The owners harvest the *Yomogi* plant and cook it with freshly made sticky rice every morning. The emerald color of *yomogi*. The softness of sticky rice cake. You'll surely want not just one but two or three.

Finally, I arrived at the Soni Plateau. When you come here in the autumn, the entire field is covered in golden *susuki* and it is a very popular tourist destination, but I went there in summer so there were not too many people around. But that suited me perfectly. I got to see a different view of the Soni Plateau when the *susuki* was still green and it looked silver under the bright summer sun. In the middle was a white path. It was as if I was walking amidst the light and wind. Or maybe I was walking on the surface of the sea, or the clouds. It felt so perfect. This, too, is the path one should walk if you are in Nara.

坂本大三郎（山伏[12]）
Daizaburo Sakamoto

奈良县的长青祭典

『面白』的庆典

据说能剧起源于奈良。更早的时候，"散乐"由遥远的东亚大陆经海上传来日本。到了平安时代，散乐和本地的民间艺术融合，形成了"猿乐"与"田乐"。表演者聚集在寺庙和神社的庆典上，演出祭典仪式。日本南北朝时代结束后，室町时代开始时，这种艺术形式得到了朝廷和上层阶级的保护，表演者的技艺也因此有机会得到磨炼和精进。其中，大和猿乐剧团之首观四座的演员、剧作家世阿弥，经历了各种曲折，终于使"能"的艺术性得到确立，将猿乐改革为我们今天所熟悉的能剧。

世阿弥在其所著的《风姿花传》中，记录了他对技艺的领会和理解。传说天照大神将自己关进天岩户的洞窟里闭门不出，于是大家在洞口跳起"神乐"，将歌舞奉献给神。太阳之神被人们的表演吸引，于是再度现身洞外。就在这时，聚集在洞口的人们突然被神的光芒照亮，众人欣喜，脸上都映射出白光。所以后来日语

Long Lasting Festival in Nara

An "Amusing" Festival

By Daizaburo Sakamoto

Nara is said to be the birthplace of Noh. Noh has its origins in *sangaku*, an ancient Chinese art, which came along distance from the West of Japan, Asia. Once in Japan, it was combined with local native arts to become *sarugaku*, which was centered on humorous wordplay and impersonation, and *dengaku*, which consisted primarily of songs and dances performed with wind instruments and percussions as agricultural ceremonies. Their practitioners are said to have congregated and performed at shrine and temple festivals. When the Period of Northern and Southern Courts ended and the Muromachi Period began, the same practitioners gained the support of the shogunate and other influential figures and their art became more refined. The art, which came out of Yamato sarugaku practiced by the Yuzaki-za sarugaku troupe and established by Zeami, turned, after many twists and turns, into what we know as "Noh" today.

里"有趣"的意思，就用"面白"两个汉字来表达。

　　我总认为庆典艺术是以宗教和信仰为背景，在自然和乡土的结合中被创作出来的。而在信仰和宗教被弱化变得淡薄的今天，我又在思考应该如何重新审视表演艺术和传统庆典。我认为世阿弥的话也许蕴含了重要的提示。

　　太阳给予生命力量和养分，是自然的象征。在我看来，世阿弥的话是想说明，人内心的欢乐，源自与自然的交流和共鸣，艺术和表演也都应以此为根本。

　　我虽然未曾信仰任何宗教，但当我亲近艺术，参加表演或庆典时，内心和身体都能切实地体会到快乐。如果像世阿弥所述，能剧、表演和庆典都是为了让人们亲近自然而诞生的艺术，那我也愿意信仰这种艺术。

Zeami wrote about the secrets of his art in his classic text *The Flowering Spirit*. This art was carried out as Shinto music and dance, which took the myth of the sun as its theme, at "Amanoiwato" (the heavenly rock cave). By dedicating these performances to the sun god hiding in the cave, the performers lured the sun out of hiding. The faces of the people who had gathered to watch the performance were suddenly exposed to light. The faces were thus white, and hence amusing (the two Chinese characters that constitute the word "amusing" in Japanese are "face" and "white").

I believe that festivals produced connections, through religious contexts, between people and their land, that is, their local natural environment. When I think about what the arts and festivals can provide in the contemporary period, in which religious faith has been all but dismantled, I feel Zeami's words are pregnant with important meaning.

The sun is a symbol of nature that gives and nurtures life. I think that in the words above, Zeami is saying that in finding the arts "amusing", we can see that the arts are fundamentally connected to nature. I don't accept religion uncritically, but I do believe in my emotional and physical "amusement," which is a response I have when I see or create some artworks, festivals, and performances.

奈良县的民艺

富本宪吉的

『做花样不耍花样』

高木崇雄（「工艺风向」创办人）

Takao Takaki（Foucault）

Mingei of Nara

Kenkichi Tomitomo's "Making Invisible Patterns"

By Takao Takaki（Foucault）

已故陶艺家富本宪吉先生 1886 年生于奈良县生驹郡安堵町（出生时为安堵村）。安堵村靠近法隆寺，丰饶的土地培育了少年富本。自幼学习画画的富本，长大后去了东京美术学校（现东京艺术大学）深造。上学时他得知了威廉·莫里斯领导的、倡导手工艺回归生活的"艺术与工艺美术运动"，热心于此的他最终选择自费去英国留学。

在学成归国的船上，富本又通过英国陶艺大师伯纳德·里奇结识了柳宗悦。两人在关于新手工艺发展的话题上一拍即合。1926 年 4 月，富本宪吉、柳宗悦、滨田庄司和河井宽次郎联名发表了《日本民艺美术馆创办意向书》。后来富本先生作为彩绘陶瓷艺术家被认定为"重要非物质文化遗产保有人"，也就是大家所说的"人间国宝"，所以他也被誉为"日本民艺之父"。

富本先生留下过这样一句名言："做花样不耍花样。"这句话与《d 设计之旅：京都》中提到的河井宽次郎先生所说的"工作本身会工作"有异曲同工之妙。一个简单词语，在同一个句子中却有不同的含义，似是艺术家在尝试参透世间的深意，两句都是精彩的金句。也正是遵循着自己的理念，富本先生创作的纹样，都是借鉴自然中

The pottery maker, Kenkichi Tomimoto, was born in Ando-cho, Ikoma-gun in Nara Prefecture in 1886. He grew up near Horyuji Temple in Ando Town; his childhood was spent drawing pictures, which later led him to go to Tokyo School of Fine Art, where he was influenced by William Morris. He learned of the Arts and Crafts Movement, which led him to study abroad in England to learn more about it.

Through Bernard Leach, whom he met aboard the ship on his way home, he connected with Muneyoshi Yanagi, one of the founding fathers of the Japanese *Mingei* Movement.

When *Nihon Mingei Bijutsukan Setsuritsu Shuisho* (*The Proposal for Establishment of Mingei Museum*) was published in April of 1926, Tomimoto's name was alongside Yanagi's, together with Shoji Hamada and Kanjiro Kawai. Tomimoto, who was later named the Living National Treasure for his contribution to ceramic painting, was indeed one of the founding fathers of the *Mingei* Movement.

When Tomimoto painted patterns on pottery, he wasn't coming up with anything new or shocking. For Tomimoto, all the new patterns could be found everywhere in nature. (→p. 094)

已有的样子，将自然的纹理融入自己的设计中，并不断地延展，使之成为更丰富的新的纹样。

然而，在创作新的纹样时，富本先生绝不会刻意地加入毫不搭界的元素，也不会异想天开地创作一些单纯满足自我表现的东西。反倒是像柳宗悦对他的评论那样："一个好的陶艺作者就是要相信自然中涌动的力量。""在这个信仰崩塌的时代，富本先生的作品唤醒了人们对自然的崇敬。"为了创作出全新的原创作品，富本先生反其道而行之，从原本就存在于我们周围却最容易被忽视的自然环境中去寻找灵感。

有一次滨田庄司去富本家做客，家中突然飞进了一只漂亮的蛾子。富本先生即刻画起了草图，不一会儿就完成了一个新的花纹样式，这使得滨田先生对富本先生的功力赞不绝口。从这件逸事可以看得出，对于生活环境中的花草、动物，还有人们在日常生活中的样子，富本先生不仅了解，更是用自己的双眼细致入微地去观察。然后，他用手将双眼所见画出来，再加入自己的审美，便将隐藏在自然中的美的元素通过纹样表现了出来。

正因为如此，富本先生创作的纹样并不只是

Shoji Hamada tells a story of how when a beautiful and unfamiliar moth flew into Tomimoto's house, Tomimoto started sketching and created a new pattern. From this anecdote, we can see how Tomimoto observed and took in everything from his everyday life, things that people may ignore from familiarity — plants, flowers, animals, and people. And whatever he saw, he sketched, and by reorganizing them in his head, he brought out the beautiful essences of nature to transform them into "patterns."

For that reason, Tomimoto's patterns aren't just ornaments. His patterns embody the rhythm of nature, the very essence of life. Every life has rhythm, and it transforms into visual pattern in Tomimoto's hand. These patterns are what Tomimoto and Yanagi pursued all their lives. Therefore, patterns can't be created out of thin air. A thing taken for granted from its familiarity must be noticed, must be observed, and reduced down to its essence in our heads, and recreated it into patterns.

Tomimoto wove together the history of Nara, people's lives, and nature to create "patterns," and his words reflect

单纯的装饰图案。正如柳宗悦先生所说："纹样记录了生命的样子，没有生命感就不成为纹样。"自然中的所有生物都有生命的律动。截取这律动中的一帧帧画面，就成了纹样。无论富本先生还是柳宗悦先生，他们的作品都是对此最好的实践。

所以说，纹样图案不是简单地一拍脑袋就能做出来的。就算看似妙手偶得、信手拈来，但其实最稀松平常的事物才最容易被忽视，所以只有靠每天的细致观察才能有所发现。

富本先生曾经用"安堵久左卫门"这个笔名，将安堵这个地方称作"产土"，即出产美物

的沃土。富本先生在这里终其一生，用自己对这片土地的爱，将奈良的历史、人们的生活，以及大自然的律动，编织成历久弥新的美丽纹样。从富本先生的话里也能读出他的生活原则：从他人那里获得知识时从不会投机取巧，而是脚踏实地靠自己的眼睛去捕捉世界，活出自己的生命节奏。

从纹样中，人可以看到一个比人类社会更广阔的世界。从美丽的纹样中，我们开始接触到美之奥义的冰山一角。

我也要去寻找和创造我生命中新的"纹样"。

his down-to-earth philosophy that could only be earned through observation and experience.

Through patterns, people observe the world bigger than humanity.

Through beautiful patterns do we get a glimpse of the mystery of beauty.

I, too, need to discover new pattern.

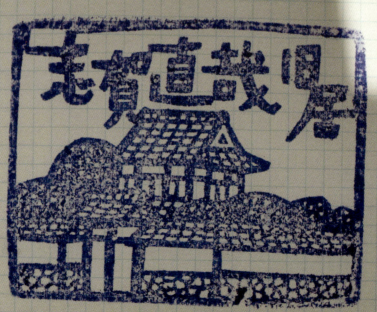

NIPPON VISION

野口忠典（d47 design travel store）

日本视野

NIPPON VISION

Tadanori Noguchi

奈良县的长效设计产地巡礼

我首先来到的是三乡町和御所市附近。从江户时代起，这里的农家就会在农闲时制作草履[13]和鼻绪[14]，现在，这里也是麻制拖鞋、塑料成型凉鞋及草履的重要产地。最让我感兴趣的是，在三乡町乃至全国的幼儿园及中小学都普遍推广的一款朴素的草履——Kenko Misatokko[15]，这款鞋是由倡导"足育"，即"促进健康要从脚下做起"的兵库教育大学名誉教授原田硕三先生和Misato鞋业联合会共同开发的，从1982年延续至今。校园中每天用到的东西，传承着本地的故事，这种古为今用的尝试真是了不起。

我还去了三乡町的Cafe Funchana，那里卖的Design Setta Sango雪驮[16]华丽又可爱，深得我心。咖啡店的主人星田和彦先生和妻子纯子女士正是雪驮的设计者。为了促进本地产业长久持续的发展，夫妇俩在设计上费尽心思，例如选用富有时尚感的复古土布来做鼻绪等。

第二天的目的地是吉野。奈良县政府的林业职员野口贵士先生，还有致力于宣传吉野地方文化和产业的Re: 吉野生活会的桝谷纪惠女

A Pilgrimage Tour of Nara Prefecture's Long-Lasting Designs

NIPPON VISION

By Tadanori Noguchi

The first thing I did was to head toward Sango and Gose. During the Edo period, farmers in this area were known to have made woven sandals and sandal thongs when not farming. Today, they make plastic sandals and casual sandals.

Another place I was curious to go see was "Design Setta Sango," a company that makes *setta*-sandals of lovely design, and to "Café Funchana" in Sango town, where they sell these sandals. Junko and Kazuhiko Hoshida, the designer couple who also owns the cafe, worked with the local *setta*-sandal makers to create a new line of sandals that featured vintage cloth for thongs as well as their design, creating a business model that will sustain the local artisanal industry.

On the second day, I headed toward Yoshino to meet with Takashi Noguchi, the Nara Prefecture Forestry Department official, and Norie Masutani, who is the member of "Re: Yoshino to Kurasu (→p. 100)

DESIGN SETTA SANGO
复古系列
GERMAN SCHOKOLADE　中码　6 480日元
DESIGN SETTA SANGO
Vintage Series
GERMAN SCHOKLOADE Size M ¥6,480

DESIGN SETTA SANGO®
CAFE FUNCHANA & WASABIYA   MADE IN JAPAN

士接待了我，带我走访了川上村等地。

　　吉野的林业发展可以追溯到室町时代，这里每公顷土地上种植有约一万棵杉树（是一般种植密度的两倍以上）。高密度的种植迫使木材笔直而缓慢地生长。一棵杉树长成可用之材需要五百年，即使是提前采伐的间伐木也有两百年树龄，是可以用来筑屋建楼的珍贵木材。

　　吉野杉被用作建材之前，是制作酒桶的樽丸。木桩被切割成弧形的小木条，待用的木条被捆成圆筒形，故而得名"樽丸"。做樽丸剩下的边角料后来被加工成筷子，并发展成产业。d47 食堂所用的一次性筷子就来自这里的芳本制作所。芳本昭德先生说，虽然周围漫山遍野都种着杉树、桧木，但由于日本对建筑木材和酒桶的需求减少，边角料也正随之变少，很难在本地找到制作筷子的原料。因此，在一次性筷子几乎全靠进口的现状下，我们特地选择吉野产的筷子，就是想为扶植吉野的林业出一份绵薄之力。

　　第三天，我来到了日本袜子产量第一的广陵町。这里的袜业发端于江户时代中期的 1910

Kai," the group that promotes the culture and industry of Yoshino. They showed me Kawakami Village, the forestry industry in Yoshino that started nearly 1,000 years ago. They have nearly 10,000 pines on one hectare of land (twice the usual number), which forces the pines to slowly grow straight. It takes nearly 500 years for each pine to grow. Even the 200-year-old trees that were cut down and made into lumber are considered a rarity, and are well-regarded as lumber to build houses and building.

Even before the lumber industry existed in Yoshino, there was the *tarumaru* (sake barrel) industry. Barrels were made out of specially cut lumber, and whatever was left over was used to make disposable chopsticks. I went to see Akinori Yoshimoto, the president of "Yoshimoto Seisakujo," which makes chopsticks for our *d47 Shokudo* (Restaurant d47). He said that even though pines and Japanese cypresses are abundant on the surrounding mountains, it's hard to get one's hands on them. Disposable chopsticks were originally born out of the need to do something with leftover lumber pieces, but because the need for wooden houses and sake barrels has decreased, the materials to make chopsticks have decreased as well. Perhaps using the disposable chopsticks made in Yoshino will

年。广陵町是大和木棉的原产地，从种植到纺织都在本地完成。

由于广陵町的制袜工艺是用"编织"，而不是用"针织"，所以这里的袜商又被叫作"编织屋"。我采访了其中的山屋株式会社的野村佳照社长。山屋从 1820 年开始经营棉花生意，随着时代的变革又转做袜业，1993 年建立了自己的品牌 Hoffmann，并使用当时还未普及的有机棉作为原材料。但即使自主品牌的销量增加，他们也没有将订单外包，而是一视同仁，继续为客户生产高质量的袜子。

由广陵町往南，我来到了大和高田市的棉线批发商萱泽商店。社长萱泽成一先生不追求单一品种的销售数量，而是为各家袜厂寻找他们想要的棉线，且专业意识极高，绝不会转卖给别家袜厂。受他的影响，儿子有淳先生和儿媳良子女士借助奈良袜业传承下来的优良的技术，开发了自有品牌 saredo，还做起了零售。saredo 的原材料都是纺线时剩下的回收棉。"虽为足下产品，却是顶上功夫。"我认为这句话很好地概括了奈良所有手工制造者的初心。

help the Yoshino lumber industry.

On the third day, I headed to Koryo Town, the biggest producer of socks in Japan. I visited with Yoshiteru Nomura, the president of "Yamaya Corporation." The company, when it was established in 1820, was in the cotton business, but with the passing years, they changed to sock making, establishing Hoffman, a new brand in 1993. At about the same time, they started making socks out of organic cotton, which was not so common back then. By creating their own lines, the company has been making socks of high quality.

From Koryo Town, I headed toward Yamatotakada City and visited "Kayazawa Shouten," a thread distributor. Seiichi Kayazawa, the president of the company, doesn't sell just any thread; he only sells thread that he is sure sock makers would want. Growing up watching his father's business model, his son Ariatsu, with his wife Ryoko, established *saredo*, a sock brand that embodies the best of the Nara sock-making technology and skills. They also sell them. For the fabric, they use unused cotton left over when making thread and recycle them into socks. I have a feeling that everything about Nara's craftsmanship is embodied in these words, "These may only be socks, but still, they are important."

ORGANIC GARDEN（有机花园）

"Garabou" 棉袜

上　短袜　　1 728日元
中　踝袜　　1 728日元
下　长袜　　2 376日元

ORGANIC GARDEN

Garabou

Upper: Middle

Unbleached Cotton ¥1,728

Middle: Ankle-length

Unbleached Cotton ¥1,728

Lower: Sneaker

Unbleached 、Cotton ¥2,376

saredo

"Tortoise" 回收棉混纺线袜

上　S48卡其色　　2 160日元
中　S22明黄色　　2 160日元
下　S18炭灰色　　2 160日元

saredo

re-specked cotton rib and cable socks

Tortoise

Upper: S48 KHAKI ¥2,160

Middle: S22 YELLOW ¥2,160

Lower: S18 CHARCOAL ¥2,160

芳本制作所
桧木天削元禄免洗筷
9寸（约24厘米）
Yoshimoto Seisakujo
Hinokigenrokutensogebashi
9 *sun* (approx. 24 cm)

奈良定食

Yuki Aima

相马希辉（d47 食堂 总监）

奈良，让人重新发现质朴中的美好

　　说起奈良的美食，一定会有很多人提起"茶粥"。茶从中国传入日本，早在奈良时期仅供皇室享用，直到后来才在平民中普及。奈良县东北部的月濑是重要的茶叶产地。月濑位于京都、滋贺、三重的府县交界处，地势高，温差大，适宜种植茶叶。月濑健康茶园更是在这个区域里根据种植地的地形、方向、土质、坡度等更为细致的条件，对种植的树种、栽培方法进行调整，力求为每块茶田种上最合适的茶。为了避免机械采茶可能压过茶树根部而造成伤害，他们坚持手工采摘茶叶。另外，区域内陆续增加的退耕地块，他们也逐渐租用下来，使之重新回归茶园，这也让我印象十分深刻。在他们守护的这片茶园里，每一株茶树都有自己的个性，出产的茶虽然味道各有不同，但都是新鲜、淡雅的，是优良的土地孕育出来的味道。

　　约 1200 年前，奈良是当时日本的首都。那时虽然距离日本料理文化源头的江户时代还有很长一段时间，但也有一些当时的食物一直流传到今天，其中就包括奈良的酱菜和三轮龙须面。

Nara's "Home Grown" Meal

By Yuki Aima（Director, d47 Shokudo）

Nara: Rediscovering the Importance of Simplicity

People often associate Nara with *chagayu* — rice cooked with tea. Tea, which came from China, was consumed by aristocrats during the Nara period, and the practice eventually filtered down to the commoners. Tsukigase, situated northeast of the prefecture, is now known for tea. Tsukigase Organic Tea Farm, the tea producers, are known for their meticulous tea growing process: they plant specific tea plants according to the terrain, location, and soil and adjust the cultivation process accordingly. They also do not use machines when tending to tea plants, but use only hands for fear of destroying or hurting the roots. The tea leaves produced here are not consistent, but what's lovely is that each tea plant is unique, and its leaves are not flashy but mild in flavor.

Nearly 1,200 years ago, when Nara was the capital of Japan, *narazuke* and *miwa-somen* were both eaten. At Imanishi Honten, where the entire shop smells of *narazuke*, you can watch the last step

　　近铁奈良站附近的今西本店店内，弥漫着奈良酱菜的香味。透过玻璃，你可以看到制作奈良酱菜的最后一道程序：酒糟腌制。穿过店铺，就来到了最里面的生产区和储藏区。尽管我们是突然到访，店主今西泰宏先生还是慨然地为我们做起了向导。店里最出名的腌菜瓜最少也要腌制三年。其他的酱菜原料还包括西瓜、茄子、葫芦等等，不少都腌制了超过十年，酱菜的保质期都在两年以上。参观今西本店，我再次为日本人从奈良时代就掌握的腌制食品的技巧所感动。

　　从奈良市往南，就来到了三轮龙须面的发源地大神神社。森正龙须面铺就位于鸟居门前的小道上，那里的龙须面，面身细腻到可以顺喉直下，汤底也甚是美味。生面制成之后要放置一年，待其熟成后才拿来用。店主热情地领我到后厨参观，还教我料理中的窍门和装盘的功夫。

　　奈良县南部的吉野山区，是传说中源义经等历史传奇人物隐匿的深山险境。作为涵盖和歌山县、三重县、奈良县的纪伊半岛饮食文化圈的招牌和颜面，吉野山区种植了许多柿子和梅子。为了了解柿叶寿司的相关知识，我专程拜访了在奥吉野川上村开店的杉本雄造先生。制作柿叶寿

of bran-pickling behind the glass window. It takes nearly three years to make bran-pickled melons; there are also bran-pickled watermelons, eggplants, and gourds, and some of them take 10 years to make. Once opened, the bran pickles last two years. I was touched that this was one of the Japanese preservation food cultures that has lasted for 1200 years. South from Nara City is Omiwa Shrine, which is said to be where *Miwa-somen* was first made. I had a bowl at Morisho, the restaurant at the alley next to the shrine. The noodles were thin and went down my throat quite smoothly. The soup was quite tasty as well. They told me that they ferment the noodles for a year before they serve it.

　　The Yoshino Mountain area in the southern part of the prefecture is quite rough terrain. I went to see Yuzo Sugimoto, who owns a catering shop in Kawakami Village, to learn how to make *Kakinoha* sushi, a kind of sushi made with preserved mackerel wrapped in persimmon leaves. You put pieces of salted mackerel atop vinegared rice, wrap them up in persimmon leaves, and press them under a lid for the night. Persimmon leaves act as preservative while, at the same time, their lovely smell transfers over to mackerel, creating a very complex flavor. The pine lumber of Yoshino has long been (→p. 107)

奈良定食

主厨　加藤 惠

摄影　安永 Kentauros

※从上开始顺时针方向依次为

【柿叶寿司】
川上村的柿叶包裹的鲭鱼寿司，柿叶中富含的单宁具有保鲜防腐的效果。

【月濑番茶】
月濑健康茶园利用废弃耕地翻新的茶园自然栽培的『再造田之茶』系列茶叶。

【三轮素面的龙须面】
醇香温热的三轮龙须面，配合奈良县的名产原木香菇、炸面花碎，真是相得益彰。

【林州梅子干】
王隐堂农园的梅干由林州的梅子和紫苏制成，外皮柔软，果肉醇香。

【奈良酱菜】
今西本店采用古法精制的，经过长年熟成的奈良酱菜。

【富有柿子】
跨越奈良县和和歌山县，占日本国内七成产量的柿子产地出产的甜柿。

司，首先要将腌过的鲭鱼备好，切薄片，放到寿司饭团上后，再用柿叶细心包裹，然后压上重石，摆放一夜之后味道刚刚好。

柿叶不仅有保鲜的作用，其清新的香味还会和鲭鱼的鲜味叠加，为寿司增添丰富的口感。秋天的时候，柿叶也会由青变红，用红色的柿叶包裹的寿司颜色尤为鲜艳，真可谓色味俱佳。

说到奈良的美食，也要提一吉野的杉树。吉野杉年轮细致、香气淡雅，长久以来就是制作日本酒酒桶的优质原材料。虽然现在多数酒厂已经改用不锈钢或搪瓷的储酒罐，但同在吉野町的酒厂美吉野酿造，还是坚持使用吉野杉制成的酒桶，这样即使不特别控制温度，也可以利用乳酸菌的力量抑制其他杂菌的繁殖。当地具有代表性的"花巴"等著名品牌都是用这个方法酿造出来的。这些本地酒芳醇中略带酸味，更适合搭配腌制食品、味噌、酱油味的食物。例如吃柿叶寿司时，喝这些酒就再合适不过了。吉野除了有杉树，还种植着许多桧木，这些木材的边角料也被用来制作一次性筷子。d47食堂自2013年开业以来一直在使用吉野桧木制成的一次性木筷。

朴实无华的奈良人，用自己的双手取材于自然，又慷慨地回馈给这片土地。在我构思"奈良定食"时，透露着他们这份质朴的各种美食就自然而然地出现在了我的脑海中。

used in making barrels for Japanese sake. Today, many breweries use steel tanks but Miyoshino Jozo K.K., a brewery in Yoshino Town, still uses barrels made out of Yoshino pine when making their top brand sake, *Hanatomoe*. It's the perfect sake to accompany *Kakinoha* sushi. Yoshino is also known for their Japanese cypress, which is the wood used to make disposable chopsticks.

Made from what is around them, Nara products tend to embody simplicity. I came up with the best *teishoku* — the set dinner — for Nara.

Kakinoha sushi: Sushi made out of mackerel and wrapped in persimmon leaves from Kawakami Village. The tannin in the leaves acts as a preservative. ***Tsukigase Bancha-tea***: One of the most famous teas from Tsukigase Organic Tea Farm, produced in the most innovative farming style. ***Miwa-Somen no Nyumen***: Miwa-somen noodles in thick soup broth with *Shitake* mushrooms from Nara and fried *age-tama*. ***Rinshu-ume (Rinshu Plums)***: Pickled plums made by Oindo Noen. The skin is soft and the fragrance lovely. ***Fuyugaki***: Persimmons grown in Nara and Wakayama, which account for about 70% of the persimmon market.

奈良县的伴手礼

编辑部诚意推荐

柿子酱、柿子干 两样都凸显了柿子本身的美味，精心制作的成品中包含着制作者对食材的热忱。透明包装能显出柿子本身的颜色，也是商品的一大亮点。（佐佐木）柿子酱150g、柿子干60g，各540日元 柿的专门店 三条通店 ☎0742-22-8835 ♀奈良县奈良市上三条町27-1 村田大楼1楼 **Persimmon jam, Kakibiyori**（Dried persimmon） 150g / 60g ￥540 each Kaki no Senmon Sanjodori Store ♀Kamisanjocho 27-1, Nara, Nara

小鹿土铃 著名旅店"江户三"位于小鹿聚居的奈良公园，这家旅店的纪念品也是憨态可掬的小鹿造型。（空闲） 一套 1 728日元 江户三 ☎0742-26-2662 ♀奈良县奈良市高畑町1167 **Earthen Bell**（Deer） 1 set ￥1,728 Edosan ♀Takabatakecho 1167, Nara, Nara

风之森林 阿尔法(ALPHA)-1型 用奈良县产的纯米秋津穗酿造的日本酒。清爽口感令人惊喜，深受大众的喜爱。酒标的设计也很有特色。（神藤） 720ml 1 242日元 油长酒厂 ☎0745-62-2047 ♀奈良县御所市中本町1160 **Kaze no Mori ALPHA TYPE 1**（Sake） 720ml ￥1,242 YUCHO SHUZO CO., LTD. ♀Nakahonmachi 1160, Gose, Nara

K咖啡的轻便烘焙挂耳包 用捞金鱼的袋子装着，收到这个小礼物的人，都会忍不住想去大和郡山的金鱼街走一趟。（空闲） 一袋5包 700日元 K咖啡 ☎090-6986-3255 ♀奈良县大和郡山市 柳4-46 **K Coffee's Drip Bag Coffee** 5 bags ￥700 K Coffee ♀Yanagi 4-chome 46, Yamatokoriyama, Nara

熊野古道周边传承下来的铁锅炒茶 几片茶叶就能泡出满溢的清香。小瓶包装是送礼的最佳选择。（空闲） 70g 1 836日元 奈良自然茶专门店 TE＝CHA mail@teandcha.com ♀奈良县奈良市神功3-3-2 **Pan-roasted Tea Handed down in Kumano Kodo area** 70g ￥1,836 Organic Tea Shop Tea and Cha ♀Jingu 3-chome 3-2, Nara, Nara

Tumi-isi 本地手工匠人和高中生利用吉野杉木、桧木制成的积木。玩起来会上瘾，连工作都被抛到脑后了。（神藤） 一套 8 964日元 A4 ☎050-5856-9856 ♀奈良县吉野郡东吉野村 小708 **Tumi-isi**（Building block made of Japanese cedar and cypress） 1 set ￥8,964 A4 ♀Higashiyoshinomura omura 708, Yoshino-gun, Nara

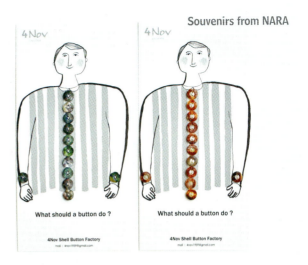

小鹿酥饼 说到奈良一定会联想到鹿，就连美味的小酥饼也做成了形状弯曲的可爱的小鹿模样。(神藤) 一盒15个 1 080日元 横田福荣堂 ☎0742-33-0418 ♀ 奈良县奈良市二条町1-3-17 **Deer Cookies** **15 per box** **¥1,080** Yokota Fukueido ♀ Nijocho 1-chome 3-17, Nara, Nara

11月4日的贝壳纽扣 用天然贝壳制成的纽扣折射着美丽的光泽，佩戴于身，自己顿时也时尚起来。(佐佐木) 一套 1 296日元起 信夫贝壳纽扣制作所 ☎0744-22-5239 ♀ 奈良县橿原市十市町800 **Shell button** **1 set** **¥1,296 ～** Shinobu Kaibotan Seisakusho ♀ Toichicho 800, Kashihara, Nara

纯麻奈良晒[19]手帕 每天使用手帕的时候，脑中就会浮现出奈良晒的传统织法，也回想起自己在奈良学到的点点滴滴。(神藤) 3 780日元 冈井麻布商店 ☎0742-81-0026 ♀ 奈良县奈良市中之庄町107 **Hon Asa Nara Zarashi Handkerchief** **¥3,780** Okai Mafu Shoten ♀ Nakanoshocho 107, Nara, Nara

微笑 包装上的山茶花是从江户时代后期沿用至今的图案。盒子里圆形的糖果被摆放得好像花儿盛开一般。(神藤) 一盒 1 188日元 万万堂通则 ☎0742-22-2044 ♀ 奈良县奈良市桥本町34 **Bisho (candy)** **1 box** **¥1,188** Manmando Michinori ♀ Hashimotocho 34, Nara, Nara

Shiro Yamato意大利面 龙须面发源地生产的手工意大利面，面身有劲道，是连意大利厨师也爱不释手的国际化产品。(佐佐木) capellini (天使面)、fedelini (极细面) 各250g 各577日元 胜记高田商店 ☎0120-38-6538 ♀ 奈良县樱井市芝374-1 **Shiroyamato Pasta** Capellini / Fedelini 250g each ¥577 each Marukatsu Takada Shoten ♀ Shiba 374-1, Sakurai, Nara

奈良酱菜 乌黑的酱菜极具视觉冲击力，用清水洗净耐心等待3天后，才能见到奈良酱菜的真身。(佐佐木) 盒装腌白瓜 150g 1 296日元 今西本店 ☎0742-22-2415 ♀ 奈良县奈良市上三条町31 **Narazuke (White melon pickled in sake lees)** White melon, 150g in a box ¥1,296 Imanishi Honten ♀ Kamisanjocho 31, Nara, Nara

杉木碗 一只碗让你把吉野杉的魅力握在手中。树木年轮成了每只碗独特的纹理，散发生命力之美。(空闲) 大号 (直径约130mm，高约70mm) 3 500日元 (工厂直销价) APPLE JACK木艺工坊 ☎0746-53-2443 ♀ 奈良县吉野郡川上村东川1595 **Bowl made of Japanese Cedar** Large (diameter 130mm, height 70mm) ¥3,500 (Factory direct sales price) Kobo Apple Jack ♀ Kawakami-mura Unogawa 1595, Yoshino-gun, Nara

In–Town Beauty ② NARA

奈良：城内之美

垣谷弥生女士（白雪布巾）

摄影：西冈洁
妆发：石川衣里（bociii.）
鸣谢：白雪布巾、奈良公园
Photo: Kiyoshi Nishioka
Hair Styling & Make-up: Eri Ishikawa（bociii.）
Special Thanks to: Shirayuki-Fukin, Nara Park

奈良县的CD

推荐人鹤林万平先生在奈良市创立了 sonihouse 工作室，制作全新的音箱。他制作的音箱音质极其细腻，受到许多爱乐者和音乐人的推崇。

TOWN AND COUNTRY
It all has to do with it.

It All Has to Do with It.
城市与乡村（Town and Country）乐队

　　我在大阪出生长大，学生时代搬到了京都。提起这两个地方，脑海中都能很快地浮现出一些特定的画面和它们各自独有的地域特色。住在这两个地方的时候，我也会感觉到自己和周遭的不同，会有意识地去融入当地的氛围。

　　但在奈良，老实说，并没有这样的感觉。其实我觉得这是件好事。这也是我选择在奈良开创自己事业的原因之一。奈良的风土也好，人也好，都十分放松。这并不代表这个地方很懒散，相反大家都自顾自地在埋头苦干。不用刻意让自己变得"很奈良"这件事本身，就"很奈良"。大家都可以很放松地做自己。

　　我在这里推荐的CD在发行时可算是革命性的存在了，但乐队在那之后也只是一直默默地制作好音乐。他们的音乐也是启发我创业的重要契机。

CDs of Nara

Manpei Tsurubayashi, the owner of "sonihouse" and designer of innovative speakers, has chosen some CDs that best embody the spirit of Nara. His speakers have a huge fan base amongst performers and audiences.

It All Has to Do with It.
Town and Country (Thrill Jockey, imported version)

For me, there is no "Nara-ness" but I think that's what makes Nara special. People and cities in Nara aren't in hurry to go anywhere or get anything done, but that doesn't make us lazy. We just know how to live our lives according to our own rhythm. In the end, no one can force "Nara-ness" onto anyone, because there is no such thing. When Town and Country first produced the album *It All Has to Do with It*, it was quite innovative and revolutionary, but that didn't make them famous and for many years they have been making innovative music. This album is the reason why I became a speaker designer in the first place.

奈良县的书

推荐人砂川昌广先生在大和郡山市旧城区的柳町商店街上开了一家名为 Tohon 的书店。他在书店中注入对各色事物的思考，店内有他精心挑选的"杂货与书""城市与书"等系列。

《言之森》
西尾胜彦（BOOKLORE出版社）￥1 620日元

"奈良
这个城市本身
似乎不会老去
她好像
总是置身事外"

这首诗的作者西尾先生在京都住了25年，又在大阪住了4年，写作这本诗集的时候刚搬来奈良不久。在作者从新移民的新鲜视角创作的关于这个城市的诗作中，处处传达着这里慵懒淡然的氛围，令人感到放松。除了"淡然"，也常见到"平和""安稳""宁静""踏实"等形容，都是谦逊低调的词语。

诗人所用的淡然低调的修辞，与奈良本身的性格也颇为相似。虽然奈良有非常悠久的历史值得夸耀，却不见住在这里的人常常把这些事挂在嘴边。西尾先生形容奈良"像是睡着了一般"，他的诗作中也常将自己写成是在睡梦中。读他的诗集，让我觉得这样入定般的淡然和谦逊，要比大张旗鼓的夸耀更有价值。

Books of Nara

Masahiro Sunagawa, the owner of Tohon, a bookstore in the Yanagimachi Shopping Area in Yamatokoriyama, has chosen books that best embody the spirit of Nara. He is known to curate books thematically: stationery and books, cities and books.

Koto no Mori (Forest of Words)
Written by Katsuhiko Nishio (BOOKLORE ¥1,620)

"I sometimes think / that Nara / is absentminded / the city is / old / maybe too old," writes Nishio, who wrote this poem when he first moved to Nara. As a newcomer to the city writing about this new place, he wrote pages permeated with this "absentmindedness" but it's an astute observation about this city. And this absentmindedness is what makes this city a very easy place to live, and this collection an easy collection to read. The poet calls this city "a sleeping city," and he himself is often portrayed asleep in his poems. Whenever I read this collection, I think that there is more value in sleeping and being absentminded than being fiercely proud about something.

Osamu Kuga

空闲 理

奈良县的日用佳品

「白雪布巾」的『豆腐』与『蛋糕』

Amazing Tools Found in Nara

Shirayuki Fukin's "Tofu" and "Cake"

By Osamu Kuga

趁着为筹备这期内容去奈良出差采访的机会，我在当地为自己重新置办了一堆袜子和手帕。我总觉得，用料上乘的贴身衣物或手帕，会让用的人内心不自觉地自信起来。而且，在一天结束，或是新的一天开始的时候，用水把它洗干净、晒干，就好像自己的一部分也在这个过程中被洗净了一般，焕然一新。所以就算是出差，我也经常在住处自己用手洗。并不是担心投币式洗衣机、干衣机会损伤织物（虽然实际上应该是会有些损伤的），只是觉得用不到那么强力的清洗方式。温水手洗的洗净力已经足够了，室内自然晾干也完全没问题。为旅行而设计的用品，给生活带来便利，可以说是"在旅行中创造生活感"。我从奈良市的白雪布巾（以前的垣谷织物厂）购入的三块我最常用的旅行手帕就是这样令人爱不释手的日用佳品。

其实，早在我开始为《d 设计之旅：奈良》做采访之前，我家里厨房擦餐具的布、桌布、浴室的毛巾浴巾，几乎用的都是白雪布巾的产品。它吸水性好，轻盈速干，经久耐用，就算用旧了也可以作为擦鞋布甚至抹布，或用于园艺发挥余热。每块布巾从全新开始，经历每个阶段，到最后都能物尽其用，而且价格合理，让人容易一冲动就买多了。我妻子比我更爱买他们的产品，常常买来作为礼物送给亲朋好友，体面又实用。

这次借着去奈良采访的机会，我第一次有幸参观了白雪布巾的工厂。工厂里还新设了商品展示区，有许多别的店没有的限量商品，只要有存货，还可以直接在这里购买。我的那几块手帕就是在那时买的。

"白雪布巾"这个名字既是公司的商标，也是由现任社长垣谷欣司先生的祖母在不经意间开发的具有品牌代表性的商品。当时，垣谷先生的祖母将制作蚊帐过程中余下来的边角料缝制在一起，做成大小不一的抹布使用。

没想到大家都觉得十分好用，于是才在昭和四十年（1965 年）决定把它商品化，这就

In my home, almost all cloths, from our kitchen cloth and dishcloth to bath and face towels are made by Nara's "Shirayuki Fukin Co., Ltd." They are light, absorbent, and dry quickly. When they get tired after long-term use, we use them as rags for gardening and shoe polishing. They can be used to the end for different ends at various stages. They're also very affordable.

In researching this volume dedicated to Nara, I visited the "Shirayuki Fukin" factory for the first time. The product gallery newly established on the factory premises offers all their products (depending on available inventory), including limited and exclusively available ones.

"Shirayuki Fukin" [white snow cloth], the product after which the company is named, was invented by CEO Kinji Kakitani's grandmother, who layered and sewed together scraps of textile, which were an inevitable byproduct of Nara's local mosquito net production industry.

Another feature of "Shirayuki Fukin" is its graphic design. Surprisingly, Kakitani draws all the patterns adorning the company's various products himself. He explains, "We don't want to become a big corporation because we want to continue (→p. 116)

有了从蚊帐材料中诞生的白雪布巾。时至今日，白雪布巾仍在继续生产蚊帐。虽然现在大多数日本家庭都很少用到蚊帐了，市场需求也在逐年递减，但白雪蚊帐的追随者反倒有增无减。祖母秉持的信念是"绝不出产无用的商品"，所以品牌一直保持着稳定的高品质。也许就是这份对品质的坚持让公司能坦然面对时代的变迁。

白雪布巾另一个亮点是它的设计。也许有人会觉得日常用品普普通通的就好，不用添加特别花哨的设计，但白雪布巾偏偏是在普通的用品中加入了更明快的设计使之更贴近时代。如果用陶瓷碗来打比方的话，白雪布巾就像白山陶器森正洋设计的平茶碗（一款口广身浅的碗）。《d设计之旅：佐贺》曾经介绍过白山陶器如何与时俱进地开发出深受现代人喜爱的设计美观的饭碗，我觉得"白雪布巾"可以说是布巾界的白山陶器。而更令人惊叹的是，"白雪布巾"众多的设计图案全部是垣谷总经理亲自设计的。不过垣谷先生并不喜欢被称作设计师，而是以匠人自居。他

说："我们并不想，也不会变成大公司。因为我们只想踏踏实实地制作高质量的产品。打个比方的话，我们更像是豆腐作坊，或者是蛋糕店。"把自家的产品比作豆腐和蛋糕，是垣谷先生独创的、富有诗意的诠释。垣谷先生解释道："用雪白、精致、柔软的抹布去擦拭洒到桌上的酱油，这种日常中的讲究可说是日本文化的一种体现。但它终归是块抹布，所以质量再好也得是抹布的价格。"所以就价格而言，产品要和豆腐一样便宜。"但另一方面，每天在厨房忙碌、洗衣打扫的主妇们，都会想要用上设计好看的布巾。你看，如果用这个毛巾包着小宝贝该多可爱呀。所以从愉悦人心的角度来说，我们的产品要和蛋糕一样可人。"垣谷先生微笑着说道。

设计上既像豆腐一样实用亲民，又能像蛋糕一样为日常的家务时间增添一份轻快愉悦的心情，这种两全其美的设计不正是我们每个人生活中都需要的日用佳品吗？这样的奈良白雪布巾，请你有机会一定要试一下，亲自体验它的妙处。

making good products. What we do is similar to what a tofu maker or baker does." The comparison shows Kakitani's creative, poetic spirit. "Japanese people," he continued, "wipe the soy sauce they spilled on the table with a fine, fluffy white cloth. That's culture. That means the quality has to be high, but the cost low enough so that you can wipe soy sauce with it." That, in a sense, is "tofu." "The housewife standing at the kitchen, cleaning and washing daily dreams about cute cloths. Look, you could wrap your baby with this towel, it's very cute. That's what I mean by 'cake'", he said with a smile.

"Shirayuki Fukin's" products combine practical "tofu-like" design with "cake-like" design that brightens the home or workspace and makes them more fun. As consumers, we need both and the combination of the two makes for a truly superior tool. Try Nara's "Shirayuki Fukin" and see for yourself.

東大寺御用達
白雪ふきん しらゆき

美味的柿叶寿司

编辑部推荐

【表太郎】 位于日本有名的赏樱胜地——吉野山。古色古香的店铺，就在世界文化遗产金峰山寺参道上的"铜之鸟居"旁。寿司的包装用吉野杉木精制而成，精美得让人舍不得拆开。一口下去，那香糯柔软的寿司饭让你惊呼不已。来奈良赏花时，记得一定要尝尝这里的柿叶寿司啊！（8个/1 050日元起）

表太郎
奈良县吉野郡吉野町吉野山429
0746-32-3070
9:00～16:00（赏樱期间 9:00～17:00）周一休息
从索道吉野山站步行5分钟

Hyotaro
Yoshino-yama 429, Yoshino-cho, Yoshino-gun, Nara
9:00–16:00 (during the cherry blossom season 9:00–17:00) Closed on Monday
5 minute walk from Yoshinoyama Ropeway Station

森正龙须面铺
Morisho
165
三轮站
Miwa Sta.
大和上市站
Yamato-Kamiichi Sta.
166
吉野山站
Yoshinoyama Sta.
370
表太郎
Hyotaro
大泷茶屋
Otaki Chaya

自从开始做"d设计之旅"，我们已经品尝过的寿司，有稻荷寿司、鲭鱼寿司、鲋寿司、江户前寿司等等，这次来到奈良，我们要向大家隆重介绍的是"柿叶寿司"。江户时代，人们一般用盐给鲭鱼杀菌并防腐，然后用随手可得的柿子叶把鱼肉包起来。后来，鱼肉加上米饭，就成了寿司……像这样关于柿叶寿司的来源，流传着各种说法。这些且不去管它，总之，如今无论是去赏花还是去兜风，大家都要带上柿叶寿司。秋天时，把包裹寿司的叶子换成红叶，颜色也会更为鲜艳！柿叶寿司就是如此既讨人喜爱又美味可口！下边为大家介绍三家柿叶寿司的名店。

Recommended Dish by the Editorial Team

Delicious *Kakinoha Sushi* (Sushi Wrapped in Persimmon Leaves)

For the Nara issue, our recommendation without doubt is *kakinoha sushi*. The dish is said to have been created during the Edo period to wrap salted mackerel with persimmon leave to preserve it, and they later added rice... Whatever the origin, it doesn't change the fact that it's a perfect picnic food to take along when driving to see autumn foliage. Even the persimmon

【大泷茶屋】 在大泷水库附近的断崖上建造的吉野风格[17]的建筑物里，有姐妹三人，亲密地坐在矮桌旁，悉心地包裹柿叶寿司（8 个 /870 日元起）。她们使用的柿叶是几位店主从当地的山上亲自摘来的，青翠欲滴。寿司入口的瞬间，清新甘凛，回味无穷。你也可以把寿司稍微放一会儿，然后把寿司放在柿叶上，放进烤箱里烤一烤，也十分美味。

大泷茶屋
📍 奈良县吉野郡川上村大泷 420-1
☎ 0746-53-2350
🕐 约 8:30 ～ 17:30 周三休息（12月～3月中旬休息）
🚃 距大和上市站车程约 15 分钟

Otaki Chaya
📍 Otaki 420-1, Kawakamimura,Yoshino-gun, Nara
🕐 8:30–17:30 Closed on Wednesday and from December to mid March
🚃 15 minute by car from Yamato Kamiichi Station on Kintetsu Yoshino Line

【森正龙须面铺】 如果你将这家寿司店的柿叶寿司（5 个 /700 日元）买回去送人，对方一定会非常开心。寿司用竹皮包裹，上边印着美观的芋版画[17]图案。店家还会附送一点腌菜，叮嘱你配着寿司一起吃。请记得，参拜大神神社时一定要顺路拜访这家名店。

森正龙须面铺
📍 奈良县樱井市三轮 535
☎ 0744-43-7411
🕐 10:00 ～ 17:00（周日、节假日 9:30-17:00，冬季 10:00-16:30）周二休店（逢节假日营业，每月 1 日营业），周一不定期休息
🚃 从三轮站徒步约 5 分钟

Morisho
📍 Miwa 535, Sakurai, Nara
🕐 10:00–17:00 (On Sunday and national holidays, 9:30–17:00, Winter 10:00–16:30)
Closed onTuesday, but open if its's a national holiday
Open on the first day of every month
Occasionally closed on Mondays
🚃 5 minute walk from Miwa Station, JR Sakurai Line

leaf wraps change color in autumn! Here are the three best restaurants known for their *kakinoha sushi.*

Kakinoha sushi by Morisho
This might be a wonderful gift to take home — a box of *kaki nohasushi* (5 for 700 yen). Wrapped in a stamped bamboo skin, the packaging is quite lovely. A pinch of pickles is included — do be sure to eat them with the sushi.

Kakinoha sushi by Otaki Chaya

Three sisters run this restaurant and make their sushi together (8 for 870 yen). Persimmon leaves used here are personally picked by the sisters from the nearby mountain. They are deep green and smell refreshing. You can heat up the sushi in the oven as well.

Kakinoha sushi by Hyotaro
Located on Mount Yoshino at the world heritage Kinpusenji Temple, next to the bronze *tori*. This sushi comes in a beautiful lunch box made out of Yoshino pine. Take one bite, and you'll be surprised by how soft the rice is. If you are going cherry blossom viewing in Nara, this is a must-buy place for *kakinoha sushi* (8 for 1050yen) here!

西冈 洁　1976 年生于大阪。二十几岁时学习过服装设计, 后来为了探寻自己所学习的那些服饰的发源地, 花费两年时间, 徒步探访了亚洲和大洋洲的村落, 之后成为摄影师。2015 年起, 将奈良县东吉野村和东京作为活动据点, 活跃于两地间。

🏠 www.nishioka-kiyoshi.com

Kiyoshi Nishioka　Kiyoshi Nishioka was born in 1976 in Osaka. He traveled to Asian and Oceanian villages for two years in search of the origins of clothing and fashion, which he had studied in his early 20s. Later, he became a photographer and in 2015, he began working in Higashi Yoshino Village, Nara Prefecture in addition to Tokyo.

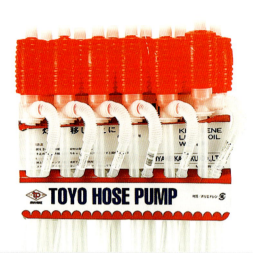

TOYO HOSE PUMP

上／Toyo Pump BD 型
现在售价 218 日元
左／在店铺销售时悬挂用的纸板

长效设计案例

三宅化学的"Toyo Pump BD 型"

 获 2013 年 Good Design·Long Life Design 奖

每一件能长期保持销量的"设计性很高的商品",都有着"除了设计性之外的长销理由"。总公司设在矶城郡的三宅化学株式会社所生产的"Toyo Pump BD 型",是 1959 年发售的家庭用灯油泵。用户不用举起沉重的油罐,也不用弄脏双手,就能方便地为煤油炉加油。这是一个利用物理原理的简单器械,比电动的泵要便宜,也不会发生机械故障。虽然家庭工具中电器的比例正逐渐增加,它却有着能够让人看见工具的工作原理这一趣味性,而且,无论小孩还是老人,都能够放心地使用,这也是它能够长期保持销量的另一个原因。(撰文:前田次郎)

Long-Lasting Design Case Study
"Toyo Pump Type BD" by Miyake Kagaku Co., Ltd.

"Toyo Pump BD," produced by Miyake Kagaku Co., Ltd., headquartered in Shiki, Nara Prefecture, is a kerosene pump designed for domestic use and released in 1959. It allows users to easily add oil to their kerosene stove. Because it is a simple device that functions using the laws of physics, it rarely breaks and is more affordable than electronic pumps. "Toyo Pump BD" remains popular even as our tools in the home are increasingly electrified, because it is safe for users of almost any age and because the logic of its operation is transparently visible. (Jiro Maeda)

Recipient of 2013 Good Design
Long Life Design Award

Above: "Toyo Pump BD" is
currently sold for ¥218.
Left: Paper hanger mount for
in-store display

空闲之旅 II

主编的奈良之旅

空闲 理

Osamu Kuga

Kuga Travel 2: Editor's Travel Notes

By Osamu Kuga

这一期"空闲之旅"的主题，是"从南至北再向北，穿越奈良！"到了旅途后半段，我来到了奈良县北部，终于可以坐下来写一写奈良市和大和郡山市。

在奈良市的旅行中，我没有感受到太多所谓的"大和文化"或是"日本特色"。相反，我的心情更像是来到了外国。提起和奈良一样或是更甚于奈良的"古都"，那就要数京都了，可奈良和京都，实在是大不相同。更确切地说，我觉得奈良与保留了浓厚琉球王朝文化的冲绳有着更为相似的地方。奈良人和鹿等动物们共同生活，也保护树木和森林。佛像、寺庙和神社坐落其中，它们与其说是庄严而神圣，倒不如说是华丽而优雅。这里是观光胜地，来自海外的游客比当地人还要多，可是这里却没有那么多引人注目的料理，只有当地产的蔬菜还算丰富新鲜。与其说奈良不以美食来吸引外人，倒不如说奈良并没打算特意准备任何东西诱人前来。在这里旅行的时间越长，我也愈发爱上了这样的奈良。

从近铁奈良站步行前往奈良町

从京都站出发，坐上近铁特快前往近铁奈良站，在即将到达目的地时，会从平成宫遗迹中间穿过。透过车窗，能看到右手边是朱雀门，左手边是大极殿（都为修复后的建筑）——葱葱郁郁的草木中有着红色的建筑物，像是枕词[19]"青丹"所描绘的风景。我喜欢近铁的"Vista Car"号特快列车，如果碰巧坐上了就很高兴。橙色（或者应该称其为柿色）的车身，与奈良县的山和田间的绿色形成鲜明的对比，列车行驶的样子就像一幅画。

近铁奈良站的站台在地下，从地下来到地面，你也完全感觉不到什么"日本屈指可数的观光胜地的电车总站"之类强势的存在感。这样就很好。商店街从车站周边延伸开来，观光客众多，热闹而拥挤，附近却没有很高的楼房（高于兴福寺五层塔的建筑物只有奈良县政府大楼而已），就算是在市区，除了有拱顶的商

Now we are going to focus on Nara City and the northern part of the prefecture.

Kyoto, along with Nara, are called ancient capitals but that's where similarities end. I am always reminded of Okinawa, with its history of the Ryukyu Kingdom, whenever I am in Nara because locals here live and protect nature and animals. There are many Buddha statues and temples and shrines around, but they seem to blend in with the natural world around them. Though this is a tourist spot, their local dishes are nothing flashy — they're made using simple ingredients that are in season. The residents are not trying to draw people here with food, nor do they have any desire to. Maybe this modesty is what attracted me to Nara the longer I stayed there.

Walking From Kintetsu Nara Station to *Naramachi*
Platforms in Kintetsu Nara Station are underground, but there's no sense that you are at the station of one of the most popular tourist spots in Japan. Though there are shopping
(→p. 126)

店街之外，到处都能看到开阔的天空，让人心情舒畅。

我穿过拱形屋顶的东向商店街（其由来是原来所有的建筑物都是朝着兴福寺所在的东边而修建的），向奈良町走去。在东向商店街，还有猿泽池附近，各有一间冈井麻布商店的分店。采访时遇到的很多人都向我称赞道："这个小伙子做事好认真呢！""他把奈良晒继承得真好！"他们所说的就是三十出头就独当大任，把事业继承下来的冈井大祐先生。店铺里摆放的各种制品当中，最显眼的就是手工纺线、织造的奈良晒"MAFU A MANO"系列。这是冈井先生亲自经手的系列，价格非常亲民。就算没有"手工制作"或是"遵循传统"这一类的宣传口号，我想，今后也一定会有越来越多的年轻人因为那简洁的设计、舒适的触感而对它爱不释手。

说到奈良传统制造业当中其他具有代表性的东西，那就是墨了。书法、绘画、和歌、信件、随手的涂鸦……奈良县之所以保有这么多留存了千年以上的贵重、美丽和有趣的东西，正是因为它们是用墨写成的。说到奈良的制墨，那是在室町时代，人们收集起兴福寺二谛坊佛堂天井里点着的佛灯的炭灰，用胶使其凝固，这就是墨的起源。古梅园直到现在还保留着这种传统制法——以菜籽油点灯，将盘子覆盖其上，收集附着在上边的烟尘。店铺的格局有些严肃，说不定会让某些想要进店的人望而却步。其实没关系，您大胆地进店便是了。店铺的第十六代传人松井晶子女士，会用易懂、细致且令人愉快的方式来讲解有关奈良墨的知识。副主编神藤秀人很喜欢软笔（尤其爱用奈良出产的吴竹品牌的软笔），想借这次的机会来体会一下正牌的奈良墨汁，于是来到店里，轻松地跟店主说明自己"喜欢偏蓝的色调"。松井女士指着颜色展示表，在种类繁多的墨当中，为他选出了加入了本蓝的青墨"道风"（Michika-ze）——它能极美地表现出深浅，也适用于绘画。

arcades around the station and it is thronged with tourists, there are no high rises (the only building taller than the Kofukuji Gojunoto is the Nara Prefectural Office Building). Though you are in the middle of the city, you can see the sky above you — unless you are in the arcade.

"Okai Mafu Shoten" shops can be found in the Higashimuki Shopping Arcade as well as near Sarusawa-ike. Everyone I met during my trip praised Daisuke Okai, the young owner of "Okai Mafu Shoten, K.K.," as someone who is professional and

passionate about *Nara zarashi* — fabric. Even in the shop, my eyes were drawn to the bleached handspun handwoven *Nara zarashi* from among the many other products. The "MAFU A MANO" series was designed and produced by Daisuke Okai himself, but the price is rather low for the amount of energy and time put into its conception.

Another traditional product Nara is known for is calligraphy ink, which is said to have first been made during Muromachi Period, nearly eight hundred years ago. "Kobaien" is one of the

我经常投宿的奈良 SunRoute 酒店在猿泽池附近，办理好入住手续，我向南走去。我先去看了看元兴寺，那里屋顶的一部分瓦来自日本最为古老的飞鸟时代。之后，我前往专卖袜子的店铺丝季（SiKi）。这是来自广陵町的山屋（Yamaya）的直营店，以有机棉为主，使用天然素材制作高品质的袜子。袜子的穿着感非常舒适，只要穿过一次，就再也不想穿回大量生产的 1000 日元三双的袜子了。

和鹿一起在奈良公园和东大寺散步

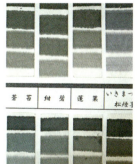

很多当地人都告诉我，奈良公园附近风景最好的展望台，其实是奈良县政府的楼顶（已故设计师片山光生的作品，他生前曾参与旧国立竞技场的设计）。我正在暗自琢磨是不是要混进去，忽然听到一个爽朗的声音："免费开放，请这边走！"抬头一看，警备员正在热情地为我指出电梯的位置。来到楼顶，奈良的 360 度美景尽收

makers of ink who still makes it in the traditional way. Shoko Matsui, the sixteenth generation shop owner, is always happy to explain the history and usage of Nara ink if you ask.

I checked into the "Hotel SunRoute Nara" near Sarusawa-ike and walked south. I stopped by Gankoji Temple and looked at the roof tiles, which are said to be among the oldest in Japan, made during the Asuka period. Then I kept walking toward "SiKi," the sock specialty shop run by "Yamaya," the company that makes high quality organic cotton socks. Their socks are so good that once you wear them, you can never go back to wearing socks you can buy at three for a thousand yen.

Walking with a Deer Toward Nara Park and Todaiji Temple
The locals told me that the best view around Nara Park is the rooftop of the Nara Prefectural Office. The security guard showed me the way from the elevator, telling me that admission was free. From the rooftop, I could see Mount Wakakusa and the Great Buddha Hall of Todaiji Temple, the entire panorama of (→p. 128)

眼底，若草山、东大寺、大佛殿、兴福寺、五重塔等风景名胜一览无遗。仔细一看，这里还设置了长椅供人休息，我突然心生后悔——要是把柿叶寿司便当带来该多好啊。

紧邻县政府北边的是奈良县立美术馆，我去探访的时候，这里正在举办生驹郡安堵出生的已故画家富本宪吉的画展。看过这个画展，我才知道，富本的画所独有的题材"羊肠小路""竹林月夜""大和川急雨"，原来就是安堵的风景。富本出生的房子，作为富本宪吉纪念馆留在了安堵，在2012年闭馆。不过，听说有关方面正在筹划，准备再次将其开放利用。

从县政府出发，无论是前往正在举办正仓院展的奈良国立博物馆，还是东大寺、春日大社，路程都不远，走过去很快就到了。可是在白天，这些地方到处人挤着人，鹿挤着鹿，根本走不快。在刚开始采访的7月，牡鹿的角尚短，到了8月将尽的时候，鹿角已经长得很漂亮了。不经意间在森林里与它们相遇，它们身

上那种庄重与威严的气氛，令人完全不会想伸手去摸一摸它们的脑袋，反而会主动让出道路，请它们先走。在那之后，鹿角本应长得更大、更尖、更硬，可是考虑到鹿和人的安全，奈良公园的管理员们会再次将牡鹿的角锯短。

奈良的鹿不起早。我早上散步走到东大寺时，它们都还趴在树荫下纹丝不动。令我深感佩服的是，卖鹿仙贝的人会把南大门前的参道打扫得干干净净，不留一丝鹿的粪便。石板路上洒着清水，反射着清晨的阳光。

我先参拜了安放着四天王像的东大寺戒坛堂——据说这四天王十分灵验；然后穿过后门，来到让人神清气爽的内参道，走向大佛殿。抬头看，正好看到一间咖啡店，名叫"工场旧址事务室"，据说他家的三明治远近闻名。低层的木造建筑带有一些现代感，店如其名，这里曾经是制造乳酸菌饮料的工厂。与外侧熙熙攘攘的大路不同，这里很安静，就连窗外偶尔经过的鹿，看起来也那样彬彬

Nara. When I saw benches, I regretted not bringing lunch.

Just north of the Prefectural Building is Nara Prefectural Museum. When I was there, Kenkichi Tomitomo's work was being exhibited. I learned that his works, such as *Curving Road*, *Moonlight in Bamboo Forest*, and *Sudden Rain over Yamato River*, are the landscapes of Ando Town where he came from.

From the Prefectural Building, I walked toward Nara National Museum, Todaiji Temple, Kasuga Taisha Shrine, but everywhere I went was full of people and deer. When we started researching for this issue in July, the horns of the stags were still short, but by end of August, they had grown intimidatingly long. No matter how friendly the deer were when I came across them in the forest, I didn't dare scratch their heads — they looked that dignified and that intimidating. I stood on the side and let them pass me. Horns are supposed to grow bigger, sharper, and harder, but in order to keep other deer and people safe, the city files them down every year.

I also found out that deer don't wake up early.

(→p. 131)

有礼（大概是我的错觉）。

从咖啡店步行到正仓院正仓，很快就到了。站在稍远一些的地方，可以欣赏建筑物的整体外观。这座建筑物，我们已经在历史教科书里小小的照片上看过好多次了，但是当我身临此处，面对着这座用传统工法"校仓造法"所建造的、划时代的建筑物时，它那巨大、壮观、黑黝黝的实体，仍然令我深受震撼。在校仓造法的宝库当中，正仓院是最大的，其他还有比如唐招提寺等等，都有一些能近距离欣赏的地方。这生动而有力的设计，是现代建筑所不具备的，并且和所谓的"日式建筑"也不一样，希望大家能尽情欣赏。

若草山和春日山原始森林

距离东大寺不远，有一家旅馆武藏野，大家一定要住一晚。它位于二月堂和春日大社的中间，无论去两者中的哪一个，徒步都可以很快到达。并且，最值得一提的是，颜色青翠欲滴的大斜坡——若草山的入口，就近在眼前。天气晴朗时，店家提供早餐外带服务，手提的藤篮里会一并送上味噌汤、茶和野餐垫，用钥匙打开尚未开放的若草山的大门，便能像包场般尽情享受。这是其他地方绝对无法模仿的、完美得令人嫉妒的服务。房间里放着的池田含香堂的奈良团扇也非常漂亮，用简洁的透雕描绘着若草山、春日大社等很有奈良风格的主题图案。

若草山的别名是三笠山，据说是因为形状如同三个斗笠重叠起来的样子而得来的名称。山顶有古坟，光是听到"有古坟"，就令人不由得感叹："不愧是奈良啊……"并且，这个古坟还是出现在《枕草子》里的莺冢古坟，当我在解说牌上读到这里时，更是一边点头一边感叹："不愧是奈良"了。

想去若草山山顶的话，可以沿着奈良里山观光公路开车上去。若不在山顶的观光公路上

When I went for walks to Todaiji in the morning, I saw them curled up under the trees. What impressed me was how the sellers of deer food cleaned up after the deer every morning. There was no deer waste found anywhere by the southern gate of the temple. The path gleamed with water in the morning.

I stopped by the building that has the Shitenno Statue (the statues of Four Heavenly Kings) and then went around the back to a path leading toward the Great Buddha Hall of Todaiji Temple. Be sure to stop by "Café kojoato Jimushitsu," a café that sells delicious sandwiches. Just as the name suggests, it used to be a factory that made drinks. Compared to the busy roads and path in front, this is quiet; even the deer that walk by the window once in a while seem to take note of how quiet they must be.

From "Café kojoato Jimushitsu," Shosoin Shoso is only a few steps away. You can look at the building from afar. This is one of the most cited buildings in Japan—for its innovative architecture that used the cutting edge technology of the time. When seen close up, though, it is huge and dark and thrilling to

(→p. 132)

掉头，继续往前开下去，便是一条无法回头的单行道。当柏油路变成碎石路，你就进入了世界遗产——春日山原始森林。距离奈良市区 20 分钟车程的地方就有原始森林，这样的环境令人惊讶。这里也是河濑直美导演的《殡之森》里最后一幕的拍摄场地。

穿过日影斑驳摇曳的森林，回到大道上，从稻田、茶林间穿梭而过，到达田原。这里是拍摄《殡之森》的两位主人公相遇时的取景地，周边的茶园给人留下非常深刻的印象。能在盛夏时节来到这里，真是太幸运了，你眼里所看到的风景，跟电影里一模一样。

设定导航，可以把奈良公共交通的日笠巴士站作为目的地。

去大和郡山看金鱼。去生驹山品尝茶粥

说到奈良的特色产业，绝不能不提大和郡山市。为了养殖金鱼，市内修建了密密麻麻的水池。这里的金鱼产业繁荣到每年都会举办捞金鱼大赛的程度。我们的"奈良 d 标总览"中介绍过的那家位于柳町商店街入口处的 K 咖啡，非常值得一看，也希望大家看完了 K 咖啡，顺便在周围走一走，看一看。咖啡店近旁 Tohon 书店的店主砂川昌广先生，推荐了这期的"奈良县的书"。店里收藏着与金鱼相关的独特的书和杂货，品类齐全。我在那里找到了库尔特·冯古内特的《泰坦的女妖》的二手文库版，立刻毫不犹豫地买了下来。尽管还没有开始读，但在这个故事中也出现了金鱼，让我十分惊讶。听了 Tohon 店主夫妇的推荐，我走完整条柳町商店街，来到了日式点心老店本家菊屋。这里有一种小小的日式点心，在琼脂上涂着砂糖、做成金鱼的形状，名字就叫作"捞金鱼"，非常可爱。这是只有大和郡山才能买到的特产，送人的话，收到的人一定会很开心。

说到奈良特有的乡土料理，能与三轮龙须面、柿叶寿司齐名的，要数茶粥了。这种食物

look at. There's no building like this now — not quite Japanese architecture — this really is an amazing building to behold.

Wakakusayama and Kasugayama Genshirin
If you have a chance, I strongly encourage you to stay at "MUSASHINO" if you are near Todaiji. Without a doubt, the most impressive thing about this hotel is its view: the light green slope of Mount Wakakusa. When the weather is good, the hotel staff can pack up breakfast to go and will open the locked gate of

Wakakusayama so you can have a picnic breakfast before anyone comes in. This is a unique service only they can do. The Nara fan by Ikeda Gankodo in the room is also lovely—each is of different design, one with Wakakusayama and another with Kasuga Taisha Shrine.

You can drive along the Nara Okuyama Driveway to get to the top of Mount Wakakusa. If you keep going on this driveway, it becomes a one-way unpaved road, leading you to Kasugayama Genshirin, a World Heritage site. If you think about

与东大寺二月堂的修二会（汲水节）有着很深的关联，至少在 1200 年前，奈良人就已经吃上了这样的食物。在今天的奈良，既有"平时都会吃""喜欢吃，所以经常吃"的人，也有"完全不吃""没吃过"的人。当我看到超市里就有茶粥专用的茶包在销售时——我买了一包，在三奇楼的厨房里做好之后吃掉了，算是留下一份美好的回忆吧——我不禁想，看来这种食物还是在这里生了根嘛。茶包还按照口感喜好分了类别，比如"浓稠口感""清淡口感"等等。

令我为其着迷、朝思暮想的店，是那家鬼之茶屋西本，位于生驹山脚的鬼取町那如同过山车般急促的坡道上。那一带还有一些很受欢迎的咖喱店和比萨店。这家店是奈良自然茶专门店 TE = CHA，店里的人告诉我的，它的设计具有都市感，兼营批发和零售业务，不遗余力地向游客传递着大和茶的魅力。在鬼之茶屋西本的店铺里，摆放着茄子、黄瓜、辣椒等蔬菜，闪闪发亮，看上去令人垂涎欲滴。店里的人告诉我，这些全都是自己栽种的。听到这里，我抬头四顾，发现这里被田地包围，田里生长着各种农作物，硕果累累。道路的另一侧设有带着屋檐的户外座位，在那里能品尝到茶粥午餐，午餐的内容相当丰富，以茶粥为主食，附带用自家栽种的蔬菜所制作的种类繁多的配菜。正当我为套餐的量和美味程度感到震惊时，店员一边说着"请慢用"，一边又端来了满满一盘新鲜蔬菜炸成的天妇罗。我在刚炸好的、香脆的天妇罗上撒上盐，然后大快朵颐，一边呼呼地吹着气，一边喝下凉凉的茶粥——真是无比幸福的时刻。这样一顿饭，却只要 600 日元，令我喜出望外。坐在店里，抬起头，还能远远地看见若草山。餐厅的环境如此令人心旷神怡。将自己亲手栽培的美味的蔬菜提供给客人，店家的美意直截了当地传递到了我的心里，让我非常满足。真是一家不可多得的好店啊。

it, it's amazing that there's a primitive forest only twenty minutes away from the city center. This is the place where the last scene of *The Mourning Forest*, the movie directed by Naomi Kawase, was filmed.

Driving through the sunlight dappled forest to a paved road through rice fields and tea farms, you reach a place called Tawara. This is where the two main characters from *The Mourning Forest* met. Just like in the movie, I was there in mid-summer, and I had the chance to see the exact location of the movie. Keep your eyes open for Higasa Bus Stop.

Driving to Yamatokoriyama to see Goldfish and to Mount Ikoma to Eat *Chagayu*

We cannot fail to mention Yamatokoriyama City when talking about Nara's special products. The entire city is filled with fish tanks and ponds to raise goldfish. Each year, they hold Goldfish Competitions to see who can fish out the most goldfish. Do come if you have chance — and don't forget to go to "K COFFEE" (a *d mark* café) right near Yanagimachi Shopping

(→ p. 134)

奈良就是道路，我们从那里走过。

在奈良之旅的最后阶段，我再一次前往东大寺二月堂。在"奈良d标总览"的文章中我提到过，当地人曾向我推荐说"那里早晨的风景最美"。可如果我要是跟当地人说"二月堂最美的时候是早晨"，所有的奈良人一定都会摇着头说，"不对不对，那里晚上才是最漂亮的"……我觉得奈良人好像就是这样的。

夜里去二月堂时，你也可以按照"奈良d标总览"的文章中所提到的路程前往，不过路上有不少地方会漆黑一片。春日大社的参道深处完全没有路灯，如果月亮没有露面，连鹿的眼睛也不透一丝光亮，那可是真正的伸手不见五指，光是看着就让人心里发毛。这还不算，黑暗之中还会有啪嗒啪嗒的脚步声逐渐靠近。有鬼啊！——当然没有这种事（真

Arcade. Close to the café is "Tohon," the book shop, whose owner wrote the column "Books of Nara" for this issue, but he also sells goldfish-related books and knickknacks. I came across a used copy of *The Sirens of Titan* by Kurt Vonnegut Jr., and purchased it on impulse. Goldfish appeared in this novel (of course), but I haven't had the chance to finish the book yet. On the recommendation of the owners of "Tohon," I stopped by "Honke Kikuya," the Japanese sweet shop nearby. I bought a box of *Kingyo Sukui* (Goldfish fishing), a gummy sweet in a goldfish shape, to take home as a gift.

Along with *Miwa-somen* and *Kakinoha sushi*, *Chagayu* is another local dish of Nara, which is said to have been around locally for nearly 1200 years. My favorite restaurant is "Oni no Chaya Nishimoto," which is atop a very steep hill in Onitori Town in the Ikoma Mountain Range. There's a terraced veranda where you can eat lunch, but the dishes are amazing. With chagayu as its main dish, there are many side dishes of vegetables and others. The staff bought out more vegetable tempura as I sat there, surprised by the quantity. And the lunch came out to 600 yen. When I looked up from my food, I could see as far as Mount Wakakusa.

碰上鬼好像也蛮好玩……），那是胆子很大的当地人，正若无其事地散着步。良好的治安是奈良市极具魅力的一点。虽说"事无绝对"，可就算在深夜时分，一个人走在一片漆黑里，想到有鹿在看着，有佛祖在看着——这样的威慑力，仿佛给人带来了安心感。奈良人的信条是"不需要多余的灯火""夜本来就是黑的"——真希望不管到了什么时候，奈良永远都能如此。

深夜的二月堂果然美不胜收。回廊里吊着的灯笼在白天也让人感觉很美，到了夜里全都被点亮，熊熊燃烧着，散发出光辉。在抬头看灯笼时，耳边隐约听到虫鸣声、不知是哪儿的水沟里流动的水声，以及掠过林间树叶的风声。背后，山脊线隐入了黑暗之中，轮廓难辨，二月堂的光如同悬浮在半空，看起来就像是星空一样。你可以用自己的双腿，亲自走入那星空所在之处。任谁都会为这气氛所陶醉吧。有人或许会觉得，这是人生所经历的至高无上之

美……且慢，不单单如此，当你踏上梦幻般的回廊，蓦然回首，奈良城里的万家灯火尽收眼底，那才是更为迷人的风景——身临此处，三生有幸矣。

奈良就是道路——沿路前行，所到之处必有美景。然而，偶回头，看看自己一路走来的足迹，以及自己出发的地方，你会发现，现实的情景，或者说过去的足迹，更美、更可爱。她吸引着我们，让我们有朝一日重返她的怀抱。我一定会回来。奈良的山水，奈良的道路，无论何时，无论何地，总在提醒我，记起这一切。

Nara Is Like a Path — The Path We Took

For the end of the Nara trip, I went back to Todaiji Nigatsudo once again. You can follow the path that is mentioned in the "d mark" article, but at night, there are many dark areas. One good thing about Nara City is its safety. Maybe people know that even at night, the deer and Buddha are looking after you, and that's what stops people from committing crimes.

Nigatsudo in the middle of the night is beautiful. The path is lit with lanterns, creating a dream-like feel. Even though the mountains have disappeared in the dark, the floating light from Nigatsudo makes it look like stars in the night sky. Maybe some people may say that this is the most beautiful sight in the world. However, what we discover is that when we turn around, there is light from Nara City, and what is more beautiful is the lights of the daily lives of people living in reality.

Nara Prefecture is a road. The destination is beautiful but when we look back and see the road we have walked on, where we came from, that is equally as beautiful. The past is as real as the present. And we are reminded that we can always go home—that we must go home eventually. I was reminded of this throughout my travels through Nara.

不变的美味

编辑部哪怕放弃采访也要去吃一顿的奈良县餐厅

对奈良公园里的鹿儿来说，若被问到"什么东西最好吃啊？"，鹿一定会回答说："鹿仙贝，咩——"而我们编辑部发掘的名产美味就更多了。在这里，我们给大家介绍一下编辑部成员亲身体验过好多次的、想要推荐给大家的 8 种美味。

Favorite Dishes From Nara

If one were to ask the deers of Nara Park what the most delicious local food was, they would indubitably answer, "Deer Senbei!" In the editorial department, however, we encountered many more tasty local foods. Below are the eight foods we ate repeatedly and recommend.

1 黄豆面团子
Kinako Dango (Rice dumpling in a roasted soybean flour)

我一向害怕早起排队，可是为这个团子却在所不惜。可以依据个人喜好沾上黄豆面。(空闲) 1串70日元

团子庄 坊城本店
- 📍 奈良县橿原市 东坊城町860
- ☎ 0744-27-4340　● dango.kir.jp
- 🕐 8:30～17:00 (售完即止) 周二以及每月第一个周三休息

Dangosho Bojo Main Store
📍 Higashibojocho 860, Kashihara, Nara

2 抹茶 (附带红豆馅茶点Mimuro)
Matcha with bean-jam wafer

大神神社大鸟居旁边的老店。店内设有日式茶房，可在此享用有名的红豆馅点心Mimuro。(空闲) 550日元

白玉屋荣寿
- 📍 奈良县樱井市三轮660-1　☎ 0744-43-3668
- ● www.begin.or.jp/mimuro
- 🕐 本店8:00～19:00 茶房 10:00～18:00 周一、每月第三个周二休息

Shiratamaya Eiju
📍 Miwa 660-1, Sakurai, Nara

3 茶粥套餐
Chagayu Set (Green tea porridge set)

用新鲜采摘的蔬菜做成的料理，数量丰富。这价格，太值了！餐厅在颇为急促的坡道尽头，请注意安全驾驶。(空闲) 600日元

鬼之茶屋 西本
- 📍 奈良县生驹市鬼取町413　☎ 0743-77-8476
- 🕐 11:30～15:00 (14:00截止点单) 每周四及每月第二、第四个周三休息

Oni no Chaya Nishimoto
📍 Onitoricho 413, Ikoma, Nara

4 土灶早餐
Kamodo no Asagohan (breakfast set)

清晨在东大寺二月堂散步后的享受。8点钟新鲜出炉的土灶蒸饭。(佐佐木) 550日元

鹿之舟 灶
- 📍 奈良县奈良市井上町11　☎ 0742-94-5520
- ● www.kuruminoki.co.jp/shikanofune/kamado
- 🕐 8:00～18:00 周三休息

Shikanofune Kamado
📍 Ionuecho 11, Nara, Nara

5　吞拿鱼和鸡蛋的三明治
Tuna and Egg Sandwich

非常有名的三明治，可以在乳酸菌饮料（商品名FUTORUMIN）工厂原址改建的宽敞的店内品尝到它。炸土豆饼三明治在当地也很有人气。（佐佐木）850日元

工场旧址事务室
📍 奈良县奈良市芝辻町543　☎ 0742-22-2215　🌐 kojoato.jp
🕐 11:00～18:00（周六、周日及节假日9:00～18:00）
　　周一到周四休息
Kojoato Jimusitsu
📍 Shibatsujicho 543, Nara, Nara

6　石窑盐味烤面包
Ishigama Shiopan (Salted bread)

店里的面包和三明治，你一看就想买回来送人。要品尝盐味面包，请看准石窑里出炉的时机（上午7点30分）。（佐佐木）194日元

Alpenrose总店
📍 奈良县奈良市神功4-6-6　☎ 0742-72-4183　🌐 alpenrose.jp
🕐 面包店 7:30～18:00　咖啡店、餐厅 8:30～16:00　全年无休
Alpenrose Main Store
📍 Jingu 4-chome 6-6, Nara, Nara

7　鸡肉饭做成的蛋包饭
Chicken Rice no Omurice
(Omelette made with fried chicken rice)

在我常住的奈良SunRoute酒店旁边。采访之前来一份，精神百倍，提神就靠它了。（神藤）810日元

Hisago食堂
📍 奈良县奈良市鹤福院町32　☎ 0742-22-3795
🕐 午餐 11:00～15:00　周一休息
Hisagoya Shokudo
📍 Tsurufukuincho 32, Nara, Nara

8　彩华拉面（小份）
Saika Ramen Small-size (Stir-fried vegetable and pork over spicy noodle soup)

夕阳西下时出现在巨大的停车场上的小面摊。在辽阔的停车场上来一碗拉面，那叫一个畅快。（神藤）670日元

彩华拉面 流动推车
📍 奈良县天理市别所町223 Price Cut天理北店停车场内
🌐 www.saikaramen.com
🕐 17:30～1:00（周六、周日及节假日 16:30～1:00）　全年无休
Saika Ramen Yatai
📍 Besshocho 223, Tenri, Nara（in the parking area of Price Cut Tenri Kita Store）

奈良町宿

THE 4th
NARA INTERNATIONAL
FILM FESTIVAL 2016

Sep. 17.18.19.20.21.22

しろ	くれない花	蒼苔	紺碧	蓬莱	いきまつ 松煙墨	おちまつ 松煙墨	宮

CONTRIBUTORS
撰稿人与信息提供者

相马夕辉 Aima Yuki
D&DEPARTMENT PROJECT
每次出差都要有奈良产的香茗傍身，
朝早才能醒神。

冈本友纪 Okamoto Yuki
la forgerone 铁铺
制作灯和各种物件，也参演过资生堂和
金麦啤酒的广告。forgerone.com

木本好美 Kimoto Konomi
proyect g oficina
位于 Casadecha 1472。

阿部里奈 Abe Rina
D&DEPARTMENT 福冈店 店长
承蒙大家的支持，福冈店今年 11 月迎
来三周年的店庆啦！（注：日文刊的发
行时间为 2016 年 11 月）

桶田千夏子 Okeda Chikako
Luft 设计师
奈良酱菜、日本酒，就着大和油菜，
让我想要融进大和山水的怀中。

熊谷太郎 Kumagai Taro
正酒屋 六根净 主理人
坚持 "一日一食" 的断食已有 9 个月。
对绳文文化突然感兴趣。

井冈友美 Tomomi Ioka
奈良民宿 纪寺之家
愿您享受到原汁原味的奈良町屋生活。

垣谷欣司、垣谷弥生
Kakitani Kinji, Kakitani Yayoyi
白雪布巾
以后也要不断创作新的花样。

熊坂充 Kumasaka Mitsuru
富山店主厨
向你介绍富山美味的酒家。

石川衣里 Ishikawa Eri
bociii 美发师
经营着祖母创办的发廊，
向顾客们传达着奈良的魅力。

加藤惠 Kato Megumi
d47 食堂 主厨
向全国的母亲们学习，将 "妈妈的味道"
传递出去。

黑江美穗 Kuroe Miho
d47 博物馆
通过展览会和 d47 落语（注：类似相声）
大会重新发现奈良。

井上香织 Inoue Kaori
京都造型艺术大学的 D&DEPARTMENT
京都项目成员
我享受骑着自行车漫游京都。

加藤由美 Kato Yumi
农悠舍王隐堂 企划负责人
奈良人文风土的深刻和有趣
触动了我。

坂本大三郎 Sakamoto Daizaburo
山伏
月山即将迎来更艰苦的季节。

岩井翼 Iwai Tatsumi
无印良品
本人好像是不受鹿儿青睐的类型。

萱泽有淳 Kayazawa Ariatsu
萱泽商店 saredo
想带着这本书重新认识一下奈良
不为我们所熟知的一面。

泽田央 Sawada Hiro
d47 design travel 商店
决定从早上开始熬汤底做味噌汤。

岩田文明 Iwata Fumiaki
月濑健康茶园 主理人
利用奈良月濑的特殊地势制出好茶。

喜多和夫 Kita Kazuo
工场迹 主理人
终于等到了奈良号！
工场迹也成长了许多哟。

清水美香 Shimizu Mika
Sannichi-YBS 的 D&DEPARTMENT 山梨县
喝着山梨产的酒，品尝着本地蔬菜料理，
度过一个美妙的山梨之夜。

上原丽 Uehara Rei
撰稿人
感觉到夏天结束的时候，离红叶的季节
就不远啦。这也是游览四国喀斯特县立
自然公园的最佳时节。

北岛真由美 Kitajima Mayumi
Perhaps 艺廊
非常喜欢佐贺。在艺廊中和人聊天是
人生中最快乐的时光。

白崎友美 Shirasaki Tomomi
Naramagane 副主编
向大家传达奈良的惬意、悠闲、
怀旧气息。

卫藤武智 Eto Takenori
日语校阅负责人
奈良的蓝天、大和文华馆，即使是长大
以后也一定要再到奈良来看一看。

北室淳子 Kitamuro Junko
手拉素面 "北室白扇"
在四国德岛制作美味的素面。

进藤仁美 Shindo Hitomi
d47 design travel 商店
这次去了心心念念的阿波晚茶的产地，
下次要去哪里呢？

大野瞬 Ohno Shun
FUKUBU INC.
正对着在院子里嬉戏的小猫们发呆。

Kifumi
插画师
橿原市出身。对奈良号万分期待！
kifumiweb.com

渡边真也 Shinya B
Temple 大学艺术系高级副教授
教授已经开始经营自己的博客了：
ShinyaB.com

大道刚 Oomichi Go
D&DEPARTMENT PROJECT
翻到残的书，穿到烂的鞋。

金贞姬 Kim Junghee
3KG 的 D&DEPARTMENT 北海道店
想要跟 d design travel 去旅行！

砂川昌广 Sunagawa Masahiro
Tohon 店主
在大和郡山市柳町商店街上经营着一家
小小的书店。

砂川美穗子 Sunagawa Mihoko
书籍杂货集合店 Furukoto 的店员
兼编辑作者
每天都觉得奈良有说不尽的好。

那须野由华 Nasuno Yuka
d47 食堂的啤酒主管
幻想着自己有一天能在秋筱之森
举行结婚典礼。

丸川龙也 Marukawa Tatsuya
istgraph 总裁（注：公司现已改名
为 DragonBlooms）
用心去做美丽而令人愉悦的设计。

取访木之实 Suwa Konomi
MARUYA 的 D&DEPARTMENT
鹿儿岛店的店员
十几岁时第一次独自旅行，
去的就是奈良。

新山直广 Niiyama Naohiro
TSUGI 设计总监
总觉得和奈良很有缘分。
时隔多年又想再去奈良看看了。

御子柴泰子 Mikoshiba Yasuko
半月舍 员工
位于城下町彦根的旧书店。

关纱代子 Sayoko Seki
d47 食堂
夜不饮，不成活。

西冈洁 Nishioka Kiyoshi
摄影师
移居仪式的奈良之后反倒有种
回到家的感觉。

村木谕 Muraki Satoshi
制作人
这次拿起照相机叨扰了奈良。

园部晓子 Sonobe Akiko
d47 design travel 商店
会怀着对吉野杉的感谢来使用一次性
筷子。

**野口明日香 Noguchi Asuka,
渡会奈央 Watarai Nao**
发条堂
热爱漫画、喜剧，和吉野的二人组。

村田敦 Murata Atsushi
蔬菜咖啡馆 Toy Toy
在山口用蔬菜烹制午餐。
（此外，也深爱着咖啡。）

高木崇雄 Takaki Takao
工艺风向 店主
那些每天在平城宫遗址放风筝的老人
就是我对晚年的向往。

野口贵士 Noguchi Takashi
奈良县政府 林学职员
奈良的森林和树木都与我们每一个人
息息相关。欢迎大家到奈良来！

卖豆纪拓 Mezuki Taku
YUTTE
YUTTE 的分店已经开到松江啦！
（注：说的是岛根县的松江市）

田代淳 Tashiro Jun
d 金缮部顾问
金缮部成员们修缮一新的食器又重新
回到 d47 食堂中发光发热。

野口忠典 Noguchi Tadanori
d47 design travel 商店
奈良的故事就是对人和材料的细细
斟酌。

森山胜心 Moriyama Katsushi
Kan-kaku Inc. 主理人
向岛根县的隐岐岛出发！
oki-islands.com

田中那津美 Tanaka Natsumi
TOWN 情报 par-ple 编辑部
奈良县内唯一的地区情报杂志，
在奈良县可谓无人不知。

野口学 Noguchi Manabu
D&DEPARTMENT 大阪店 店长
为了了解（奈良），就要买（这本书）
并加以利用。

安永 Kentauros Yasunaga Kentauros
安永摄影事务所
kentaurosyasunaga.com

田部井彰基 Tabei Akinori
d47 design travel 商店
器物和茶类主管。

原茂树 Hara Shigeki
日田 Liberte 主理人、
电影技术人员等等
在大分县日田市经营着私人影院。

山崎修平 Yamazaki Shuhei
d47 design travel 商店
作为奈良人，希望大家都能感受到
奈良的魅力。

鹤林万平 Tsurubayashi Manpei
Soni House
被编辑部诚意满满的采访所感动，
也很期待以后的各期。

渊上凉子 Fuchikami Ryoko
D&DEPARTMENT PROJECT
小目标是了解各种事情的背景资料。

山田藤雄 Yamada Fujio
NOOK & CRANNY 主管
强力推荐骑单车游览名古屋。
NOOK 也提供租赁单车服务。
nookandcranny.nagoya

寺崎美绪 Terasaki Mio
URBAN RESEARCH DOORS
本部媒体部
悠闲的奈良时光和亲切的奈良县民，
都让人觉得美好。

桝谷纪惠 Masutani Norie
Re: 吉野生活会
在吉野住着很多有趣的人呢！

横山七绘 Yokoyama Nanae
阿拉斯加文具店 店主
希望不断有好的产品能渗透到岐阜县。

中村千晶 Nakamura Chiaki
d47 design travel 商店
List：
喝着斑鸠牌牛奶长大的奈良小孩，
喜欢夜里一片漆黑的奈良。

松井知子 Matsui Tomato
List：
第 4 届长崎巡礼在 2016 年
11 月举行！

渡边美穗 Watanabe Miho
d47 食堂
热衷收集各种冷门的小知识。

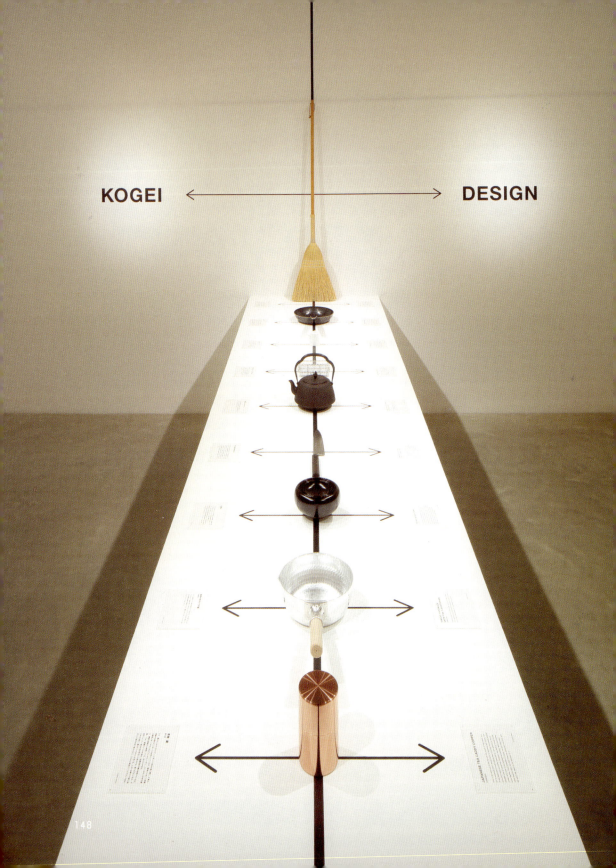

KOGEI ←——————→ DESIGN

Naoto Fukasawa
深泽直人

寻常

工艺和设计的界限

"工艺和设计的界限"这一展览（编辑部注：2016年10月8日～2017年3月20日）正在石川县的金泽21世纪美术馆展出。在金泽这个盛行手工艺而且设计也很好地融入其中的地方，我认为现在正适合进行这样的展览，于是想到了这个主题。无论是从思考"工艺"这个角度，还是从思考"设计"这个角度，我认为都是一件很有意义的事。

展览的契机，源于我经常被问到的一个问题："这是属于手工艺品，还是属于设计作品？"我知道，工艺与设计的界限是很模糊的。

可是，当艺术家本身也是制作者，即他会亲自用手做东西，那么制作出来的就是"工艺品"；如果艺术家不亲手参与制作，而是用机器来制作，甚至进行量产，这样制作出来的东西则被称为"设计作品"。这时，两者之间存在的差异是很明显的。

我突发奇想：在展厅的正中间纵向画一条线，右侧摆上设计作品，左侧摆上工艺品。从那条中心线出发，两端离得越远的，就越是"典型的工艺品"和"典型的设计品"，中心的线上放置的东西，自然也就很清楚了——正

Futsuu (Normal): Boundary Between Craft and Design

By Naoto Fukasawa

I curated an exhibition called "The Boundary between Kogei and Design" at the 21st Century Art Museum, Kanazawa, in Ishikawa Prefecture, which is showing now (October 8, 2016–March 20, 2017). In the city that is known for craftwork and that has a high level of graphic and product designs, I thought this was a very fitting theme to explore.

The initial idea came from questions I am often asked, such as, "Is this craft or is this designed object?" Of course, I knew that the boundary between these two things is vague. However, I can't deny that with traditional craftworks, the artist is the producer and the object is handmade by the very artist, whereas designed objects are almost never made by designers themselves.

I came up with an idea to draw a line in middle of the floor of the exhibition space and to place designed objects on the right side and craftworks on the left side. The farther (→p. 150)

是那些既能称之为工艺品也能称之为设计作品的"原型的极致"。比如苹果公司的 MacBook Pro、开化堂的茶筒等等，就被放在了中心线上。我想，既是工艺品，也是现在仍持续使用的物品，不恰恰是既能被称为工艺品也能被称为设计作品吗？

相对于画在"工艺"和"设计"界限上的纵轴，我对其他的东西应该放置到横轴上的哪个位置怀有更深的兴趣。与放置在中心的 MacBook Pro 相对照，我把 Olivetti 公司生产的打字机 Valentine 放到了工艺的一侧。它是设计史上的

名品，作为现在已经很少使用的物件，我们仿佛常常能听到对它的赞美："这个设计作品已经可以归入工艺品的领域了。"相反，有不少绝佳的工艺品，在如今的生活中除了鉴赏之外很少有其他用处，我因此思考了这样的配置。

我请石川的漆器匠人做了一个用便宜的聚氨酯涂装的塑料碗，并且制作了一个与它形状完全相同、在木质的碗上重复涂漆的漆碗。涂装和涂漆的过程也对比着做了展示。这个展示并不是想根据物品所放置的位置来追究它的好坏，而是想俯瞰在制作过程中所倾注的匠心。

away an object was from the line, the more "traditional" they were — traditional craftworks, traditionally designed objects — and the closer they were to the line, the boundary was less unclear. *MacBook Pro* by Apple and a Cylinder Tea Canister by Kaikado are placed atop the line; my thinking is that if these objects are used, they are both designed products as well as craftworks. I was curious to see which objects ended up farther away from the line. I placed a Valentine typewriter by Olivetti on the craftwork side, in contrast to the *MacBook Pro*. Even though this machine is known for its high quality design, it is no longer in use so I could almost hear people praising it as the

craftwork for its design. By contrast, enough crafts are no longer used, and I kept that in mind while I placed objects here and there.

I had a lacquer artisan make me a plastic bowl with cheap varnish and a wooden bowl with lacquer in the same exact shape. The step-by-step processes for each bowl are on display at the exhibition. I did not do this so that people can judge whether this is good or bad; I wanted to show people the passion and thoughts that are put into the creation of an item. I am beginning to think that maybe a highly designed object can be seen as a craft. The closer designed objects get to the

深泽直人 工业设计师。为欧洲、亚洲多家知名企业进行过品牌设计，并为日本国内著名大型制造商提供设计咨询。曾于日本国内外多次获奖，被英国皇家艺术协会授予"荣誉皇家工业设计师"。著有《设计的轮廓》（TOTO 出版）等。2012 年起担任日本民艺馆的馆长。

Naoto Fukasawa Product designer. Fukasawa has designed products for major brands in Europe and Asia. He has also worked as a consultant for major manufacturers in Japan. Winner of numerous awards given by domestic and international institutions, including the Royal Designer for Industry Award, honored by the British Royal Society of Arts. He has written books, most importantly *An Outline of Design* (TOTO). Since 2012, he is the Director of Nihon Mingei-kan（Japan Arts and Crafts Museum）.

P.148、P.150的图片为"工艺和设计的界限"展览现场（2016年10月8日～2017年3月20日，金泽21世纪美术馆） 摄影：木奥惠三 图片提供：金泽21世纪美术馆

一些成为精湛名品的设计作品也可以被称为"工艺品"，不是吗？那些无法再做改变的、实用之美的设计结晶，早就已经是工艺品了。也就是说，我能感受到这种看不见的引力——好的设计会逐渐接近工艺的领域。我甚至认为，例如精湛的手表或是 iPhone，被称为"工艺品"也毫不为过。

在我心里，"工艺"也好，"设计"也好，同样都在"制作"这条线上。我认为是没有界限这类东西的。可是，因为我们有"设计"这样的定义，有"工艺"这样的现象，在"制造"活动中才产生了界限的概念。

我觉得，"d"品牌也是正在那分界线周围进行摸索的活动体。人类感知"好"的感觉器官处于不断变化中，环境与物质之间的关系，或许为人类的感知提供了与过去不一样的刺激。但是，人类感知"美"的器官，是不会有什么变化的。

我觉得，让我们安静下来，思考一下"到底是什么让我们感受美好"，也是很有必要的。

boundary of the category of craft, the more utility they have. Take, for example, an *iPhone*: reduced down to its essence, it has reached the category of craftwork, I think.

For me, craftsmanship and designed objects are in the same line of what it means to create things. Maybe there is no boundary, but because we have definitions of "design" and "craft", we have divided them needlessly.

This magazine and the company, "d" is an attempt to rethink about the boundary as well, I think. What people think of as "good" is changing. People are demanding new sensations, new stimuli, because the contemporary relationship between environment and things have changed. But our need for beauty, our sense of beauty, hasn't really changed much.

It is, indeed, a good time to think about what is ordinary, what is natural to use.

D&DEPARTMENT PROJECT
FRIENDS

47
REASONS
TO
TRAVEL
IN
JAPAN

001
北海道
HOKKAIDO

北果楼 札幌本馆
- 北海道 札幌市中央区北1条西5-1-2
- 0800-500-0318
- www.kitakaro.com

Kitakaro Sapporo Honkan
- Kita 1-jo Nishi 5-chome 1-2, Chuo-ku, Sapporo, Hokkaido

002
青森
AOMORI

八户 Portal 美术馆 hacchi
- 青森县八户市三日町11-1
- 0178-22-8228
- hacci.jp

Hachinohe Portal Museum "hacchi"
- Mikka-machi 11-1, Hachinohe, Aomori

在这家点心店里，你能感受到北海道的文化和历史的气息 北果楼 札幌本馆今年25岁了。它所在的建筑物，是修建于大正十五年（1926年）的旧县立图书馆。店门口那棵刺楸树，树龄已经有140多年；玄关大厅的台阶，在保留着建造初始风貌的同时，依照建筑大师安藤忠雄的方案进行了改建。书架一直延伸到交叉拱顶顶高高的天井上，令人震撼。书架上排列着与北海道历史、文化、文学相关的书籍，可自由阅览，令人开心。回去时别忘了买一盒巧克力夹心饼干"北海道 厅立图书馆"回去送朋友，这在别处买不到的！（金贞姬／D&DEPARTMENT 北海道）

属于八户市民的"像社区文化馆一样的美术馆" 八户 Portal 美术馆 hacchi 建于2011年，不仅设有专门售卖东北地区特色产品的 Kaneiri 美术馆商店，还能阅览与艺术相关的书籍，是一个文化观光交流的场所。馆内还设有传统工艺品和特产的展示厅如南部裂织，以及使用大屏幕和模型进行的观光展示。那天，当地的商店街正在举办"三日町感谢之夜"活动，热闹非凡，我则趁机观看了当地的汽水"三岛橘汁"制作过程的影像，对八户的街道有了一些深层的了解。我希望，这样的美术馆，不仅八户有，每个地方都应该有一个才好。（泽田 央／d47 design travel store）

A confectionery store where the culture and history of Hokkaido can still be found The structure of the Kitakaro Sapporo Honkan, now celebrating the 25th anniversary of its establishment, is the former municipal library, built in 1926. By the entrance stands a kalopanax tree over 140 years old, and while the staircase in the entrance hall preserves the charm of the past, the building's renovated interior was designed by renowned architect Tadao Ando. Impressive bookshelves extend all the way to the high cross vault ceilings. Feel free to pick up a book to read during your stay from the extensive collection of books about the history, culture, and literature of Hokkaido. On your way home, purchase some Kitakaro Sapporo Honkan chocolate sandwich cookies as a souvenir of the old Hokkaido municipal library. (Kim Junghee, D&DEPARTMENT HOKKAIDO)

A community-centered museum for Hachinohe residents The Hachinohe Portal Museum, known as "hacchi" and completed in 2011, is an interactive cultural and tourism facility where visitors can browse art-related books, and is also home to the exclusive Tohoku regional Kaneiri Museum Shop. It features several sightseeing exhibitions using panels and models of traditional crafts and specialty products such as *nambu sakiori* cloth. Among the crowds of people at the "Mikkamachi Appreciation Evening" event venue along a local shopping street, I got to know a little more about the city of Hachinohe by watching video footage of the manufacturing process for the local Mishima citron cider. More places like this should exist—not only in Hachinohe, but all across Japan. (Hiro Sawada, d47 design travel store)

003

岩手
IWATE

卡尔塔咖啡店
⚲ 岩手县盛冈市内丸 16-16
☎ 019-651-5375
🏠 kissa-carta.com
Cafe Carta
⚲ Uchimaru 16-16, Morioka, Iwate

这里的面包如米饭，每天吃也不会厌 卡尔塔是一家只有十张座位的小咖啡厅。它家有一种圆形面包，是每天早上在店里新鲜烘焙的。点单后，店家会用烤箱加热，让面包皮变得脆脆的；用它做的三明治，也非常好吃。到了冬天，店内会推出红豆面包，里面是市内的日式点心老店梅月堂的红豆馅。——"卡尔塔开始卖红豆面包了"，这对我来说就是冬天开始的标志。点一份三明治套餐，盛汤的碗是我做的。看到自己亲手制作的漆碗在这里用了三年依然光泽明亮，很开心！（田代 淳／ Urushinuri Tashiro）

Bread you'll never tired of eating, just like rice! Carta is a small cafe that seats ten. It uses rounded loaves for sandwiches and toast that are baked at the shop every morning. After each order is taken, the bread is toasted in the oven to produce a delicious crisp crust. In winter, *anpan* with the red bean paste from the city's long-established Japanese confectionery shop "Baigetsudo" make an appearance. Hearing "Carta has started its *anpan* buns" truly evokes winter for me. You also can order sandwiches as a set meal, and the soup is served in lacquer bowls that I painted. These bowls have been in service for three years now and have grown shiny with use, which makes me happy to see. (Jun Tashiro, Urushinuri Tashiro)

004

宫城
MIYAGI

八濑咖啡
⚲ 宫城县气仙沼市台 229-1
☎ 0226-55-2307
Yasse Coffee
⚲ Dai 229-1, Kesennuma, Miyagi

文化遗迹上的咖啡店 三陆的地形是沉降式海岸，海的后边临山。在气仙沼市的八濑地区，海岸边至今还保留着不少旧时美丽的渔村和后山并存的风景。在后山上，八濑咖啡店沿袭八濑这一地名，于 2013 年开业。这是一家很受欢迎的店，现在也有不少人专程从远方前来。这家店修建在绳文时代的古迹上，据说，你从这里挖下去，就能挖到原始时代的石器。立足于这块人类居住历史如此长久的土地，被那悠久的历史感和安全感围绕，难怪店家自己烘焙的咖啡，喝起来也变得十分特别了。不过，对我来说，说到气仙沼，我更喜欢这里的咖喱饭。（熊谷太郎／正酒屋 六根净）

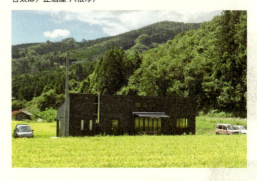

A cafe on the ruins The ria coast of Sanriku features mountains that rise almost up from the sea. Even now, the Yasse district of Kesennuma is home to many remnants of beautiful fishing villages existing in harmony with woodlands since the old days of the coast. Yasse Coffee, founded in 2013, was named after these woodlands. These days, people come from far away to visit this large, popular cafe. It's situated on top of the ruins of the Jomon era; it's said that if you dug here, you'd uncover ancient pottery. The fact that people have lived in this place since ancient times envelops you in a sense of security and history, and the in-house roasted coffee is exceptional. Kesennuma is for me, even more than the fish, about the curry served here. (Taro Kumagai, Rockonjo)

005
秋田
AKITA

全国烟花竞技大赛
📍 秋田县大仙市雄物川河畔 特设赛场
☎ 0187-62-1262（大曲商工会议所）
🏠 www.oomagari-hanabi.com
All-Japan National Fireworks Competition
📍 Special stage on the banks of the Omono River, Daisen, Akita

006
山形
YAMAGATA

桐佳丽大楼
📍 山形县山形市七日町 2-7-23
☎ 023-679-5433（株式会社MARUR）
🏠 www.tongari-bldg.com
TONGARI BLDG.
📍 Nanoka-machi 2-chome 7-23, Yamagata, Yamagata

日本顶级烟花匠人聚集于此，各显神通 被誉为日本三大烟花大赛之一的"大曲烟花"，又名"全国烟花竞技大赛"，每年八月举办。赛事始自 1910 年，原本是烟花匠人们自发开展的烟花赛事，后来逐步成为全国的烟花师们比试手艺的地方。观众在雄物川对岸的看台上抬头观看，满眼都是飞入夜空的流光溢彩，目光所及之处，立刻被那恢宏的气势震撼。在约 6 分钟的时间里，连续升空的烟花让人惊叹到无法用言语形容，在高潮时升空的"垂柳"规模宏大，漫天的火花经久不散，在夜空中展示着绚丽的身姿。（园部晓子／d47 design travel store）

一边追求特立独行，一边努力与周边共存 这里曾经同时拥有 11 家电影院，矗立于山形的文化巅峰，被称为"电影院大道"。后来，这些电影院都销声匿迹。到 2016 年，这座 40 岁的大楼重获新生。大楼里边有十三时，摆放着修行僧人坂本大三郎先生的书籍和山里的特产；还有名为"nitaki"的餐厅，向游客介绍腌菜等山形特有的食文化，为大家提供着新鲜的味觉体验；更有画廊 KUGURU 等等。负责施工和平面设计的创意工匠们也在这里设立了办公室，同时这里也是 2016 年"山形美术展"的主会场。（岩井巽／良品计画株式会社）

The work of Japan's ultimate fireworks artisans Held in August every year, the Omagari Fireworks display is one of Japan's three largest fireworks displays, and is also known as the All-Japan National Fireworks Competition. This event, launched in 1910, is a contest where the nation's fireworks experts show off their expertise by launching fireworks on their own. The audience, watching from the balcony seating across the Omono River, is captivated and overwhelmed by the colorful lights and ever-changing shapes that burst ceaselessly into existence. The fireworks which continue for about six minutes strike viewers speechless, and the fiery blossoms of the climactic *shidare-yanagi* (weeping willow) display remain beautiful long after they are launched, with their sparks slow to fade. (Akiko Sonobe, d47 design travel store)

Edgy building coexisting with community Once lined with 11 movie theaters, the avenue once known as "Cinema Street" was the pinnacle of culture in Yamagata. Although all have gone out of business now, in 2016 this 40-year old building was reborn as the Tongari Building. It is now home to "Jusanji," lined with old books and gifts from the mountains selected by the "mountain hermit" Sakamoto Daizaburo; restaurant "nitaki," which takes advantage of the unique food culture of Yamagata, such as pickles, to create new tastes; and the "KUGURU Gallery." The creators who worked on the building's renovation and graphics also have offices here, and it serves as the main venue of Yamagata Biennale 2016. (Tatsumi Iwai, Ryohin Keikaku Co., Ltd.)

007

福岛
FUKUSHIMA

仁井田本家
- 福岛县郡山市田村町金泽字高屋敷139
- ☎ 024-955-2222
- ⌂ www.kinpou.co.jp
- Niida-Honke Co., Inc.
- Tamura-machi Kanezawa Takayashiki 139, Koriyama, Fukushima

008

茨城
IBARAKI

撞舞
- 茨城县龙崎市 3710
- ☎ 0297-64-1444 （龙崎市撞舞保存会）
- ⌂ www.city.ryugasaki.ibaraki.jp
- Tsukumai
- 3710, Ryugasaki, Ibaraki

与自然共存的酿酒厂 山形市"正酒屋 六根净"的熊谷太郎先生精心挑选了产自东北地区的日本酒，每种都如此美味，令人不禁啧啧赞叹。其中，1711 年创立的福岛县"仁井田本家"，使用的是不施任何农药和化肥所栽培出的大米，并用自家农田的井水和自家山间涌出的地下水来酿造，做出了日本第一款使用100% 自然米的纯米酒。我非常喜欢金宝自然酒的"浊酒"。这款纯白色米酒甘甜而酸爽，冰镇一下喝起来甘爽可口，温酒同样回味无穷。这样的口感源自"自然米"所蕴含的原始芳香。(神藤秀人／d design travel 编辑部)

美丽的舞蹈，预示着夏日已经来临 夕阳西下，观众灼热的视线集中在了两位男性舞蹈演员身上。这就是持续了四百多年的"撞舞"。每年 7 月下旬，在龙崎市的八坂神社祇园祭最后一天，祈求五谷丰登、消灾祛病的祭典在撞舞大道上正式上演。带着雨蛙面具的男性舞蹈演员，在高达 14 米的撞柱上，不佩戴安全绳，或倒立，或在绳上滑行，高超的技巧令人目不暇接。那景象，令我深受震撼。他们身穿漂亮的唐草纹样的窄袖汗衫和日本传统的武士灯笼裤，戏剧般的演出引起观众的阵阵惊呼。等你回过神来，夏日的夜空早已悄然在眼前展开。(加濑千宽／D&DEPARTMENT PROJECT)

Sake brewery in harmony with nature The Tohoku regional *sake* variants carefully selected by Taro Kumagai at the "Seishuya Rokkonjo" store in the city of Yamagata are truly delicious. These include "Niida Honke," founded in Fukushima Prefecture in 1711, which uses brewer's rice grown without any chemical fertilizers or pesticides, blended with natural water from the company's own mountain fields and spring water from their own well. This was Japan's first pure rice *junmai sake* made from 100% natural rice. Personally, the Kinpo Shizenshu cloudy *nigorizake* is my favorite. This sweet, white pure rice sake with a hint of acidity can be enjoyed chilled, but it can be heated too. This is the original taste and power of natural rice. (Hideto Shindo, d design travel Editorial Team)

A beautiful dance heralding the coming of summer At dusk, all eyes are firmly fixed on the two dancing men. For over 400 years, the Tsukumai ceremony has been held in late July every year on the last day of the Gion Festival at Yasaka Shrine in the city of Ryugasaki. This ritual, held on Tsukumai Street, is conducted to pray for rain and good harvests and to ward off illness. The dancers, who wear masks shaped like tree frogs, leap about atop 14-meter poles, performing a series of feats such as handstands and rope sliding without safety nets or lines. I was overwhelmed by this performance. Their costumes of traditional swirl-patterned undershirts and tattsuke-hakama pants are also fantastic. It makes me feel as though I've watched an entire stage play—then I suddenly notice that the summer sky has darkened to night. (Chihiro Kase, D&DEPARTMENT PROJECT)

009
栃木
TOCHIGI

矢野津津美
ynttm.tumblr.com
Tsutsumi Yano

010
群马
GUNMA

baimai
群马县富冈市上高尾29
0274-67-1188
baimai
Kamitakao 29, Tomioka, Gunma

一位对"土祭"始终不离不弃的摄影家 我在益子町的祭典"土祭"上结识了矢野津津美先生——一位豁达而体贴的摄影家。他本人是土生土长的当地人，每年举办的祭典他都会积极参与，那些转瞬即逝的东西很自然地定格在他所拍摄的照片里，显得弥足珍贵。这是他2015年所拍摄的一张照片，当地人身穿造型家泽村木绵子的作品。听着西明寺的川流声，被绿色浸润的神秘风景在脑海中苏醒，让人仿佛能感受到人们平静祈祷的情景。同时，他还负责益子町发行的画册《MICHIKAKE》的摄影工作，每一幅作品都真挚地传达着益子町地域文化的魅力。（黑江美穗／d47 MUSEUM）

品尝群马的当季蔬菜 baimai店里不用肉，只以蔬菜为主料，制作咖喱和辛香料理。店主春山若木先生将自家古旧的住宅加以改建，成为现在的店面。七月酷热的日子里，我点了一个色彩丰富的"蔬菜咖喱套餐"，包括青茄子、四叶黄瓜、甜玉米等蔬菜，辣味不会过于强烈，清爽的调味非常可口，很快就被我一扫而光。因为店家只使用固定几种当地农家培育的当季蔬菜，所以这里的菜单每周才更换一次。下次能吃到什么呢？……我不知不觉拿起画册，想查一查蔬菜的收获时令。（田部井彰基／d47 design travel store）

A photographer supporting the Hijisai festival I met Tsutsumi Yano at the Hijisai festival in the town of Mashiko, and he had a great, easygoing nature. He was deeply involved in creating the festival, since he also lives locally, I think that is the reason why his photographs, both of nature and of events that people are likely to miss, were shot with such care. In 2015, he took a photograph of local people wearing pieces by sculptor Yuko Sawamura. You can sense the sound of the stream running near the Saimyoji Temple, the revitalizing green of the mystical landscape, and the gentle prayers of the people. He was also responsible for the photography in the *Michikake* booklet issued by the town of Mashiko, which truly conveys the charm of Mashiko. (Miho Kuroe, d47 MUSEUM)

Taste the seasonal vegetables of Gunma Restaurant baimai serves vegetable-centered curries and other dishes using spices, all made without meat. Owner Wakako Haruyama created the store by renovating an old residence on her own. During an extremely hot day in July, I ordered the colorful vegetable curry set meal, featuring green eggplant, Suyo cucumbers, sweet corn, and more. It was not too spicy, with simple and delicious seasoning, and I ate it with delight. The menu changes weekly, since baimai uses only certain varieties of seasonal vegetables grown by local farmers. I have already researched the vegetable harvest thinking about what I might be able to enjoy the next time I go. (Akinori Tabei, d47 design travel store)

011
埼玉
SAITAMA

伯爵邸
📍 埼玉县埼玉市大宫区宫町 1-46
☎ 048-644-3998
Hakusyaku Tei
📍 Miyacho1-chome 46, Omiya-ku, Saitama, Saitama

012
千叶
CHIBA

吕久吕
📍 千叶县千叶市中央区中央 3-4-10
☎ 043-224-5251
🏠 rokuro.cafe
Rokuro
📍 Chuo 3-chome 4-10, Chuo-ku, Chiba, Chiba

在这里，时光仿佛为你停留 伯爵邸是一家 1975 年开业的咖啡店。店内布置着鲜红的窗帘和沙发、古典式样的瓷器等物品，彩画玻璃灯具中透出的光线柔和而舒适。店里有名的大宫那不勒斯面，搭配上埼玉县产的蔬菜精心制作而成。为了"能让附近专门学校的学生用低廉的价格在这里度过悠闲的时光"，一份面的分量相当于别处的三份，令人惊喜不已。店主选用的食材即使冷了也不会变硬；用这里的咖啡豆做成的咖啡，即使变凉也依然可口。这份待客的诚意在菜单中尽得体现。（渡边美穗／d47 食堂）

没有拿手菜，岂敢自称名店 时隔久远，我再次拜访了学生时代再三犹豫才敢进门的咖啡店吕久吕。这家店 1976 年开业时是一家画廊，为了能让人更轻松地接触陶艺作品，又开设了咖啡店。咖啡店里使用了各种各样的餐具，比如在千叶很少见的萩烧、笠间烧等，卖咖啡的同时，也展示和销售这些餐具。最有名的是这个"咖喱大吐司"，在一整个特别定制的吐司面包中注入店家引以为傲的咖喱而成。连面包边儿都那么美味，我总是忍不住再点一份奶酪和鸡蛋。这家千叶市的名店，从开业伊始一直坚持做这道费时费力的料理，美味流传至今。（进藤仁美／d47 design travel store）

Forget the passing of time in this coffee shop Coffee shop Hakusyaku Tei was founded in 1975. With its bright red curtains and sofa, classical ceramic art objects, and stained glass lighting, the store has a soft, comfortable feel. Its famous "Omiya Napolitan" spaghetti dish uses vegetables from Saitama Prefecture. The servings are of surprising volume, enough to serve three people, help ensure that the many full-time students nearby can spend some leisurely time at an affordable price. The fresh ingredients and the coffee beans are carefully selected to remain delicious even after they cool down. The owner wants customers to spend some leisurely time here, and this mentality is evident in the menu. (Miho Watanabe, d47 SHOKUDO)

Its famous dishes are testimony to this venerable store After a very long break, I revisited the Rokuro café where I spent some time in my student days. Although it opened in 1976 as a gallery, the owners reopened it as a cafe so that customers would feel free to touch and handle the ceramic wares. Rokuro exhibits and sells a variety of pottery wares, such as Hagiyaki and Kasamayaki ceramics, which are quite rare in Chiba. Its famous "Curry Jumbo Toast" dish, available by special order, consists of a full loaf of toasted bread filled with homemade curry. Delicious down to the crust; I like it topped with egg and cheese. Ever since its founding, Rokuro has earned its place as one of Chiba's most famous cafes by naturally continuing to invest good deal of time on service. (Hitomi Shindo, d47 design travel store)

013

东京
TOKYO

天野屋
⚲ 东京都千代田区外神田2-18-15
☎ 03-3251-7911
🖥 www.amanoya.jp
Amanoya
⚲ Sotokanda 2-chome 18-15, Chiyoda-ku, Tokyo

014

神奈川
KANAGAWA

大浪
⚲ 神奈川县川崎市高津区新作3-3-2
☎ 044-888-6361
🖥 onami-sibori.com
Onami
⚲ Shinsaku 3-chome 3-2, Takatsu-ku, Kawasaki, Kanagawa

传承自江户时代的甘酒 天野屋开在神田明神参道入口处，是创建于弘化三年（1846年）的甘酒屋。来到这里的人，可以喝上一杯甘酒。你当然可以在店内的甘味屋里品尝甘酒，但天气好的时候，我建议大家端着甘酒悠闲地散散步。甘酒使用在地下室发酵而成的曲（一种发酵后的谷物）制成，据说开店时的制作方法一直沿袭到了现在。我去的那天非常炎热，我喝了杯冰甘酒，没放糖，却有爽口的甜味，燥热的身体瞬间得到滋润。店里也销售曲，你不妨试从江户时代延续而来的发酵工艺所带来的力量。（大野瞬／作家）

在这里，我第一次见识了金属旋压 金属旋压，是将金属板装在模具上，像转盘那样一边转动一边用旋轮施加压力进行加工。大浪家1982年在川崎创立了相和鲜榨工业，与设计师山崎义树先生一起设立了生活用品品牌"大浪"（Onami）。杯子上特意留下旋压制法的痕迹，能让人想象到制作过程，很有意思。"因为经常制造大型的制品，非常费力，因此机器的底座是埋在地下的。"店主谈笑自如，我们却感受到了他们把技术代代传承下去的决心。（黑江美穗／d47 MUSEUM）

***Amazake* handed down since the Edo era** The Amanoya store, which stands at the entrance to Kanda Myojin Shrine, was established in 1846 as store for *amazake*, a sweet, thick fermented rice drink. When you visit, first try the *amazake*. You can enjoy it at the sweets shop on the same property, but if the weather is good, you should take your *amazake* to go and wander around as you like. The *amazake* is made in the basement here using *koji* (sake starter), and the recipe has remained unchanged since the store's founding. The *amazake* is clean and refreshing, even on very hot days, and since no sugar is used, it refreshes the overheated body naturally. Since Amanoya also sells *koji*, you can try your hand at the power of fermentation, handed down since the Edo era. (Shun Ohno, writer)

Encountering *hera shibori* for the first time *Hera shibori*, or metal spinning, is a type of metal processing whereby a metal workpiece is fixed in place upon a metal form and rotated like a potter's wheel, while being worked with a spatula-like tool called a *hera*. The Onami homeware brand was launched by the Onami family of "Aiwa Shibori Co., Ltd.," founded in Kawasaki in 1982, together with designer Yoshiki Yamazaki. It is interesting to imagine the manufacturing process of these cups, which intentionally leave the *hera* marks as part of the design. With a smile, the experts explain that, "Since quite a bit of force is applied when manufacturing large-scale products, the base of this machine needs to be buried in the ground." Here, such technical expertise is passed down from father to son. (Miho Kuroe, d47 MUSEUM)

015
新潟
NIIGATA

岚溪庄
📍 新潟三条市长野1450
☎ 0256-47-2211
🏠 www.rankei.com
Rankeisou Inn
📍 Nagano 1450, Sanjo, Niigata

016
富山
TOYAMA

内脏煮乌冬 丝庄
📍 富山县富山市太郎丸本町1-7-6
☎ 076-425-5581
Motsu-nikomi Udon ITOSHOU
📍 Taromaru-Honmachi 1-chome 7-6, Toyama, Toyama

尝尽新潟的四季之味
第一次拜访这里是在春天。那次，我品尝了从当地深山里摘来的野菜天妇罗，清香四溢，一看就很新鲜，还有我从没见过的粗大的煮紫萁。下田乡的当季料理——富有弹性的鲤鱼刺身、盐烧鳟鱼等等，一道接一道，陆续上场。岚溪庄地处三条市的深山里，是依傍着溪谷而修建的温泉旅馆，晚餐的每一道菜都很

鲜美。我会选在季节变换时造访。本馆的绿风馆是昭和初期的歇山顶式建筑，深茶色的木质墙壁令人放松而惬意。到那儿别忘了品尝一下用温泉水做成的早餐粥！（中村千晶／d47 design travel store）

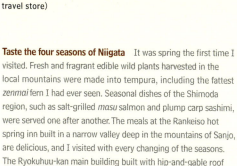

富山值得排队拔草的名吃　招牌料理"内脏煮乌冬"使用的是冰见乌冬[21]。厨房设在店中央，围绕着厨房的是18个吧台座位，另外还有桌席和日式宴会席，大约能容纳40人。即便如此，到了午餐时间，门口仍然会大排长龙。16个土锅一齐放在灶上，厨师像匠人一样精确地用锅盖检查着食物的烹饪进度，技术高超，动作娴熟。进店稍等片刻，店员就会把咕嘟咕嘟冒着泡的内脏煮乌冬端到你的面前。锅里是扁扁的、软糯的乌冬和满满的内脏，还有把它们调和在一起的味噌，令你胃口大开！（熊坂充／D&DEPARTMENT 富山）

Taste the four seasons of Niigata　It was spring the first time I visited. Fresh and fragrant edible wild plants harvested in the local mountains were made into tempura, including the fattest *zenmai* fern I had ever seen. Seasonal dishes of the Shimoda region, such as salt-grilled *masu* salmon and plump carp sashimi, were served one after another. The meals at the Rankeiso hot spring inn built in a narrow valley deep in the mountains of Sanjo, are delicious, and I visited with every changing of the seasons. The Ryokuhuu-kan main building built with hip-and-gable roof architecture, constructed during the early Showa period, has wooden walls in deeply calming shades of brown. The morning rice porridge made with hot spring water is my recommendation. (Chiaki Nakamura, d47 design travel store)

There's always a queue for this Toyama specialty　The signboard menu says "Motsu-nikomi udon," Himi udon noodles with stewed meat. The central kitchen is surrounded by an 18-seat counter and more than 40 table seats as well as Japanese style seating. Despite all this, in daytime there is always a queue of eager locals. 16 varieties of stew are all simmering over the heat at once, constantly checked by efficient movements of the staff using the pot lids. Wait for a bit and your udon noodles with stewed meat will arrive, piping hot and bubbling. Served with plenty of meat and plump, soft udon noodles, the appetizing flavor is finished off perfectly with the addition of miso. (Mitsuru Kumasaka, D&DEPARTMENT TOYAMA)

017
石川
ISHIKAWA

轮岛 KIRIMOTO 本町店
📍 石川县轮岛市河井町1-172
☎ 0768-22-7494
🏠 www.kirimoto.net
WAJIMA KIRIMOTO Honmachi Store
📍 Kawaimachi 1-172, Wajima, Ishikawa

018
福井
FUKUI

"旧店新生"集市
☎ 0778-65-0048（"旧店新生集市"执行委员会）
🏠 kawada-t.jp/renew
RENEW

漆器革命　日本各地有众多漆器产地，我家每天使用的餐具主要是轮岛漆器。我家使用轮岛的漆器名牌"KIRIMOTO"十多年了，有时早上不得不匆忙出门，餐具上的水也来不及擦干，放着直到晚上回家，就这样，一直用到现在，也没有任何问题。而且，特有的莳地加工方法使它具有独特的亚光质感，就算在露营时你也可以放心使用，漆器不会留下明显的擦伤。此外，

这种漆器还非常轻便。2016 年，我偶遇了设计师大治将典先生设计的汤匙，每次这把汤匙与我心爱的漆器、瓷器或玻璃等餐具轻轻碰撞，发出叮咚之声，我都不禁感叹：这汤匙真是做到了极致。（神藤秀人／d design travel 编辑部）

工房里的新发现　靖江市河和田地区，是一个聚集了漆器和眼镜制作者的小村落。每年十月，这里会举办体验型市集"旧店新生"，可以自由参观制造现场，也可以当场购买。逛完市集上的二十几家店铺后，你会发现好几家简洁洗练的店铺，店主都是年轻的手艺人。在一座普通民居似的工房里，有一位面相看上去有点吓人的工匠，给我解说商品时却热心而亲切。我与这些仿佛距离自己很遥远的匠人聊得开心，在回去的路上，心中对于手工艺的认识已经悄然发生了变化。两天之间，我感受到了工艺品产地与时代相配的节奏，以及它们不断发展变化的深度。（新山直宏／TSUGI）

A revolution in lacquerware　Many regions across Japan produce lacquerware, but for the tableware that my family uses every day, I choose mainly Wajima lacquerware. I first encountered KIRIMOTO lacquerware more than 10 years ago — and I've never had any problem with it even if I rush out in the morning, leaving the lacquerware in water all day until I return home. In addition, the unique *makiji* matte finish keeps any scratches inconspicuous, even when used roughly in the camp. As a bonus, they are ultra-lightweight. For 2016, designer Masanori Oji has been working on his *renge* ("lotus") — the ultimate spoon, designed to strike softly on precious glass, porcelain, or lacquerware dishes. (Hideto Shindo, d design travel Editorial Team)

Studio tours give rise to new awareness　Creators of lacquerware and glasses gather in the Kawada district in the city of Sabae. Every October, the hands-on Renew market is held here, where it is possible to watch creators at work and buy their creations. Visiting the 20 or so participating stores, including many sophisticated stores launched by young creators themselves, as well as workshops that resemble ordinary houses, one will hear artisans who may have seemed rather intimidating at first glance discuss their creations with great reverence. Through conversations with these artisans who previously seemed rather distant to me, my awareness of creative work had changed by the time I returned home. Over two days, I really felt the depth of this district, which continues to change with the times. (Naohiro Niiyama, TSUGI)

019
山梨
YAMANASHI

曲之仓 咖啡店
📍 山梨县北杜市白州町台原 2283
☎ 0551-35-2236
🌐 www.kouji-is.com/#!cafe/clyrv
Kura Cafe Kouji's
📍 Hakushu-cho Daigahara 2283, Hokuto, Yamanashi

020
长野
NAGANO

阿尔卑斯读书营地
📍 长野县大町市平森 9707-1（木崎湖露营场）
🌐 alpsbookcamp.jp
ALPS BOOK CAMP
📍 (Lake Kizaki Campsite) Hiramori 9707-1, Omachi, Nagano

使用曲糖的甜品店 山梨名酒"七贤"创立于 1750 年，在酒窖里的酒仓咖啡店里，可以品尝到用曲糖制作的甜品。曲糖是用发酵米和米粉制成的天然甜味料。这也正是只有"七贤"才能做到的。它用来造酒的水是被选为"日本 100 个著名水源地"之一的甲斐驹岳的潜流水。用曲糖和县内产的蔬菜、水果做成的冰沙很受欢迎。这个店里专设了一个书架，摆放着春光堂书店为《d 设计之旅：山梨》推荐的书籍。徜徉其间，可以悠闲地享受恬静的时光。（清水美香／D&DEPARTMENT 山梨）

阿尔卑斯山脚下的书市 这是松本市内的书店"刊日"的店主菊地彻先生所主办的书市。在木崎湖的露营场里，由书店和出版社牵头，另有 80 多家食品店、饰品店、杂货店，从日本各地前来参加。从会场可以看见湖泊和北阿尔卑斯的雪山，不仅有音乐演出、脱口秀、朗读会、放映会，到了夜里还会燃起篝火。制作者亲口告诉你每一本书的故事，这是这书市最有意思的地方。我买了奈良县的诗人西尾胜彦先生的诗集，静坐在湖畔，一直读到日落。（大道刚／D&DEPARTMENT 策划）

摄影: Yukihiro Shinohara

A sweet store that uses *koji* sugar Shichiken, by Yamanashi Meijo Co., founded in 1750. At the Kura Cafe, you can enjoy sweets made with koji sugar (*kouji tou*) in a sake brewery. Koji sugar is a natural sweetener made from fermented rice koji and rice flour. Shichiken uses the subterranean water of Mt. Kai-Komagatake, selected as one of Japan's 100 best water sources, to perform sake brewing. "Kouji," the store's smoothies made from koji sugar and locally grown fruit and vegetables, are popular. The store also houses a book shelf produced by "Shunkodo" Bookstore, which also selects books for the D&DEPARTMENT YAMANASHI project—so enjoy some leisurely time browsing these. (Mika Shimizu, D&DEPARTMENT YAMANASHI)

A literary event at the foot of the Alps This literary event is organized by Toru Kikuchi, who runs the "sioribi" bookstore in the city of Matsumoto. Held at the Lake Kizaki campsite, the event features exhibits by over 80 stores from around Japan—including bookstores and publishers, of course, as well as food, accessories, and miscellaneous goods stores. The venue, which overlooks the lake and Japan's Northern Alps, plays host to live music, talk shows, reading sessions, screenings, and a campfire at night. The best part of this literary event is hearing stories about the books directly from their authors. I bought a collection of poetry by Nara poet Katsuhiko Nishio and read it by the lake until dark. (Go Oomichi, D&DEPARTMENT PROJECT)

021
岐阜
GIFU

千代保稲荷神社
⚲ 岐阜县海津市平田町三乡 1980
☎ 0584-53-1374（海津市商工观光科）
Chiyobo Inari Shrine
⚲ Hirata-cho Sango 1980, Kaizu, Gifu

022
静冈
SHIZUOKA

沼津 KANEHACHI
⚲ 静冈县沼津市千本港町 109
☎ 055-954-0008
🏠 numazu-kanehachi.com
Numazu KANEHACHI
⚲ Senbon Minatomachi 109, Numazu,
Shizuoka

特产：进贡油炸豆皮 这个神社被人亲切地称为 "Ochobo -san"，深受大家喜爱。因为举行祈愿生意兴隆和家宅平安的 "月越参拜"，所以每到月末的深夜至次月初，这里都会特别热闹。这个神社是日本三大稻荷神社之一，建于室町时代，虽然规模不大，每年也有 200 万人前来参拜。我小时候，每年正月也会来参拜。我记得自己对神社里供奉的炸豆皮特别感兴趣，每次来到这里都像逛庙会一样，既开心又兴奋。如今我已经长大成人，仍然会为了祈愿生意兴隆而去参拜。参拜完毕之后，还一定要去尝尝参道上的炸串、草饼、河鱼等料理。（横山七绘／阿拉斯加文具）

渔港之城・沼津的食堂 熙熙攘攘的沼津饮食店街上，我被黑白的标志吸引，掀开暖帘，来到了 "沼津 KANEHACHI"。骏河饭装在接近脸盆大小的木桶里，里边有樱花虾、鲱鱼等骏河湾捕获的鱼类，摆得满满当当，整整齐齐，吸引着食客的目光。吃完后，还有鱼肉高汤做成的味噌汤。店内的墙壁像一块大黑板，画着沼津港卸货的景象和金枪鱼的图解插画。这个体现着沼津自豪感的店铺设计，来自当地的建筑设计事务所剑桥森林。（佐佐木晃子／ d design travel 编辑部）

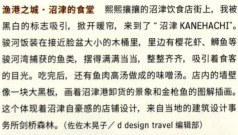

Oage fried tofu at Chiyobo Inari Shrine This shrine, which is nicknamed Ochobo-san, is especially crowded late at night at the end of each month when countless people come to pray for prosperity in business and safety at home for the coming month. Built in the Muromachi period, Chiyobo Inari is said to be one of Japan's three major Inari shrines, with two million people coming to worship at the shrine every year, despite its small size. As a child, I visited the shrine every New Year's Day, and I remember the novelty of offering the *oage* fried tofu to the deity — it was as exciting as visiting the fair. Even now as an adult, I still pray there for prosperity in business, after which I'm sure to enjoy a delicious meal of *kushikatsu* skewers, *kusamochi* rice cakes, or river fish on the path leading to the shrine. (Nanae Yokoyama, Alaska Bungu)

A dining hall in the fishing port of Numazu In the bustling restaurant district of Numazu, attracted to a monochrome sign that reads "Numazu Kanehachi," I part the *noren* curtain and boldly enter. Their *suruga-don* rice bowl is filled to the brim with seafood such as sakura shrimp and amberjack caught in Suruga Bay, prepared with great care. I finish my meal with the miso soup made with fish broth. Using the walls as blackboards, illustrations of tuna and pictures of the port of Numazu decorate the interior. The restaurant design conveys great pride in Numazu, and was created by local architectural design firm Cambridge-no-Mori. (Akiko Sasaki, d design travel Editorial Team)

023
爱知
AICHI

Y.市场酿造厂
- 爱知县名古屋市中村区名站4-17-6
- ☎ 052-533-5151
- 🔗 craftbeer.nagoya

Y.MARKET BREWING
- Meieki 4-chome 17-6, Nakamura-ku, Nagoya, Aichi

024
三重
MIE

拟革纸
- 三重县伊势市宇治浦田1-5-2
  [革工艺 雷屋(KAMINARIYA)]
- ☎ 0596-26-1333
- 🔗 www.okageyokocho.co.jp/tenpo.php?no=18

GIKAKUSHI
- (KAMINARIYA Leather Crafts) Ujiurata 1-chome 5-2, Ise, Mie

名古屋的啤酒，来自名古屋的名水

Y.市场酿造厂开在柳桥，是名古屋第一家精酿啤酒坊，距离名古屋站很近。三层楼的建筑物里，一楼是酿造作坊，二楼开设了啤酒餐厅，供应新鲜酿造的精酿啤酒。我去过好多次，在品尝着品种丰富的高品质啤酒的同时，我总是会为市区里能酿造出这么好喝的啤酒

而感到大惑不解。其实，这里的水质非常优良，一些大型啤酒公司也在这个地区拥有啤酒厂。出产于名古屋的美味，现在也正被送往日本各地。（山田藤雄／NOOK&CRANNY）

江户的精华所孕育的高雅之杰作

在三重县，有一项曾在1900年巴黎世博会上获得金奖的传统工艺："拟革纸"。它将和纸加工成与真皮极其相似的质地。第一次看到"拟革纸"的时候，无论怎么看它都像是真皮，而拿到手里的瞬间会让你为那轻盈而惊讶不已，这才回过神来：它原来是纸！拟革纸曾经一度销声匿迹，志愿者们正在为了它的复兴而积极活动。2016年6月，在OKAGE横丁开设了展示和销售拟革纸的"革工艺 雷屋"。这种江户时代才有的精美风格，让人心动不已。（丸川龙也／丸川商店）

Nagoya beer, supported by Nagoya water Y. Market Brewing is Nagoya's first craft beer brewery to set up shop in Yanagibashi, right next to Nagoya Station. The three-story building features the brewery on the ground floor and a beer restaurant on the second floor that serves fresh-brewed craft beer. I've visited several times to enjoy the rich variety of high-quality beer, and it always surprises me to see such delicious beer brewed in an urban area. A leading beer company has also set up a facility in this region, which is known for the quality of its water. The fantastic taste of this region is starting to spread across Japan. (Fujio Yamada, NOOK & CRANNY)

Ethical products created in the Edo era Mie Prefecture is home to the traditional craft of *gikakushi*, in which Japanese paper is processed to appear exactly like leather. *Gikakushi* was awarded a gold medal at the Paris Exposition of 1900. When I first saw *gikakushi* imitation leather paper it resembled leather in every way, but the moment it picked it up I was surprised by its lightness — a reminder that it is, in fact, paper. Although production of *gikakushi* paper stopped for a time, the craft is re-emerging thanks to the efforts of volunteers. In June 2016, the Kaminariya leathercraft studio was opened in Okageyokocho to exhibit and sell *gikakushi* imitation leather paper. I'm thrilled to see the stylish, elegant tastes of the Edo era kept alive until now. (Tatsuya Marukawa, Marukawa Shoten)

025

滋贺
SHIGA

湖北 OHANASHI
📍 滋贺县米原市米原中町 米原站内(井筒屋)
☎ 0749-52-0006
🌐 www.izutsuya.cc
Kohoku no Ohanashi
📍 (IZUTSUYA) Inside Maibara Station, Maiharanakamachi, Maibara, Shiga

026

京都
KYOTO

平井常荣堂药房
📍 京都府京都市左京区孙桥町15
☎ 075-771-4963
🌐 www.jjyoeido.com
Hirai Joeido Yakubo
📍 Magohashi-cho 15, Sakyo-ku, Kyoto, Kyoto

湖北的故事,藏在便当里 每次乘坐电车前往东京时,在米原站购买"湖北的 OHANASHI"便当都是一个小小的奢侈和期待。打开唐草纹样的包装,掀开盒盖,腌渍樱花叶那独特的香味立刻飘散开来。便当里有烤鸭肉、琵琶湖产的虾所做的虾豆、醋拌鱼肉、腌渍芜菁等,味道很朴素。从 1987 年开始销售以来,便当的内容、样式乃至放在骰子形纸盒里的糖果,几乎没有变过。吃便当的时候,我脑海中总会想起湖北的老奶奶。"记得常回来看看啊!"她说。(御子柴泰子/半月舍)

代代传承的 300 年老店 沿着鸭川散步时,一间画着药草的古老建筑物会在不经意间映入眼帘:平井常荣堂药房。它创立于 1701 年,最初侍奉幕府和大名的医生,明治之后成为专卖和汉药材的店铺。店铺建于江户时代,天井里满满地挂着药草袋,第八代店主平井正一郎先生笑脸相迎。和汉药是将中药方依照日本人体质修改调配而成,根据客人的身体状况开出处方。店里有独创的入浴剂和茶,用制作汤药的药草所调配,推荐给初次接触和汉药的人。(井上香织/D&DEPARTMENT 京都)

Listen to your lunch — the tale of Kohoku Whenever I travel by train toward Tokyo, I look forward to the modest luxury of a *Kohoku no Ohanashi* bento lunch box purchased at Maibara Station. Open the lid of the decorative spiral-design packaging, and out wafts the unique aroma of salted cherry leaves. The rustic flavors include roast duck, simmered beans with tiny shrimp caught at Lake Biwa, *nuta*, salad seasoned with miso and vinegar , red pickled turnip, and more. Since its launch in 1987, the content and form of this bento have remained almost unchanged, right up to the piece of candy included in a tiny dice-patterned box. Every time I eat one, I imagine the old lady of Kohoku saying, "Please visit us again." (Yasuko Mikoshiba, Hangetsusha)

A store with 300 years of tradition Walk along the Kamogawa River and an old building advertising herbal remedies will catch your eye. Founded in 1701, Hirai Joeido Yakubo began as a medical clinic serving the Japanese Shogunate and feudal lords, becoming a vendor of Japanese-style traditional Chinese medicine after the Meiji era. The store itself was built in the Edo era, and still has herb bags hanging from the ceiling. Eighth-generation shopkeeper Shoichiro Hirai will greet you with a smile. The medicine is based on traditional Chinese medicine altered to better suit Japanese requirements, and is formulated depending on the state of the body. The store's original blends of bathing tonics and herbal teas are recommended for those new to herbal medicine. (Kaori Inoue, D&DEPARTMENT KYOTO)

027

大阪
OSAKA

HS
 大阪府大阪市西区新町 4-3-4 3F
 06-6538-0055
 hs-hayashishoten.com
HS
 3rd floor, Shinmachi 4-chome 3-4, Nishi-ku, Osaka

028

兵库
HYOGO

南京町
 兵库县神户市中央区荣町通 1-3-18
 078-332-2896 南京町商店街振兴组合
 www.nankinmachi.or.jp
Nankinmachi
 Sakaemachidori 1-chome 3-18, Chuo-ku, Kobe, Hyogo

美，源于根基 西区新町的精品店"HS"，由林佑治先生的妻子由纪女士于 2011 年开设。这里既有民艺，也有艺术与时尚，你能感受到她对所有美的事物一视同仁的态度，以及她对于美的事物贪婪而一往无前的姿态。"看，很美吧？"佑治先生这样问道。从他的语调中，你也能体会到，对于店铺里展示的那些商品从最深处所散发出来的美，他的追求是多么执着。最近我在这里看到冲绳的大岭实清制作的咖啡杯碟，以及和歌山的森冈由利子烧制的白瓷，感动不已，当即买下，爱不释手。（野口学／D&DEPARTMENT 大阪）

神户的中国"南京町" 在贸易都市神户，有着日本三大唐人街之一的南京町，这条街上有超过 100 家店的餐厅和杂货店。春节、中秋节等各种活动贯穿一整年，一直深受神户人的喜爱。作为标志性的留影地，我向大家推荐中心广场上十二生肖像。其中我最喜欢"龙"，甚至想做一个龙的吊饰带在身边。这里的十二生肖像里有一只熊猫，关于这件事，据说还有这样一段趣闻：在中国订制生肖像亥猪时，沟通出现了问题，对方没理解清楚，于是出现了这样的结果——预定了一头猪，给了一只熊猫。（山崎修平／d47 design travel store）

A select shop selling ceramics with the essence of beauty The select shop HS, located in Shinmachi in Nishi Ward, was established by Yuji Hayashi and his wife Yuki. Their ambitious and eclectic approach to beautiful things — folk crafts, art, fashion — is evident. The root of the shop's selection criteria lies in Yuji suggesting that an item may indeed be beautiful. Recently impressed by coffee bowls by Jissei Omine of Okinawa and white porcelain by Yuriko Morioka of Wakayama, I bought them and I love them. (Manabu Noguchi, D&DEPARTMENT OSAKA)

Nankinmachi — a touch of China in Kobe In the commercial city of Kobe is situated Nankinmachi, one of Japan's three large Chinatown districts, which is lined with 100 or more Chinese eateries and general stores. Events such as the Lunar New Year Festival and Mid-Autumn Festival are held throughout the year and are well loved by Kobe locals. The Chinese zodiac images in the central square are a great photography spot — the dragon is a particular favorite of mine, so much so that I'd love to carry it with me as a charm. In addition to the usual zodiac animals there is also a panda in the mix — the backstory suggests that when these were ordered from China, the request for the zodiac's Boar was somehow muddled, with a panda being created instead. (Shuhei Yamazaki, d47 design travel store)

029

奈良
NARA

大和文华馆
⚲ 奈良县奈良市学园南 1-11-6
☎ 0742-45-0544
🏠 www.kintetsu-g-hd.co.jp/culture/
yamato/index.html
The Museum Yamato Bunkakan
⚲ Gakuenminami 1-chome 11-6, Nara, Nara

与自然和谐共处的美术馆 一边眺望着包围在美术馆周围的文华苑里的树木植物，一边沿着缓坡在花园中漫步，已故建筑师吉田五十八设计的大和文华馆就会出现在眼前。建筑物以城堡为构思原点，建有虫笼窗[22]和海鼠壁[23]，外观很美。展览室非常简洁，展示品的数量绝不算多。可是这样就正好。不用按照规划好的路线，可以时进时退，也可以来回多看几次，各人都有各自享受参观的方式。在展览室的中庭，自然光倾注而下，馆内的气氛也会随着天气的变化而改变。不经意间，已经让人体会到了奈良的四季。（渊上凉子／D&DEPARTMENT 策划）

An art museum in harmony with nature While admiring the trees and plants of the Bunkaen garden surrounding the mansion, advance up the gentle slope, the Museum of Yamato Bunkakan, designed by the late Isoya Yoshida, will appear before your eyes. The beautiful appearance of its latticed windows and the grid design of the namako-style walls evokes the image of a castle. The exhibition room is simple, and the Museum does not boast a large collection. But this is a good thing. Rather than following the usual route, you can double back or even do multiple circuits, enjoying the tour in your own way. Natural light spills from the courtyard located in the center of the exhibition room, changing the Museum's atmosphere completely depending on the weather. At this Museum, you cannot help but be aware of the four seasons of Nara. (Ryoko Fuchikami, D&DEPARTMENT PROJECT)

030
和歌山
WAKAYAMA

031
鸟取
TOTTORI

根来寺
♀ 和歌山县岩出市根来 2286
☎ 0736-62-1144
🏠 www.negoroji.org
Negoroji Temple
♀ Negoro 2286, Iwade, Wakayama

鸟取 GELATERIA
♀ 鸟取县米子市淀江町佐陀 1301-6
☎ 0859-49-1074
🏠 gelateria-ragurupo.com
GELATERIA Ragurupo
♀ Yodoe-cho Sada 1301-6, Yonago, Tottori

充满历史传奇的寺庙　根来寺由空海之后最为人所称道的觉鑁上人所开创。在安土桃山时代，根来寺的俸禄超过 70 万石，还拥有被称为"根来众"的一万余名僧兵势力，盛极一时。后来因为丰臣秀吉的天正兵火，寺庙有一大半都被烧毁了。从火中残留下来的，是大传法堂和大师堂，以及大塔。大塔是日本最大的木造塔，被定为国宝。大塔至今悄然伫立，它那木质搭建的构造所蕴含的美感，以及火绳枪弹的痕迹给人带来的视觉冲击，仿佛诉说着 900 年历史和传奇。（木本好美／proyect g oficina）

时令美味：意式冰激凌　从这家冰激凌店 2 楼的大窗户望出去，能看到伯耆富士（大山）那雄伟的身姿。店里的冰柜里，并排摆放着用当地食材做成的意式冰激凌。其中最吸引人的，当属大荣西瓜、淀江町红萝卜等用当地食材所做的只有当季才能吃到的冰激凌。你必须到当地的店里，才能体会到这种当时当季的感觉。我强烈推荐日南町番茄所做的桃太郎番茄冰激凌，这种番茄生吃也非常美味！第一次吃过之后就令我魂牵梦绕，现在已经成了夏天去大山游玩的一个理由。（壳豆纪拓／YUTTE）

A temple full of historical romance　Negoroji Temple was founded by the Buddhist priest Kakuban Shonin, said to be the most talented after Kukai. In the Azuchi-Momoyama period, the temple's territory was marked by more than 700,000 boundary stones and it was home to a force of around 10,000 *sohei* warrior monks known as the Negoro clan. However, the majority of the temple was later destroyed by fires during Hideyoshi's wars in the Tensho period. The Daidenpodo main hall and Daishido hall of Kobo-daishi were spared from the flames, as was the Daito tower. The Daito tower is the largest wooden pagoda in Japan and is a designated national treasure. Its magnificent appearance, the beauty and power of its structure and design, and traces of bullet holes said to be from matchlock firearms all convey a 900-year tale of history and romance. (Konomi Kimoto, proyect g oficina)

Even gelato has its seasons　The large second-floor windows of this gelateria open on views of Mt. Daisen ("Hoki Fuji"). The cases are lined with gelato made with local ingredients. You'll soon see that everything on the menu is created from seasonal local ingredients such as Daiei watermelon and Yodoe-cho carrot. Only a locally situated store could produce such a feeling of immediacy. I highly recommend the Momotaro tomato gelato, which uses Nichinan-cho tomatoes and needs nothing else to be delicious. After the first time, the taste becomes addictive — it's now one of the reasons I visit Daisen in the summer. (Taku Mezuki, YUTTE)

032

島根
SHIMANE

隠岐誉 杯装上撰 隠岐造酒株式会社
📍 島根県隠岐郡隠岐之島町原田174
☎ 08512-2-1111
🏠 okishuzou.com
OKIHOMARE Josen Cup, Oki Shuzou K.K.
📍 Harada 174, Okigun Okinoshima-cho, Shimane

033

冈山
OKAYAMA

Mama-chovy
📍 冈山县冈山市北区奉还町2-9-30
(Kokohore Japan)
☎ 086-259-1517
🏠 shop.kkhr.jp
Mama-chovy
📍 (Kokohore Japan) Hokan-cho 2-chome 9-30, Kita-ku, Okayama, Okayama

漂浮于日本海隐岐诸岛上的酿酒厂 在隐岐的喜庆事上不可或缺的，是当地产的清酒 "隐岐誉"。为了在隐岐留下造酒业，西乡酒造组合的 5 家公司通力合作，于 1972 年创立了隐岐造酒株式会社，同时也对酒名进行公开募集，因此就有了 "隐岐誉" 这个代表性的商标。我特别喜欢他们的杯装酒，上边画着各种富有隐岐特色的图案——民谣 "Shigesabushi"、国贺海岸的通天桥等。因为有得天独厚的适于造酒的软水和酿造用米，这里的清酒爽口而辛辣。可以一边烤着钓上来的鱼一边喝，或是在回去的轮渡上，一边品尝着清酒，一边回忆起隐岐的点点滴滴。(森山胜心 /Kan-kaku)

这里的土特产，连当地人都买 在冈山，寿南小沙丁鱼被称为 "Mamakari"。它有多好吃呢？这么说吧，一提起这个小沙丁鱼，人们甚至忍不住 "去借点 (Kari) 米饭 (Mama) 来"。这就是它的名称的由来。浅井克俊先生 2012 年从东京移居濑户内市后，就开始琢磨如何让当地的文化重新焕发活力。"Mamakari" 虽然被称为乡土料理，但当地人吃得并不多。于是，他将其与濑户内的名产柠檬、橄榄、蘑菇等容易搭配的食材进行组合，做成了像凤尾鱼罐头一样的万能调味食材 "Mama-chovy"。新的食物理念，使当地食材重新焕发出魅力。(黑江美穗 /d47 MUSEUM)

Sake brewing in the Oki Islands, floating in the Sea of Japan "Okihomare" *jizake* (local sake) is essential to the celebrations of Oki. To ensure that the brewing industry would remain in Oki, the five companies of the Saigo brewing union together founded the Oki Shuzou company in 1972. They advertised the name of the sake in parallel to the establishment, and since then, Okihomare has become a public name and the most representative brand. Personally, I absolutely love the cup sake. They are decorated with motifs of Oki, such as the folk song *Shigesabushi* and the Tsutenkyo Arch of the Kuniga Coast. Oki is blessed with soft water and brewer's rice suitable for sake brewing — giving a firm, dry flavor. It's great to drink with fish broiled over an open flame, and on the returning ferry, it's worth enjoying a drink or two while reflecting back on your memories of Oki. (Katsushi Moriyama, Kan-kaku)

Local souvenirs that even the residents buy The small species of large-eyed herring known as *mamakari* in Okayama got its name from the words *mama* (rice) and *kari* (to borrow)—meaning "delicious enough to go borrow rice for!" Katsutoshi Asai emigrated from Tokyo to Setouchi City in 2012, and started working on a regional revitalization association. While famed as the local cuisine, very few locals actually eat *mamakari*, but when combined with ingredients such as lemons, olives, and mushrooms, this setouchi specialty can be turned into a "mama-chovy" universal seasoning similar to anchovies. New ways to eat offer opportunities to review and reflect on the staples of hometown cuisine. (Miho Kuroe, d47 MUSEUM)

034
广岛
HIROSHIMA

u-shed
📍 广岛县广岛市南区宇品神田 1-5-33
☎ 082-258-5477
🌐 u-shed.jp
u-shed
📍 Ujinakanda 1-chome 5-33, Minami-ku, Hiroshima, Hiroshima

035
山口
YAMAGUCHI

尤加利与太阳
📍 山口县长门市俵山 5042-2
☎ 0837-29-0826
🏠 www.eucaly-taiyo.co
Eucaly-Taiyo
📍 Tawarayama 5042-2 Nagato, Yamaguchi

东京与广岛，在这里相连　开在港口街宇品住宅街上的 "u-shed"，是来自东京的山田泰一和山田干夫妇将祖母的房子进行改建后开设的咖啡店。菜单上，有广岛烘焙的原创咖啡，有用濑户田的无农药柠檬所制作的柠檬果汁，还有与当地很受欢迎的咖喱店 "nandi" 共同制作的帕尼尼等，致力于呈现广岛的味道。夫妇二人的朋友从东京和世界各地到访，也会开展活动，这里成为连接广岛和东京的有趣站点。u-shed 开店虽然还不到一年，已经深受当地居民和学生们的喜爱。(冈本友纪 /la forgerone)

深受当地人喜爱的烘焙店　"尤加利与太阳" 是从静冈搬迁到俵山温泉的烘焙店，于 2014 年 5 月开业。这里的主打美食是曲奇和司康，使用邻近地区出产的有机食材制作而成。店里同时也销售非常环保的日用杂货。将 butter（使用黄油）和 vegan（不使用乳制品）分开烘焙，独特的口感和丰富的口味让人欲罢不能，也令它在当地越来越受到欢迎。虽然不定期开设的邮购服务让人可以从日本各地邮购，但是如果想吃到刚出炉的热气腾腾的美味，还请您一定前往店里品尝。(村田敦 /Toy Toy)

A cafe linking Tokyo with Hiroshima　The u-shed coffee shop, located in a residential area of the port city of Ujina, was opened by Tokyo emigrants Taiichi and Miki Yamada in their grandmother's renovated house. The menu is steeped in the flavors of Hiroshima, featuring original coffee roasted in Hiroshima, lemonade made with pesticide-free Setoda lemons, and paninis created in collaboration with popular local curry shop "nandi". The coffee shop holds events with friends of the couple visiting from Tokyo and all over the world, serving as a fascinating link between Hiroshima and Tokyo. Although it's only been open a little over a year, u-shed has won a following among local residents and students. (Yuki Okamoto, la forgerone)

A bakery loved by local residents　The Eucaly-Taiyo baked goods shop, which opened in May 2014, moved its location from Shizuoka to the hot spring region of Tawarayama. As far as possible, the bakery uses organic and fair trade ingredients and ingredients produced in neighboring prefectures when baking the cookies and scones that are its main products, and it strives to deal with only environmentally considerate grocery supplies. It separates its baked goods into "butter" and "vegan" (dairy products not used) categories, and the rich flavors and textures of its creations have won over many local people, who love to eat them daily. Their products are available for purchase all over Japan by mail order, but they're best at the source in Tawarayama, freshly baked and piping hot. (Atushi Murata, Toy Toy)

036
德岛
TOKUSHIMA

037
香川
KAGAWA

亥之子点心
📍 德岛县三好市井川町辻85（岛尾果子店）
☎ 0883-78-2072
Oinoko Gashi
📍 (Shimao candy store) Ikawachotsuji 85, Miyoshi, Tokushima

MONSTER baSH
📍 香川县仲多度郡 Manno 町吉野 4243-12
☎ 087-822-2520（duke 高松）
🏠 www.monsterbash.jp
MONSTER baSH
📍 Manno-cho Yoshino 4243-12, Nakatado-gun, Kagawa

将自然与食物紧密相连的节庆食品 "亥之子" 是小麦粉中加入黑糖，拉成圆环，在炉子里稍微烘烤制成的点心。在德岛县西部，日本旧历十月的亥日被称为 "亥之子san"，人们会举行感谢收成及祈愿丰收的祭典。孩子们去各家各户巡游，可以从各个人家那里得到 "亥之子"。在节日祭典逐渐减少的今天，为了满足那些喜欢怀旧而想要一尝滋味的人，创立于1930年的 "岛尾果子店" 仍在继续制作着 "亥之子"。在我的记忆中，还保留着别人把这种点心穿在绳子上，一边说 "谢谢" 一边戴在我脖子上的情景。（北室淳子 / 手作素面 "北室白扇"）

交通便利、食物美味的户外音乐节 居住在奈良的我，和居住在福冈的朋友，在 "MONSTER baSH" 的前一天夜里在冈山站碰面，坐上一早的 "特急南风"，带着小旅行般的心情眺望着被朝霞染红的濑户内海跨过了濑户大桥。会场国立赞岐 Manno 公园，是一个群山环绕下的草地公园。从略有些高度的山丘上能看到两个主舞台，而表演也是在两个舞台交替进行的，真令人开心。午餐时能品尝到赞岐乌冬等当地美食，耳边听到四国出身的音乐人在 MC 中说着 "老妈也来看演出了……" 令人不知身在何处。（渊上凉子 /D&DEPARTMENT PROJECT）

An important festival treat linking nature with food *Oinoko-gashi* candy is made by mixing brown sugar with flour, stretching it into a wheel shape, and baking lightly in a covered pot. In the western part of Tokushima Prefecture, there is a festival known as *Oinoko-san* on the lunar Day of the Boar in October to give thanks and pray for good harvests. Children go around the neighborhood visiting houses and receive *oinoko-gashi* candy from each house. Although this tradition has somewhat declined, the Shimao candy store, founded in 1930, continues to manufacture *oinoko-gashi* for those who like to buy it with a sense of nostalgia. I have memories of wearing *oinoko-gashi* on a string around my neck as an expression of gratitude. (Junko Kitamuro, "Kitamuro Hakusen")

Outdoor music festival with great access and wonderful dining A friend who lives in Fukuoka and I (a Nara resident) met up at Okayama Station the night before MONSTER baSH. The next morning, we caught the Nanpu limited express train, traveling across the Great Seto Bridge and looking out over the Seto Inland Sea bathed in all the colors of sunrise—it felt like a mini-journey. The festival venue was Sanuki Mannou National Government Park, a grassy park surrounded by mountains. Both main stages were visible from the top of a small hill, and the alternating running timetable was perfect. We enjoyed a lunch of *sanuki udon* and other local dishes as well as a unique local talk by a Shikoku-born artist entitled "Mom is here to see us..." (Ryoko Fuchikami, D&DEPARTMENT PROJECT)

038
爱媛
EHIME

大三岛 Furusato 憩之家
📍 爱媛县今治市大三岛町宗方 5208-1
☎ 0897-83-1111
🏠 www.ikoinoie.co.jp
Rest and Relaxation House Oomishima
📍 Omishima-cho Munagata 5208-1, Imabari, Ehime

039
高知
KOCHI

岸本宪明
📍 高知县吾川郡仁淀町别枝 606（株式会社 VIVA 泽渡）
☎ 0889-32-1234
🏠 www.viva-sawatari.com
Noriaki Kishimoto
📍 (VIVA SAWATARI INC.) Besshi 606, Niyodogawacho Agawa-gun, Kochi

土佐茶产地"泽渡"的继承人 从高知市乘坐电车约 3 小时，就到了仁淀川町泽渡，一路上险峻的山谷里一排排的茶田井然有序。因为有清澈的水流与河雾，这里出产的茶叶一度广受县内外好评，是美味茶叶的产地，却因为后继无人而逐渐衰落。就在那时，岸本宪明先生回到了这里，"不想看到祖父辈辛辛苦苦创造出来的风景慢慢凋零"。为了能重新振兴茶产业，除了生产和销售泽渡茶之外，他也通过精美的设计吸引游客购买，还通过自己制作小点心以及参加县内外的活动等方式，宣传推广泽渡茶的魅力。（上原丽 / 作家）

住进"真正的小学" 附近的石头围墙里有一片广阔的橘子地，濑户内海就在眼前展开——这里有着奢侈的岛屿风光。已经废弃的旧宗方小学几乎维持着当时开校时的样子，如今已经变身为住宿设施加以利用。进了旧校舍，一直在都市里念书的我立刻光着脚在木造校舍那铺着木板的走廊上四处乱跑起来。早餐时送上来的橘子带着一小截树枝，美味得令人惊讶，酸酸甜甜，"这才是真正的橘子啊！"你可以一直吃到饱。晚饭是濑户内海的海鲜，吃得人心满意足。夕阳西下时，濑户内海那美丽的景色让人永生难忘。（那须野由华 /d47 食堂）

Stay overnight at an actual elementary school The location is a fabulous island, ringed with stone-walled tangerine groves, where the Seto Inland Sea spreads out before the eyes. The old Munakata elementary school, now closed but otherwise almost unchanged in form, is now used to provide accommodation. As soon as I arrived, I took off my shoes — although I was a child of city schools — and went running along the corridors of the wooden schoolhouse. For breakfast, I was astonished to see *mikan* tangerines still attached to the branch, boasting an authentic sweet and sour taste, of which I ate to my heart's content. For dinner, I ate my fill of seafood from the Seto Inland Sea. You'll never forget the beautiful sight of the Seto Inland Sea at twilight. (Yuka Nasuno, d47 SHOKUDO)

The heir of Sawatari, a producing center of *Tosacha* (Tosa-tea) About three hours by train from Kochi, tea plantations line up neatly in a steep valley in Sawatari, in Niyodokawa Town. This area once attracted praise from both inside and outside the prefecture as a delicious tea-producing area thanks to its clean water and river mist, but fell into decline due to lack of heirs to the industry. It was Noriaki Kishimoto who facilitated the area's turnabout, stating that he didn't want to see any changes to the landscape where his grandfather's generation worked so hard. To revitalize the tea industry, in addition to producing and selling Sawatari tea, he redesigned the packaging to make it easier to handle, started manufacturing confectioneries, and participates in events outside the prefecture to convey the excellence of Sawatari tea. (Rei Uehara, writer)

040
福冈
FUKUOKA

FRUCTUS
📍 福冈县福冈市中央区药院1-6-33 修和大厦 201
📞 092-731-8040
🏠 fructus.jp
FRUCTUS
📍 Shuwa Bldg. 201, Yakuin 1-chome 6-33, Chuo-ku, Fukuoka, Fukuoka

041
佐贺
SAGA

Higashiyoka 滩涂
（登记于《拉姆萨尔公约》[24]的湿地）
📞 0592-40-7202（佐贺市环境部环境政策科）
🏠 www.city.saga.lg.jp
Higashiyoka Tidal Flats (Designated Ramsar Site)

让 granola 麦片成为福冈早餐的必需品？ 这是一家以福冈为据点的 granola 麦片专门店。店内的用餐空间设立在加工厂里，阳光能照射进来，是一个具有开放感、让人心情愉快的空间。你可以一边看着玻璃后边的工厂，一边品尝常备的 5 种 granola 麦片。早餐 7 点开始，500 日元随便吃。这里布置的家具，比如兰迪椅等等，品味极佳，让人来了就不想走。他们的理念就是要传播 "granola ＝ 日常餐" 这样一种生活方式。真心期待着以后它会成为福冈的早餐里固定不变的一个选项。（阿部里奈 /D&DPARTMENT 福冈）

佐贺最安静的地方 在佐贺市南部，有一大片面朝有明海的滩涂，我每次都会把远道而来的客人带到那里。看着一望无际的泥地，会渐渐发现一些小生物的踪影，多如夜空之星，我们仿佛能从中感受到宇宙。其中，有当地独特的乡土料理中用到的弹涂鱼、招潮蟹、口虾蛄，还有以滩涂上的生物为食的水鸟。侧耳倾听，能听到泥地间涓涓流动的水声，小生物们行动时发出的声音，还有渔船行驶在近滩海上的引擎声。请您在退潮时来这里，体会一下悠闲的时光。（北岛真由美 / 或许 画廊）

Granola—a morning classic in Fukuoka? This granola specialty store is based in Fukuoka. An eat-in space has been established in the factory's processing area—a pleasant, uplifting space overflowing with sunlight. You can enjoy five varieties of granola while watching the factory area, separated by glass. Enjoy all-you-can-eat granola for 500 yen, starting from 7 a.m. The well-designed interior featuring Landi chairs almost makes you want to live here. The notion of granola as a daily meal is new for Japan, but I look forward to seeing it well on its way to being established as a classic Fukuoka breakfast. (Rina Abe, D&DEPARTMENT FUKUOKA)

The quietest place in Saga In the south part of the city of Saga, there are vast tidal flats facing the Ariake Sea. When guests arrive from afar, I always bring them here. If I watch the mud for long enough I see tiny creatures emerge, countless as stars in the night sky, and I start to feel part of the universe. The unique regional cuisine utilizes the creatures that live on the tidal flats — mudskipper, fiddler crab, and mantis shrimp, as well as waterfowl that live off other tidal flat creatures. If you listen hard, you'll hear the sound of water trickling in mud channels, the sound of small creatures moving, and the sound of motors of fishing boats traversing the shallow seas. Experience it slowly at the ebbing tide. (Mayumi Kitajima, Perhaps Gallery)

042
长崎
NAGASAKI

山丘上的旅行者之家
📍 长崎县长崎市西坂町 5-14
☎ 095-895-8965
🏠 www.nagasaki-route.com
Traveler's House on the Route
📍 Nishizakamachi 5-14, Nagasaki, Nagasaki

在这里就像在家里一样　Route 坐落在西坂的山丘上，此地因为日本的二十六圣人殉教而闻名。这是一间小小的胶囊式加宿舍式的旅馆。店里的床都购于无印良品，中间用隔板分隔开来，就像卧铺列车一样。从旅馆的咖啡店里望出去，能看见圣菲利普西坂教堂以及山坡上错落有致的民宅，构成了长崎特有的风景线。我喜欢楼下的家庭房。我平时在市里住，但有朋友来访，我会和友人一起在这里住下。去外边吃完饭以后，在饭厅里再喝几杯，或是骑着租来的自行车去买早饭，感觉就像融入了长崎的生活。（松井知子／画廊 李斯特）

An inn that feels like living at home　Located on the famous Nishizaka hill near the holy site of the Twenty-six Martyrs of Japan, Route is a small cabin and dormitory-style inn. Beds from MUJI are lined along both sides of a partition, something like a sleeper rail car. From the inn's cafe, look out over St. Philip's Church and rows of houses lining the slopes—a very Nagasaki-esque sight. My favorite is the downstairs family room. Even I live in the city, sometimes stay here together with friends when they visit Nagasaki. After a meal out, we may keep drinking in the dining room or rent a bicycle and head out to buy breakfast. At this inn, you can make the most of the Nagasaki lifestyle. (Tomoko Matsui, Gallery List:)

043
熊本
KUMAMOTO

马肉刺身宫本
📍 熊本县熊本市新市街 1-12 Banner 大楼
　　1 层
☎ 096-211-0108
🏠 www.basashi.jp/shop
Basashi Miyamoto
📍 Banner Bldg. 1F, Shinshigai 1-12,
　　Kumamoto, Kumamoto

家族式经营的马肉店令人安心　说到熊本县，不得不提到在典礼仪式和喜庆日子里用于宴请宾客的马肉，据说由加藤清正[25]首创。马肉的价格有些昂贵，可是既然旅行至此，就算囊中羞涩，也还是很想尝尝。精肉店马肉刺身宫本坐落在热闹的新城区再稍微向深处走一些的地方，店里有赤身（瘦肉）、后颈肉、鞍下（马鞍下方的部位）等等，马肉的种类非常丰富。我告诉店家我打算买回来吃，店家于是帮我把肉切成了大小合适的尺寸，并加上生姜和酱汁。即使一个人买，也能品尝到各个部位，每个部位一点点。这种吃法，在外边的餐厅里就不太能做得到。稍微放一会儿之后，马肉里的脂肪开始融化，刚好适合吃。再配上熊本的烧酒，一口下去，滋味超赞！（关纱代子／d47 食堂）

Peace of mind at a family-run *basashi* store　The custom of eating *basashi* (horsemeat), considered a feast for sunny days and celebrations, was apparently popularized in Kumamoto Prefecture by the daimyo Kiyomasa Kato. The price makes it something luxurious, but if your financial situation is dire, by all means enjoy it when you travel. Entering the Basashi Miyamoto butcher shop from the nearby shopping district, you will find a wide variety of cuts of horsemeat, including lean red meat, *tategami* (neck), and *kurashita* (the section of the body which comes under the saddle). When I told them I wanted to eat some as soon as I got home, they sliced appropriate amount and included a little bit of ginger and sauce for me. You just can't get this taste dining out, and eating it alone lets you compare the flavors of all the various parts. Make time to enjoy some melt-in-the-mouth fatty *basashi*, accompanied by Kumamoto shochu. (Sayoko Seki, d47 SHOKUDO)

044
大分
OITA

岳切溪谷
📍 大分县宇佐市院内町定别当
☎ 0978-42-5111（宇佐市役所院内支所）
Takkiri Valley
📍 Innaimachi Jobetto, Usa, Oita

045
宫崎
MIYAZAKI

"ONLY ONE Shiiba"
📍 宫崎县东臼杵郡椎叶村大字下福良
1762-1
☎ 0982-67-3203（椎叶村公所）
🏠 shiiba.jpn.org
"ONLY ONE Shiiba"（Shiiba Village Hall）
📍 Ooaza Shimofukura 1762-1, Shiiba-son
Higashiusuki-gun, Miyazaki

奇迹般的壮观景致　宇佐市耶马日田英彦山国家公园里的岳切溪谷，是从耶马溪溶岩形成的一块岩石上流下的涓涓细流，水深至脚踝，缓缓流淌，全长约 2 千米。因为地势起伏较缓，孩子们也可以安心地沿着溪流登山，有很多人全家老少齐出动在这里玩耍。溪谷一旁有步道，不用涉入溪水也可以欣赏到新绿和红叶时节里树林的美，独特的景观十分适合摄影。环顾这远古时代孕育出来的美景，身处其中，我的心中唯有感动。（原茂树／日田 Cinematheque Liberte）

秘境：椎叶村的现在　1910 年，民俗学家柳田国男曾到访此地，并在其著作《后狩词记》里写到了位于九州山区山岳地带的椎叶村的狩猎和烧畑习俗。我从这本书中得知，这些习俗，现在仍和"椎叶神乐"一起，作为生活的一部分在当地延续着。"小野洼设计室"的小野信介先生，用半年时间脚踏实地进行了采访。椎叶村公所发行的信息杂志，无论对于山村里人口稀少的问题，还是移居当地的年轻人，都实事求是地予以记载。书中村里人神采奕奕的笑容，以及从初夏到冬季里不断变化的椎叶村的美景，都能唤起人对旅行的渴望。（前田次郎／d design travel 编辑部）

A miraculous, magnificent object shaped by nature　Located in the Yaba-Hita-Hikosan Quasi-National Park in Usa, on top of a monolithic block of Yabakei lava, Takkiri Valley stretches about 2 kilometers in length with a stream that flows up to ankle height. Because it's so shallow, you can enjoy walking in the stream with children without worry, and you will find many families enjoying the place. To the side, a walking trail is maintained so hikers can enjoy the beauty of the seasons without entering the stream. The fresh green foliage and autumnal leaves of the trees make this unique landscape an ideal spot for photography throughout the seasons. You cannot help but be moved when taking in the superb views here, nurtured from time immemorial. (Shigeki Hara, Hita Cinematheque Liberté)

The secluded region of Shiiba today　In 1910, the visiting folklorist Kunio Yanagida wrote in his book *Nochi no kari kotoba no ki* of the hunting and slash-and-burn agricultural traditions of Shiiba Village, located in an alpine district of the Kyushu mountain range. These traditions have been kept alive to this day, together with *Shiiba kagura* dancing, which I learned about by reading this book. Shinsuke Ono of "onokobo design" took half a year of time to complete the interviews for "ONLY ONE Shiiba." Although this informative magazine is issued by the Shiiba village authorities, it clearly spells out the truth about depopulated mountain villages and the emigration of young people. It captures the lively smiles of the villagers and the superb views of Shiiba as it transitions from early summer through to winter. This is a volume to put you in a traveling frame of mind. (Jiro Maeda, d design travel Editorial Team)

好街坊露营节
📍 鹿儿岛县南九州市川本町本別府
3728-2 Kawanabe 森林学校
🌐 goodneighborsjamboree.com
GOOD NEIGHBORS JAMBOREE
📍 Kawanabe Forest School, Kawanabecho
Motobeppu 3728-2, Minamikyushu,
Kagoshima

具志川城遗迹
📍 冲绳县丝满市喜武屋 1730-1
☎ 090-840-8135（丝满市政府商工观光科）
🌐 www.city.itoman.lg.jp/kankou-navi/
Gushikawa Castle Ruins
📍 Kyan 1730-1, Itoman, Okinawa

露营如节日庆典，全员参与 在川边森林学校举办的"好街坊露营节"，到 2016 年是第七届。这个露营不是用来观赏的。在这里，你可以亲手触摸手工艺品和文学书籍，吃到美味的食物，在森林中如同沐浴般聆听音乐。垃圾需要自己分成 20 个类别；而当地作家制作舞台时，需要大家齐心协力帮忙。人人都在参与准备这个露营活动。雨后，森林里的绿色闪闪发亮，大家在欢笑声中融为一体，那种感觉，令人难以忘怀。（取访 KONOMI D&DEPARTMENT 鹿儿岛）

时光，在此停留 丝满市喜武屋，位于冲绳本岛的南端。在甘蔗田的尽头，三面临海、高约 17 米的断崖上，有沿着断崖修筑的"具志川城遗迹"，仅仅留下石墙。准确的修建年代无法考证，推测是在 13 世纪修建的。这里没有过多的修补，你只要站在这里，就会感到仿佛有一条时间的线轴，将往昔的岁月和活在当下的你连接起来。你可以任由思绪驰骋，感受这土地所拥有的美丽印记，以及仅仅在 70 年前这里发生的激战所带给人的悲伤记忆。靠在石墙上，你可以一边聆听翻涌的海浪声，一边深深地呼吸，感受生命的宝贵。（桶田千夏子 / Luft）

Created with all participants, like a festival The Good Neighbors Jamboree event will be held at the Kawanabe Forest School for the seventh time in 2016. This jamboree is not simply for viewing. Encounter crafts and literature, have delicious food, and immerse yourself in listening to music in the forest. Everyone helps out — participants sort waste into 20 different types, or help local writers create stage decorations. I think each and every person contributes to making the Jamboree. The forest sparkles green after the rain, with everyone's laughter giving an unforgettable sense of unity. (Konomi Suwa, D&DEPARTMENT KAGOSHIMA)

It's the time you spend there The village of Kyan is in Itoman City, on the southern tip of the main island of Okinawa. At the edge of sugar cane fields, surrounded by sea views on three sides, only a stone wall remains of the ruins of Gushikawa Castle, as though a part of the 17-meter high cliffs. Although it is not known for how many years the castle was inhabited, it is said to have been built in the 13th century. Simply being in this place, without doing a thing, you can feel your own life connecting with ancient times and the way it used to be. Remember the beautiful memories of this land as well as tragic memories of savage battles fought here just 70 years ago. Take a pause to breathe in this significant place and listen to the gentle sound of lapping waves. (Chikako Okeda, Luft)

首尔
SEOUL

首尔店在 2016 年 3 月～5 月里介绍了"二木工房"的辰砂白瓷。辰砂白瓷始于朝鲜时代（18 世纪），是以氧化铜作为颜料，在烧制时发生红色窑变的瓷器。这次展出了马克杯、面碗等主要用于日常的器皿，向观众传递了辰砂白瓷所特有的美丽的色彩和精湛的技术。(Jyon Surugi)

---

027 大阪
OSAKA

大阪店在 2016 年 6 月来到了"桶谷制皂"。这里的肥皂"Aiken"用牛油和椰子油制成，配方非常简单。他们使用自创立时起就一直延续的热制法进行制造，结合气温和湿度的变化，一天里几乎片刻不停地根据状况来进行调整，是如同对话般面对面制作而成的肥皂。来到大阪，请务必试一试"Aiken"哦！（门胁万莉奈）

---

026 京都
KYOTO

近年，京都店所在的本山佛光寺作为"标语之寺"而为人所知。寺庙为了用更加简单易懂的方式传达释迦牟尼的教诲，开始面向高辻大路展示八行标语，每个月会更换一次，至今已经持续了 50 年以上。用现代人能够理解的语言去书写也是标语的特征。店内也销售关于这些标语的书籍。请来找一找自己喜欢的标语吧。（小原龙树）

---

040 福冈
FUKUOKA

福冈店在 2016 年 6 月进行了"运动鞋之乡——久留米的月星"展，对工厂和球鞋的制作过程进行了展示。月星身处久留米，这里因为是橡胶产业之乡而备受瞩目，制作鞋履的历史已经超过了 140 年。为了能达到"提到日本的球鞋，那就是久留米"的认知效果，他们还在鞋垫上印制了"MADE IN KURUMI"。我徜徉在这个围绕着产业而形成的城市里，心中感受的是制造业中所饱含的热情。（原 KANATA）

---

047 冲绳
OKINAWA

冲绳店在 2016 年 6 月举行了"冲绳玻璃——吹制玻璃工房彩砂之器"展。2015 年展出了色彩鲜艳的玻璃杯，广受好评，2016 年则在透明的玻璃制品中选择了 20 个种类的器皿。器皿形状各异，另外还带有透明、金银线、马赛克 3 种工艺所带来的阴影，客人从各个角度欣赏、享受的神态令我印象深刻。展览为炎热的冲绳带来了一股清凉。（大城贵子）

---

046 鹿儿岛
KAGOSHIMA

鹿儿岛店在 2016 年 5 月举办了集中介绍"经典好物"的市集——"鹿儿岛的 d 市场"。在销售乡土点心"Akumaki"时，我体验了将糯米在碱水中浸泡、用孟宗竹的皮包裹等准备工作，顺便对水土与智慧的关系产生了进一步的思考。今后，不仅是食品和手工艺品，我还想学习更多其他方面的与文化和生活相关的知识。（中村麻佑）

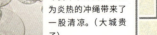

D&DEPARTMENT 计划未来在 47 个都道府县各设一家店铺作为活动据点，旨在发掘和介绍"长效设计"（可持续的、具有当地特色的设计）。目前日本国内已开设了 10 家门店，韩国开设有 1 家。

016 富山 TOYAMA

富山店于 2016 年 7 月前往被称为"五个山和纸之乡"的和纸制品工坊和小构树[25]田进行了参观。他们使用自家栽培的小构树作为原料，这在日本全国都是很少见的生产形式，并制作出了以荧光色为特征的"FIVE"系列。通常，包装外侧是灰色的，可是富山店为大家介绍的是特别定做的制品，外侧也是荧光色的。今后，我们还会陆续向大家介绍富有魅力的商品。（石井唯）

001 北海道 HOKKAIDO

北海道店邀请了"特鲁瓦田野"的发起人远藤·特鲁瓦先生作为讲师，请他推广面向成年人的食品相关知识。2016 年 5 月，我们举办了以"有机与饮食"为主题的"d 学堂"活动。此次活动以女性为中心，约有 30 人参加。"请留意一下，食物是如何被送上餐桌的？"——这番话让我留下了深刻的印象。这次活动也成为一个契机，令每个人都思考我们能够为孩子们的未来做些什么。（若林谅）

019 山梨 YAMANASHI

山梨店在 2016 年 5 月举办了"日本视野"展销（NIPPON VISION MARKET）槙田商店。槙田商店位于织物的产地——富士北麓，从事伞的制造，2016 年已经是创立 150 周年。它继承了江户时代甲斐绢[27]的"先染色""细纱织""高密度"等特征，至今仍然继续织造具有美丽光泽的伞布。展示期间，槙田商店的匠人在店里现场演示了手工组装雨伞的过程。（仙洞田知纮）

013 东京 TOKYO

东京店从 2016 年 3 月开始，接受 D&D 原创商品"LAUAN SHELVES"的订做品"LAUAN SHELVES 私人定制"的订购。利用隔板和架板、抽屉等组合而成的收纳架，组装简单，能够灵活应对生活中的各种需要，由高圆寺的"井上工业"（INOUE Industries）进行制作。如果想要寻找理想的收纳用品，请一定要来东京店看看。（杉村希咲）

022 静冈 SHIZUOKA

静冈店从 2016 年 7 月到 9 月举办了"日本视野"展销静冈的清酒。县内散布着历史悠久的酒厂，制造着具有独特风味的清酒。我们选择了 6 家酒厂制造的清酒，在 d 学堂的"简明易懂的清酒"活动中做了介绍。这次活动得到了静冈市筱田酒店店主筱田和雄先生的协助。筱田先生总是不辞辛劳，先到酿造厂那里甄选出自己发自内心想要推荐给大家的清酒，然后拿到活动上介绍，也让客人试饮，充分体现了筱田先生的一片热心。（加濑香织）

D&DEPARTMENT SHOP LIST

HOKKAIDO

SHIZUOKA

SEOUL

SAITAMA

KYOTO

OSAKA

d47 MUSEUM

TOKYO

FUKUOKA

d47 design travel store

TOYAMA

KAGOSHIMA

d47 SHOKUDO

YAMANASHI

OKINAWA

D&DEPARTMENT HOKKAIDO by 3KG
- 北海道札幌市中央区大通西 17-1-7
- ☎ 011-303-3333
- ⏱ 门店 11:00～19:00
  周日、周一休息 (逢节假日顺延次日)
- O-dori Nishi 17-1-7, Chuo-ku, Sapporo, Hokkaido
- ⏱ Shop 11:00–19:00
  Closed on Sunday, Monday (If Monday is a holiday,
  open on Monday, closed on Tuesday)

D&DEPARTMENT SAITAMA by PUBLIC DINER
- 埼玉县熊谷市肥塚 4-29
  PUBLIC DINER 屋顶露台
- ☎ 048-580-7316
- ⏱ 门店 11:00～17:00 周三休息
- PUBLIC DINER Rooftop Terrace 4-29 Koizuka,
  Kumagaya, Saitama
- ⏱ Shop 11:00–17:00
  Closed on Wednesday

D&DEPARTMENT TOKYO
- 东京都世田谷区奥泽 8-3-2
- ☎ 03-5752-0120
- ⏱ 门店 12:00～20:00
  食堂 11:30～19:00
  周三休息
- Okusawa 8-3-2, Setagaya-ku, Tokyo
- ⏱ Shop 12:00–20:00 Dining 11:30–19:00
  Closed on Wednesday

D&DEPARTMENT TOYAMA
- 富山县富山市新总曲轮 4-18 富山县民会馆一楼
- ☎ 076-471-7791
- ⏱ 门店 10:00～19:00
  食堂 工作日 10:00～17:00
  周六、周日、节假日 10:00～19:00
  不定期休息 (以富山县民会馆为准)
- Toyama-kenminkaikan 1F, Shinsogawa 4-18, Toyama,
  Toyama
- ⏱ Shop 10:00–19:00
  Dining Weekday 10:00–17:00
  Weekend, holiday 10:00–19:00
  Closed Occasionally

D&DEPARTMENT YAMANASHI by Sannichi-YBS
- 山梨县甲府市被扣 2-6-10 山日 YBS 本社
  (山梨文化会馆) 2F
- ☎ 门店 055-225-5222 咖啡厅 055-222-7793
- ⏱ 门店 11:00～19:00 咖啡厅 11:30～22:00
  周一休息 (遇节假日顺延次日)
- Sannichi-YBS (Yamanashi Culture Hall) 2F,
  Kitaguchi 2-6-10, Kofu, Yamanashi
- ⏱ Shop 11:00–19:00 Café 11:30–22:00
  Closed on Monday (If Monday is a holiday,
  open on Monday, closed on Tuesday)

D&DEPARTMENT SHIZUOKA by TAITA
- 静冈县静冈市骏河区高松 1-24-10
- ☎ 054-238-6678
- ⏱ 门店 11:30～19:30
  食堂 11:30～22:00 周二、周三休息
- Takamatsu 1-24-10, Suruga-ku, Shizuoka, Shizuoka
- ⏱ Shop 11:30–19:30
  Dining 11:30–22:00
  Closed on Tuesday, Wednesday

D&DEPARTMENT KYOTO
- 京都府京都市下京区高仓通佛光寺下新开町 397
  本山佛光寺内
- ☎ 门店 075-343-3217 咖啡厅 075-343-3215
- ⏱ 门店 10:00～18:00 咖啡厅 10:30～18:00 周三休息
- Bukkoji Temple, Takakura-dori Bukkoji Sagaru Shinkai-
  cho 397, Shimogyo-ku, Kyoto, Kyoto
- ⏱ Shop 10:00–18:00 Café 10:30–18:00
  Closed on Wednesday

D&DEPARTMENT OSAKA
店面转移, 休业中
Closed for relocation

D&DEPARTMENT FUKUOKA
- 福冈县福冈市博多区博多站前 1-28-8 二楼
- ☎ 092-432-3342
- ⏱ 门店 11:00～20:00 周三休息
- Hakata Ekimae 1-28-8 2F, Hakata-ku, Fukuoka,
  Fukuoka
- ⏱ Shop 11:00–20:00 Closed on Wednesday

D&DEPARTMENT KAGOSHIMA by MARUYA
- 鹿儿岛县鹿儿岛市吴服町 6-5 丸屋花园四楼
- ☎ 099-248-7804
- ⏱ 10:00～20:00
  不定期休息 (休息日以丸屋花园商场为准)
- Maruya gardens 4F, Gofuku-machi 6-5, Kagoshima,
  Kagoshima
- ⏱ 10:00–20:00 Closed Occasionally

D&DEPARTMENT OKINAWA
by OKINAWA STANDARD
- 冲绳县宜野湾市新城 2-39-8
- ☎ 098-894-2112
- ⏱ 11:00～19:30 周二休息
- Aragusuku 2-39-8 2F, Ginowan, Okinawa
- ⏱ 11:00–19:30 Closed on Tuesday

D&DEPARTMENT SEOUL by MILLIMETER MILLIGRAM
- 首尔市龙山区梨泰院路 240
- ☎ +82 2 795 1520
- ⏱ 11:30～20:00 每月最后一个周一休息
- Itaewon-ro 240, Yongsan-gu, Seoul, Korea
- ⏱ 11:30–20:00 Closed on the last Monday of the month

d47 MUSEUM / d47 design travel store / d47 食堂
- 东京都涩谷区涩谷 2-21-1 涩谷 hikarie 商场 8 楼
- ☎ d47 MUSEUM / d47 design travel store
  03-6427-2301
  d47 食堂 03-6427-2303
- ⏱ d47 MUSEUM / d47 design travel store
  11:00～20:00
  d47 食堂 11:30～23:00
  不定期休息 (休息日以涩谷 hikarie 商场为准)
- Shibuya Hikarie 8F, Shibuya 2-21-1, Shibuya, Tokyo
- ⏱ d47 MUSEUM / d47 design travel store 11:00–20:00
  d47 SHOKUDO 11:30–23:00 Closed Occasionally

略长的主编后记

倾听与诉说『那片土地』

Osamu Kuga

空闲理

"无论你是谁，无论那里是否有声音，你都应侧耳倾听。"我觉得，这是我在这次《d设计之旅：奈良》的采访之旅中感受最深的。就像"奈良d标总览"里关于河濑直美女士的文章中所写的那样，"侧耳倾听人声"，是为了倾听"人所发出的未成声之音"和"非人之物所发出的类声之音"。

端端正正地坐下来，倾听在那片土地上所遇到的人的诉说，那是常年扎根于那片土地的世间万物所发出的、未成声之音的代言——植物和动物，养育了它们的土壤和雨，河川里流动的水，川流下的石头和鱼，以及曾经在那片土地上生活过的人的思考和记忆。这些都似乎可以说是"那片土地的声音"。

虽然在正篇中很少涉及，但奈良时代编纂的、现存最古老的和歌集《万叶集》里所吟诵的和歌，不也正是因为倾听"那片土地的声音"，以及生活在那个时代的人的声音，才得以孕育而来的吗？《万叶集》里既收录了天皇和贵族等上层阶级和官吏，也收录了边防士兵和"无名氏"，也就是身份很低的人（平民，甚至无名之人），是来自各个阶层的人的和歌。"那片土地的声音"，是从任何人那里都可以听到的，只要你侧耳聆听，尤其是在奈良这样的地方。

Slightly Long Editorial Notes

By Osamu Kuga

Listening to the Voice of the Land, to Be Heard
Throughout my travels to research for this issue, I kept serendipitously experiencing this theme: "To listen to the voices of the voiceless, to the voices of people and non-humans." And indeed, it was one of the most important things I learned on this trip.

When I talked to people, when they opened themselves up enough to talk to me, I felt that they were speaking for the history, for nature—animals and plants, rains that cultivate the farm and streams, rocks and memories of people who once lived there. They were speaking for the land. And for the listener like me, I have to treat these stories as gifts.

I didn't get to touch upon this in the articles, but in Nara City, I met Manpei Tsurubayashi, the owner of "sonihouse," who created speakers so sensitive that all sounds in the

虽然没有在正篇当中写到，但我确实在奈良遇到了将"侧耳聆听可辨之音"这件事具象化的人。"sonihouse"的鹤林万平先生制作着具有独创性设计的音箱，并致力于企划和运营使用音箱的演出活动。鹤林先生设计的音箱，代表作之一是"scenery"，名字意为"风景"，形状是正十二面体。说到设计成这个形状的理由，鹤林先生说到，"自然界中的声音，原本就是向四面八方扩散的"。"市面上的音箱大多是塑料材质或是铝材的制品，很难自然而然地融入生活。"与此相对，他选择了天然木材作为音箱的外层材质。这台音箱无论是扩音方式还是造型的呈现，目标都是把声音表现得"自然得如同不存在"一般。

我向鹤林先生询问了开办sonihouse的契机。

2000年左右，鹤林先生深深为某支美国乐队的音乐所打动，他们细致地雕琢声音中似有若无的偏移和失真，制作了非常纤细的乐曲。可是，和年龄相近的朋友们一起聆听音乐的场所，无论俱乐部、Live House还是户外音乐节的会场，都只是用猛烈的音量播放音乐，冰箱的振动声或是酒吧的喧噪也时常干扰对音乐的欣赏。那些适合在俱乐部、音乐节上播放的乐

environment could be heard through his invention. He creates these unique speakers and produces live events around these speakers. One of the best known speakers made by this company is *scenary*, a twelve-sided speaker. It is twelve-sided because sounds in nature are transmitted all around, not just in front but in all directions. Mr. Tsurubayashi says, "Most of the speakers sold in stores are made of plastic and aluminum, and don't really fit into our homes," so all his speakers are made of wood. The vibration and appearances seem to blend into the background.

Around 2000, he came across an American band who made albums based on the principle that all sounds — even ones you can't hear — must be heard, and even inaudible noises and distortions were examined and fixed. But when he looked around, most of the musicians played in places where sounds were distorted by vibrations of refrigerators and bar noises — such as clubs — and even in outdoor concerts, they concentrated more on playing as loud as they could, not about the quality of the music. "sonihouse" was established to create a space where you can hear the pure notes of music. (→p. 184)

曲也就自然而然地大放异彩。虽然他清楚地知道，音乐的一大魅力是能够带来和他人的一体感以及让人情绪高涨，可是鹤林先生也为自己格外钟爱的纤细声响的乐曲以及制作这些乐曲的音乐家们感到不平。他坚定了想法，打算"自己来创造一个在保持自然本真的状态下聆听纤细乐曲的环境"，随之开始的活动就是 soni-house。

《d设计之旅：奈良》的采访虽然已经结束，我此刻的想法却是：一定用鹤林先生所制作的音箱去听一听他心目中理想的声音，"那片土地的声音"——"奈良的声音"。贪心一点的

话，我希望是在奈良公园的天空下，在真正的黑暗之中，来进行这样的体验，想让自己的身体和心灵都置于那绝佳的和谐之中。比如，若是能够再度侧耳倾听，体验河濑直美导演的作品，那么一定能够听到与以往都不尽相同的"奈良的声音"吧。

我在奈良，遇到了许多珍视"这片土地的声音"并为之发声的人。我真心感谢为采访提供帮助的每个人。

这本书是我从大家那里听到的"奈良的声音"，我发自内心地期望，自己能够让它尽量保持着自然的形态，传递得更远一些——哪怕只有一点也好。

Even though I am done with this issue, I do want to listen to the voice and sound of Nara through his speaker at the volume he thinks is fitting. If I can be greedy, I want to sit in Nara Park in the middle of the night — where it is pitch dark — and listen to the sound of Nara. It will be a perfect experience, I think. It'll be like listening to movies by Naomi Kawase, to really listen and hear the voice of the land — and if I listen carefully, I might be able to hear the true voice of Nara.

In Nara, I met so many people who cherish the voice of the land, and so many people who spoke clearly for the land about the land. I am grateful to all the people who helped me along this journey — I hope the gift of stories and wisdom they gave me travels far and wide in the form of this book.

KURUMINOKI

NTIQUE
&
IFE SHOP

FRENCH
STYLE
TEA
ROOM

185

朝日馆 (→ p.083)
♀ 奈良县吉野郡川上村柏木 154
☎ 0746-54-0020
🍴 一日两餐 一人 12 960 日元起
Asahikan (→ p. 083)
♀ Kashiwagi 154, Kawakamimura, Yoshino-gun, Nara

 明日香梦之自由市场 (→ p.085)
♀ 奈良市高市郡明日香村飞鸟 225-2
飞鸟梦之乐停车场
🕐 9:00 ～ 12:00 周一至周四。
周六、周日休息
Asuka Bio Marché (→ p. 085)
♀ Asuka Yume-no-Rakuichi Market parking lot, Asuka 225-2, Asukamura, Takaichi-gun, Nara

 Alpenrose 总店 (→ p.139)
♀ 奈良县奈良市神功 4-6-6
☎ 0742-72-4183
🕐 烘焙店 7:30 ～ 18:00
咖啡店、餐厅 8:30 ～ 16:00 终年无休
Alpenrose Main Store (→ p. 139)
♀ Jingu 4-chome 6-6, Nara, Nara

 今西本店 (→ p.105, 109)
♀ 奈良县奈良市上三条町 31
☎ 0742-22-2415
🕐 9:30 ～ 18:45 (周日、节日营业至 18：00)
周三、每月第三个周日休店，不定期休息
IMANISHI HONTEN (→ p.105, 109)
♀ Kamisanjo-cho 31, Nara, Nara

 A4 (→ p.108)
♀ 奈良县吉野郡东吉野村小 708
☎ 050-5856-9856
A4 (→ p. 108)
♀ Higashiyoshinomura omura 708, Yoshino-gun, Nara

 冈井麻布商店 (→ p.109, 126)
♀ 奈良县奈良市中之庄町 107
☎ 0742-81-0026
Okai Mafu Shoten (→ p. 109, 126)
♀ Nakanoshocho 107, Nara, Nara

 鬼之茶屋 西本 (Nishimoto) (→ p.133, 138)
♀ 奈良县生驹市鬼取町 413
☎ 0743-77-8476
🕐 11:30 ～ 15:00 (14:00 截止点单)
每周四、每月第二和第四个周三休息
Oni no Chaya Nishimoto (→ p.136,138)
♀ Onitori-cho 413, Ikoma, Nara

 ORIX 租车 近铁奈良站前店 (→ p.079)
♀ 奈良县奈良市高天町 38-3
近铁高天大楼 1-102
☎ 050-3537-5430
🕐 8:00 ～ 19:00 终年无休
ORIX Rent-A-Car Kintetsu Nara Ekimae Rental Site (→ p. 079)
♀ Kintetsu Takama Bldg. 1-102, Takama-cho 38-3, Nara, Nara

 柿的专门店 三条通店 (→ p.108)
♀ 奈良县奈良市上三条町 27-1 村田大楼 1F
☎ 0742-22-8835
🕐 10:00 ～ 19:00 周一休息
Kaki no Senmon Sanjodori Store (→ p. 108)
♀ Kamisanjocho 27-1, Nara, Nara

 Cafe Funchana (→ p.098)
♀ 奈良县生驹郡三乡町立野南 1-24-5
☎ 0745-73-1187
🕐 8:30 ～ 18:00 周一及每月第三个周二休息
CAFE FUNCHANA (→ p. 098)
♀ Tatsuno-minami 1-24-5, Sango-cho, Ikoma-gun, Nara

 工场旧址事务室 (→ p.131, 139)
♀ 奈良县奈良市芝辻町 543
☎ 0742-22-2215
🕐 11:00-18:00 (周六·周日、节假日 9:00-18:00)
周一至周四休息
Café kojoato Jimushitsu (→ p. 131, 139)
♀ Shibatsuji-cho 543, Nara, Nara

 Apple Jack 木艺工坊 (→ p.109)
♀ 奈良县吉野郡川上村东川 1595
☎ 0746-53-2443
🕐 8:00 ～ 17:00 周日、节假日休息
Kobo Apple Jack (→ p. 109)
♀ Kawakami-mura Unogawa 1595, Yoshino-gun, Nara

 古梅园 (→ p.126)
♀ 奈良县奈良市椿井町 7
☎ 0742-23-2965
🕐 9:00 ～ 17:00 周六、周日及节假日休息
Kobaien (→ p. 127)
♀ Tsubai-cho 7, Nara, Nara

 彩华拉面 流动推车 (→ p.139)
♀ 奈良县天理市别所町 223 Price Cut
天理北店停车场内
17:30 ～ 1:00 (周六、周日、节假日 16:30 ～ 1:00
营业) 终年无休
Saika Ramen Yatai (→ p. 139)
♀ Besshocho 223, Tenri, Nara (In the parking area of Price Cut Tenri Kita Store)

 三奇楼 (→ p.083, 084)
♀ 奈良县吉野郡吉野町上市 207
☎ 0746-39-9207
两人同行时，每人每晚 4 000 日元
SANKIROU (→ p. 082)
♀ Kamiichi 207, Yoshino-cho, Yoshino-gun, Nara

 鹿之舟 灶 (→ p.138)
♀ 奈良县奈良市井上町 11
☎ 0742-94-5520
🕐 8:00 ～ 18:00 周三休息
Shikanofune Kamado (→ p. 138)
♀ Ionuecho 11, Nara, Nara

 丝季 (→ p.127)
♀ 奈良县奈良市高御门町 18
☎ 0742-77-0722
🕐 10:00 ～ 17:30 (冬季 10:00 ～ 17:00) 不定期休息
SiKi (→ p. 126)
♀ Takamikado-cho 18, Nara, Nara

 信夫贝壳纽扣制作所 (→ p.109)
♀ 奈良县橿原市十market町 800
☎ 0744-22-5239
🕐 8:00 ～ 17:00 周日、节假日休息
Shinobu Kaibotan Seisakusho (→ p. 109)
♀ Toichicho 800, Kashiwara, Nara

 旬菜·中华 Bar Mitsukan (→ p.086)
♀ 奈良县橿原市内膳町 4-4-5 Kato 大楼 1F
☎ 0744-25-7288
🕐 17:00 ～ 24:00 (23:00 截止点单) 周日休息
Shunsai Chinese Bar Mitsukan (→ p. 086)
♀ Kato Bldg. 1F, Naizen-cho 4-4-5, Kashihara, Nara

 松月堂 (→ p.088)
♀ 奈良县宇陀市大宇陀上 1988
☎ 0745-83-0114
🕐 8:00 ～ 17:30 周三休息
Shogetsudo (→ p. 088)
♀ Ouda Kami 1988, Uda, Nara

 白玉屋荣寿 (→ p.138)
♀ 奈良县樱井市三轮 660-1
☎ 0744-43-3668
🕐 总店 8:00 ～ 19:00 茶寮 10:00 ～ 18:00
周一、每月第三个周二休息
Shiratamaya Eiju (→ p. 138)
♀ Miwa 660-1, Sakurai, Nara

 钱之花 (→ p.088)
♀ 奈良县宇陀郡曽尔村太良路 839 曽尔高原
农场花园前
☎ 090-3563-3392
🕐 10:30 ～ 17:00 (售完即止) 不定期休息
Zeni no Hana (→ p. 089)
♀ In front of Soni Kogen Farm Garden, Taroji 839, Soni-mura, Uda-gun, Nara

 sonihouse (→ p.111, 183)
♀ 奈良县奈良市四条大路 1-2-3
☎ 0742-31-5211
🖂 info@sonihouse.net 如需参观，请通过
电话或电子邮件事先联系
sonihouse (→ p. 111, 183)
♀ Shijooji 1-2-3, Nara, Nara

24 **团子庄 坊城本店** (→ p.138)
♀ 奈良县橿原市东坊城町 860
☎ 0744-27-4340
🕐 8:30 ～ 17:00 (售完即止)
周二、每月第一个周三休息
Dangosho Bojo Main Store (→ p. 138)
♀ Higashibojocho 860, Kashihara, Nara

25 月瀬健康茶園 （→ p.104）
📍 奈良县奈良市月瀬尾山 1965
☎ 0743-92-0739
🕐 8:00 ～ 12:00、13:00 ～ 17:00 周六、周日休息
※ 不是店铺
Tsukigase Organic Tea Farm（→p. 104）
📍 Tsukigase Oyama 1965, Nara, Nara

 26 Tohon （→ p.113, 134）
📍 奈良县大和郡山市柳 4-28
☎ 080-8344-7676
🕐 11:00 ～ 17:00 周四及节假日休息
Tohon（→p. 113, 134）
📍 Yanagi 4-28, Yamatokoriyama, Nara

 27 奈良县立美术馆 （→ p.128）
📍 奈良县奈良市登大路町 10-6
☎ 0742-23-3968
🕐 9:00 ～ 17:00 （16:30 起停止入馆）
※企划展 周一（逢节假日改为第二天工作日）、
年末年初、更换展示期间中休息
Nara Prefectural Museum（→p. 128）
📍 Noborioji-cho 10-6, Nara, Nara

 28 奈良自然茶专门店 TE＝CHA （→ p.108）
📍 奈良县奈良市神功 3-3-2
🕐 10:00 ～ 18:00 周三、周六营业
Organic Tea Shop Tea and Cha（→p. 108）
📍 Jingu 3-chome 3-2, Nara, Nara

 29 Hisagoya 食堂 （→ p.139）
📍 奈良县奈良市鹤福院町 32
☎ 0742-22-3795
🕐 11:00 ～ 15:00 周一休息
Hisagoya Shokudo（→p. 139）
📍 Tsurufukuincho 32, Nara, Nara

 30 表太郎 （→ p.118）
📍 奈良县吉野郡吉野町吉野山 429
☎ 0746-32-3070
🕐 9:00 ～ 16:00 （赏樱期 9:00 ～ 17:00）
周一休息
Hyotaro（→p. 118）
📍 Yoshino-yama 429, Yoshino-cho, Yoshino-gun, Nara

 31 本家菊屋 （→ p.132）
📍 奈良县大和郡山市柳 1-11
☎ 0743-52-0035
🕐 8:00 ～ 19:30 元旦休息
Honke Kikuya, K.K.（→p. 134）
📍 Yanagi 1-11, Yamatokoriyama, Nara

 32 胜记高田商店 （→ p.109）
📍 奈良县樱井市芝 374-1
☎ 0120-38-6538
🕐 9:00 ～ 17:30
Marukatsu Takada Shoten（→p. 109）
📍 Shiba 374-1, Sakurai, Nara

 33 万万堂通则 （→ p.109）
📍 奈良县奈良市桥本町 34
☎ 0742-22-2044
🕐 9:00 ～ 19:00 （周四 10:00 ～ 17:00）
周四不定期休息
Manmando Michinori（→p. 109）
📍 Hashimotocho 34, Nara, Nara

 34 Misato 鞋业联合会 （→ p.098）
📍 奈良县生驹郡三乡町立野北 1-26-23
☎ 0745-73-7822
🕐 9:00 ～ 17:00 每月第二个周六、周日、
节假日休息
Misato Hakimono Kyodo Kumiai (Misato
Footwear Cooperative Association)
📍 Tatsunokita 1-26-23, Sango-cho, Ikoma-gun,
Nara

 35 美吉野酿造 （→ p.107）
📍 奈良县吉野郡吉野町六田 1238-1
☎ 0746-32-3639
🕐 9:00 ～ 17:00 不定期休息
Miyoshino Jozo K.K.（→p. 106）
📍 Muda 1238-1, Yoshino-cho, Yoshino-gun, Nara

 36 武蔵野 （→ p.131）
📍 奈良县奈良市春日野町 90
☎ 0742-22-2739
🛏 一日一人 20 520 日元
（两人住宿时的每人平均价格）
MUSASHINO（→p. 132）
📍 Kasugano-cho 90, Nara, Nara

 37 森野吉野葛本铺 （→ p.088）
📍 奈良县宇陀市大宇陀上新 1880
☎ 0745-83-0002
🕐 9:00 ～ 17:00 不定期临时休息
MORINO YOSHINO-KUZU HONPO（→p. 088）
📍 Ouda Kamishin 1880, Uda, Nara

 38 油长酒厂 （→ p.108）
📍 奈良县御所市中本町 1160
☎ 0745-62-2047
YUCHO SHUZO CO., LTD.（→p. 108）
📍 Nakahonmachi 1160, Gose, Nara

 39 横田福荣堂 （→ p.109, 192）
📍 奈良县奈良市二条町 1-3-17
☎ 0742-33-0418
Yokota Fukueido（→p. 109, 192）
📍 Nijocho 1-chome 3-17, Nara, Nara

 40 白雪布巾 （→ p.114）
📍 奈良县奈良市南纪寺町 5-85
☎ 0742-22-6956
🕐 10:00-17:00 周日、节假日、
每月第一、三、五个周六休息
Shirayuki Fukin Co., Ltd.（→p. 114）
📍 Minami Kidera-cho 5-85, Nara, Nara

 41 奈良县政府 屋顶 （→ p.128）
📍 奈良县奈良市登大路町 30
☎ 0742-22-1101
🕐 8:30 ～ 17:30 （开放时间根据季节有所变动）
周六、周日、节假日休息另有不定期休息
Roof of the Nara Prefectural Office（→p. 126）
📍 Noborioji-cho 30, Nara, Nara

d MARK REVIEW INFORMATION (→ p. 188)

d MARK REVIEW NARA INFORMATION
奈良 d 标信息总览

 东大寺 二月堂 （→ p.026）
- 📍 奈良县奈良市杂司町 406-1
- ☎ 0742-22-5511
- 🕐 0:00 ～ 24:00 终年无休
- 🚌 JP 大和路线 奈良站乘巴士约 15 分钟后，大佛殿春日大社前巴士站徒步约 10 分钟

Todaiji Nigatsu-do（→ p.027）
- 📍 Zoushi-cho 406-1, Nara, Nara
- 🕐 Open all year
- 🚌 10 minute walk from the Daibutsuden Kasuga Taisha-mae bus stop, 15 minutes by bus from Nara Station, JR Yamatoji Line

 宇陀市立 室生山上公园 艺术森林 （→ p.028）
- 📍 奈良县宇陀市室生 181
- ☎ 0745-93-4730
- 🕐 4 ～ 10 月 10:00 ～ 17:00（16:30 后停止入场）
  3 月、11 月、12 月 10:00 ～ 16:00
  （15:30 后停止入场）
  周二休息（逢节假日则改为翌日休息）
  12 月 29 日至 2 月末休息，不定期临时休息
- 🚌 距离近铁大阪线 榛原站约 30 分钟车程

Murou Art Forest（→ p.029）
- 📍 Murou 181, Uda, Nara
- 🕐 April-October: 10:00～17:00 (admission until 16:30) March, November, December: 10:00～16:00 (admission until 15:30) Closed on Tuesday (if Tuesday is a national holiday, open on Tuesday and closed on the following day) Closed from December 29 to the end of February, Closed occasionally
- 🚌 30 minutes by car from Haibara Station, Kintetsu Osaka Line

 MICHIMO （→ p.030）
- 📍 奈良县高市郡明日香村越 13-1
  （MICHIMO Station）
- ☎ 0744-33-9090
- 🕐 9:00 ～ 18:00（营业时间随季节变动）
  年末年初休息 3 小时 3 240 日元
- 🚌 距近铁吉野线飞鸟站徒步约 1 分钟

MICHIMO（→ p.031）
- 📍 (MICHIMO Station) Koshi 13-1, Asukamura, Takaichi-gun, Nara
- 🕐 9:00–18:00 (Business hours vary with the seasons) Year-end and New Year holiday, 3 hours starting from 3,240 yen
- 🚌 1 minute walk from Asuka Station, Kintetsu Yoshino Line.

 奈良国立博物馆 （→ p.032）
- 📍 奈良县奈良市登大路町 50
- ☎ 050-5542-8600
- 🕐 9:30 ～ 17:00（16:30 后停止入馆）、周五·周六 9:30 ～ 20:00（仅限名品展，19:30 后停止入馆）
  周一休息（逢节假日改为翌日休息）
- 🚌 距近铁奈良线 近铁奈良站巴士 5 分钟

Nara National Museum（→ p.033）
- 📍 Noborioji-cho 50, Nara, Nara
- 🕐 9:30–17:00 (admission until 16:30) Open until 20:00 on Friday and Saturday (Permanent Collection only, admission until 19:30) Closed on Monday (If Monday is a national holiday, open on Monday and closed on the following day)
- 🚌 5 minutes by bus from Kintetsu Nara Station, Kintetsu Nara Line

 森正龙须面铺 （→ p.034，105，119）
- 📍 奈良县樱井市三轮 535
- ☎ 0744-43-7411
- 🕐 10:00 ～ 17:00（逢周日、节假日 9:30 ～ 17:00、冬季 10:00 ～ 16:30）
  周二休息（逢节假日营业，逢每月 1 日营业），周一不定期休息
- 🚌 距 JR 樱井线 三轮站徒步约 5 分钟

Morisho（→ p.035, 105, 119）
- 📍 Miwa 535, Sakurai, Nara
- 🕐 10:00-17:00 (9:00～17:00 on Sunday and national holidays, 10:00–16:30 on winter) Closed on Tuesday (Open on national holidays; open the 1st day of every month), Closed occasionally on Monday
- 🚌 5 minute walk from Miwa Station, JR Sakurai Line

 一如庵 （→ p.036）
- 📍 奈良县宇陀市榛原自明 1362
- ☎ 0745-82-0053
- 🕐 午餐 11:00 ～ 12:45、13:00 ～ 14:30
  晚餐 17:00 ～ 20:00（要预约）
  周一、周二休息
- 🚌 距近铁大阪线榛原站约 10 分钟车程

Ichinyoan（→ p.037）
- 📍 Haibarajimyo 1362, Uda, Nara
- 🕐 Lunch: 11:00–12:45, 13:00–14:30
  Dinner: 17:00–20:00 (Reservation is required) Closed on Monday and Tuesday
- 🚌 10 minutes by car from Haibara Station, Kintetsu Osaka Line

 竹之馆 （→ p.038）
- 📍 奈良县奈良市南鱼屋町 25
- ☎ 0742-23-6227
- 🕐 17:00 ～ 3:00 终年无休
- 🚌 距近铁奈良站近铁奈良站徒步约 10 分钟

Take no yakata（→ p.039）
- 📍 Minami Uoya-cho 25, Nara, Nara
- 🕐 17:00–3:00, Open all year
- 🚌 10 minute walk from Kintetsu Nara Station, Kintetsu Nara Line

 秋筱森林 荠菜 （→ p.040）
- 📍 奈良县奈良市中山町 1534
- ☎ 0742-52-8560（至少提前一天预约）
- 🕐 午餐 11:00 ～ 12:30、13:00 ～ 14:30
  晚餐 19:00 ～ 21:00（仅限周六·周日、节假日）
  周二、每月第三个周三休息
- 🚌 距近铁奈良线、京都线、橿原线 大和西大寺站约 15 分钟车程

Akishino no Mori Nazuna（→ p.041）
- 📍 Nakayama-cho 1534, Nara, Nara
- 🕐 Lunch: 11:00–12:30, 13:00–14:30 (reservation is required by the previous day) Dinner: 19:00–21:00 (Only on Saturday, Sunday, and national holidays; reservation is required by the previous day) Closed on Tuesday and the 3rd Wednesday of the month
- 🚌 15 minutes by car from Yamato-Saidaiji Station, Kintetsu Nara Line, Kyoto Line, and Kashihara Line

 东吉野共享办公空间 （→ p.042）
- 📍 奈良县吉野郡东吉野村小川 610-2
- ☎ 0746-48-9005
- 🕐 10:00 ～ 17:00 周二、周三休息
- 🚌 从距近铁大阪线 榛原站巴士车程约 30 分钟的东吉野村役场巴士站出发，徒步约 5 分钟

OFFICE CAMP HIGASHIYOSHINO（→ p.043）
- 📍 Ogawa 610-2, Higashi Yoshino-mura, Yoshino-gun, Nara
- 🕐 10:00–17:00, Closed on Tuesday and Wednesday
- 🚌 5 minute walk from the Higashi Yoshinomura Yakuba bus stop, 30 minutes by bus from Kashihara Station, Kintetsu Osaka Line

 中井春风堂 （→ p.044）
- 📍 奈良县吉野郡吉野町吉野山 545
- ☎ 0746-32-3043
- 🕐 10:00 ～ 17:00（16:30 截止点单）
  周三休息（冬季仅周六、周日营业）
- 🚌 距吉野缆车线吉野山站徒步约 5 分钟

Nakaisyunpudo（→ p. 045）
- 📍 Yoshinoyama 545, Yoshino-cho, Yoshino-gun, Nara
- 🕐 10:00–17:00 (Last order at 16:30), Closed on Wednesday (Open only on Saturday and Sunday during Winter)
- 🚌 5 minute walk from Yoshino Station, Yoshino Ropeway

 大泷茶屋 （→ p.046，119）
- 📍 奈良县吉野郡川上村大泷 420-1
- ☎ 0746-53-2350
- 🕐 约 8：30 ～约 17:30 周三休息
  12 月～ 3 月中旬休息
- 🚌 距近铁吉野线大和上市站约 15 分钟车程

Otaki Chaya（→ p. 047, 119）
- 📍 Otaki 420-1, Kawakamimura, Yoshino-gun, Nara
- 🕐 8:30–17:30, Closed on Wednesday, Closed from December to mid March
- 🚌 15 minutes by car from Yamato-Kamiichi Station, Kintetsu Yoshino Line

 豆铃·虫鸣 （→ p.048）
- 📍 奈良县奈良市南半田西町 18-2
- ☎ 0742-27-3130
- 🕐 12:00 ～ 19:00 周一、周二休息、另有不定期休息
- 🚌 距近铁奈良县近铁奈良站徒步约 10 分钟

Mamesuzu Chichiro（→ p. 049）
- 📍 Minami Handa Nishimachi 18-2, Nara, Nara
- 🕐 12:00–19:00, Closed on Monday and Tuesday, Other irregular closures
- 🚌 10 minute walk from Kintetsu Nara Station, Kintetsu Nara Line

 滪酒店 （→ p.050）
- 📍 奈良县吉野郡十津川村神下 405
- ☎ 0746-69-0003
- 🕐 11:30 起（售完即闭店）周三、周四休息
- 🚌 距离近铁大阪线、橿原线和八木站约 2 小时 40 分钟车程

Doro Hotel（→ p. 051）
- 📍 Koka 405, Totsukawa-mura Yoshino-gun, Nara
- 🕐 11:30– (Closes when the day's stock runs out), Closed on Wednesday and Thursday
- 🚌 2 hours and 40 minutes by car from Yamato-Yagi Station, Kintetsu Osaka Line and Kashihara Line

14 高畑茶论 (→ p.052)
📍 奈良县奈良市高畑町 1247
☎ 0742-22-2922
🕐 13:00～18:00 周二、周三、周四休息
（逢节假日改为翌日）
🚗 从近铁奈良线近铁奈良站出发，
到达巴士约 10 分钟车程的破石町巴士站后，
徒步约 5 分钟

Takabatake Salon (→ p. 053)
📍 Takabatake-cho 1247, Nara, Nara
🕐 13:00—18:00, Closed on Tuesday, Wednesday and Thursday (If either day is a national holiday, open that day and closed the following day)
🚗 5 minute walk from the Wariishicho bus stop, 10 minutes by bus from Kintetsu Nara Station, Kintetsu Nara Line

 15 K 咖啡 (→ p.054, 108, 132)
📍 奈良县大和郡山市柳 4-46
☎ 090-6986-3255
🕐 10:00～17:00 周四休息
🚗 近铁橿原线近铁郡山站徒步约 10 分钟

K Coffee (→ p. 055, 108)
📍 Yanagi 4-46, Yamatokoriyama, Nara
🕐 10:00—17:00, Closed on Thursday
🚗 10 minute walk from Kintetsu Koriyama Station, Kintetsu Kashihara Line

 16 大森之乡 (→ p.056)
📍 奈良县吉野郡十津川村武藏 487
☎ 080-2543-5552
🏠 一日一人 7 000 日元
（两人使用时的平均价格）
🚗 距近铁大阪线、橿原线大和八木站
约 2 小时 20 分钟车程

Omori-no-Sato (→ p. 057)
📍 Musashi 487, Totsukawa-mura, Yoshino-gun, Nara
🏠 Starting from 7,000 yen per person (for 2 people)
🚗 2 hours and 20 minutes by car from Yamato-Yagi Station, Kintetsu Osaka Line and Kashihara Line.

17 奈良酒店 (→ p.058)
📍 奈良县奈良市高畑町 1096
☎ 0742-26-3300
🏠 一日两餐，一人 26 017 日元
（两人使用时的平均价格）
🚗 距近铁奈良线近铁奈良站徒步约 15 分钟

Nara Hotel (→ p. 059)
📍 Takabatake-cho 1096, Nara, Nara
🏠 Starting from 26,017 yen per person, two meals included (for 2 people)
🚗 15 minute walk from Kintetsu Nara Station, Kintetsu Nara Line

 18 奈良町宿 纪寺之家 (→ p.059)
📍 奈良县奈良市纪寺町 779
☎ 0742-25-5500
🏠 一日附早餐一人 19 440 日元
（两人使用时的平均价格）
🚗 距近铁奈良线近铁奈良站约 10 分钟车程

Kidera no ie (→ p. 060)
📍 Kidera-cho 779, Nara, Nara
🏠 Starting from 19,440 yen per person, breakfast included (for 2 people)
🚗 10 minutes by car from Kintetsu Nara Station, Kintetsu Nara Line

 19 江户三 (→ p.062, 108)
📍 奈良县奈良市高畑町 1167
☎ 0742-26-2662
🏠 一日两餐 一人 19 440 日元
（两人使用时的平均价格）
🚗 距近铁奈良线近铁奈良站徒步约 15 分钟

Edosan (→ p. 063, 108)
📍 Takabatake-cho 1167, Nara, Nara
🏠 Starting from 19,440 yen per person, two meals included (for 2 people)
🚗 15 minute walk from Kintetsu Nara Station, Kintetsu Nara Line

 20 藤冈俊平 (藤冈建筑研究所·纪寺之家) (→ p.064)
Shunpei Fujioka (Fujioka Achitecture Labo/Kidera no ie) (→ p. 065)

 21 中野圣子 (奈良 SunRoute 酒店) (→ p.066)
📍 奈良县奈良市高畑町 1110
☎ 0742-22-5151
🏠 一日一人 11 340 日元 （两人使用时的平均价格）
🚗 距近铁奈良线近铁奈良站徒步约 10 分钟

Satoko Nakano (HOTEL SUNROUTE NARA) (→ p. 067)
📍 (HOTEL SUNROUTE NARA) Takabatake-cho 1110, Nara, Nara
🏠 Starting from 11,340 yen per person (for two people)
🚗 10 minute walk from Kintetsu Nara Station, Kintetsu Nara Line

 22 石村由起子 (胡桃树) (→ p.068)
📍 奈良县奈良市法莲町 567-1
☎ 0742-23-8286
🕐 11:30～17:30 （周五～周日为 11:30～21:00）
终年无休
🚗 距近铁奈良线新大宫站徒步约 15 分钟

Yukiko Ishimura (KURUMINOKI Ltd.) (→ p. 069)
📍 Horen-cho 567-1, Nara, Nara
🕐 11:30—17:30 (11:30—21:00 from Friday to Sunday), Open all year
🚗 15 minute walk from Shinomiya Station, Kintetsu Nara Line

 23 河濑直美 (→ p.070)
Naomi Kawase (→ p. 071)

编辑后记

神藤秀人　Hideto Shindo

我在旅途中有一个重要使命——选购只有在奈良这块土地上才能买到的酒具。在奈良，我看到了带有鹿等"奈良绘"图案的"赤肤烧"。这一陶器由一名职人完成连同绘画在内的所有工序，历史渊源悠久，过去曾作为茶具而流行。可我却没有买下它。我还在继续寻找着，期待着有一天能邂逅打破这层历史外壳而崭露头角的新锐赤肤烧作品。

播磨屋智子　Tomoko Harimaya

打开从奈良寄来的木盒，里边装得满满的用颜色各异的红叶包裹的手掌大小的柿叶寿司。我一边欣赏这人工无法制造的色彩，一边大口品尝，体会着手工制作的温度感。这几乎也代表了奈良。这种彻底保持自然原貌的造物精神，我也通过制作本期杂志而得以略窥一斑。

佐佐木晃子　Akiko Sasaki

我在奈良常吃的素面和饭团，非常爱用的柿子和抹布，在制作中全都倾注了"让人满心喜悦盼望收到"这一愿望，每一件都让人心情愉悦。借用"胡桃树"石村由起子女士的话来说，在仿佛和当地人一起走过的旅途上，原原本本地呈现了奈良"满载各色心意"的真实一面，完成了《d设计之旅：奈良》。

发行人 / Founder
长冈贤明　Kenmei Nagaoka　(D&DEPARTMENT PROJECT)

主编 / Editor-in-Chief
空闲 理　Osamu Kuga　(D&DEPARTMENT PROJECT)

副主编 / Deputy Editor
神藤秀人　Hideto Shindo (D&DEPARTMENT PROJECT)

编辑 / Editors
佐佐木晃子　Akiko Sasaki (D&DEPARTMENT PROJECT)
播磨屋智子　Tomoko Harimaya (D&DEPARTMENT PROJECT)
松崎纪子　Noriko Matsuzaki (design clips)
前田次郎　Jiro Maeda (D&DEPARTMENT PROJECT)

撰稿人 / Writers
渊上凉子　Ryoko Fuchikami (D&DEPARTMENT PROJECT)
坂本大三郎　Daizaburo Sakamoto
高木崇雄　Takao Takaki (Foucault)
野口忠典　Tadanori Noguchi (d47 design travel store)
相马夕辉　Yuki Aima (D&DEPARTMENT PROJECT)
鹤林万平　Manpei Tsurubayashi (sonihouse)
砂川昌广　Masahiro Sunagawa (tohon)
深泽直人　Naoto Fukasawa

设计师 / Designers
加濑千宽　Chihiro Kase (D&DEPARTMENT PROJECT)
高桥惠子　Keiko Takahashi (D&DEPARTMENT PROJECT)
中川清香　Sayaka Nakagawa (D&DEPARTMENT PROJECT)
村田英惠　Hanae Murata (D&DEPARTMENT PROJECT)

插图 / Illustrator
Kifumi

摄影 / Photographers
安永Kentauros　Kentauros Yasunaga (Yasunaga Photography)
西冈浩　Kiyoshi Nishioka

日语校对 / Copyediting
卫藤武智　Takenori Eto

翻译・校对 / Translation & Copyediting
永井真理子　Mariko Nagai (Temple University Japan)
Nettleto・太郎　Taro Nettleton
T.G.Kubota　Takayuki Kubota
Shinya B (Temple University Japan)

制作支持 / Production Support
加藤惠　Megumi Kato (d47 SHOKUDO)
针谷茜　Akane Hariya (D&DEPARTMENT PROJECT)
d47 design travel store
d47 MUSEUM
d47食堂　d47 SHOKUDO
D&DEPARTMENT FUKUOKA
D&DEPARTMENT HOKKAIDO by 3KG
D&DEPARTMENT KAGOSHIMA by MARUYA
D&DEPARTMENT KYOTO by Kyoto University of Art and Design
D&DEPARTMENT OKINAWA by OKINAWA STANDARD
D&DEPARTMENT OSAKA
D&DEPARTMENT SEOUL by MILLIMETER MILLIGRAM
D&DEPARTMENT SHIZUOKA by TAITA
D&DEPARTMENT TOKYO
D&DEPARTMENT TOYAMA
D&DEPARTMENT YAMANASHI by Sannishi YBS
GOOD DESIGN SHOP COMME des GARÇONS D&DEPARTMENT PROJECT
Drawing and Manual

宣传 / Public Relations
松添みつこ　Mitsuko Matsuzoe　(D&DEPARTMENT PROJECT)
清水 睦　Mutsumi Shimizu (D&DEPARTMENT PROJECT)

发行销售 / Publication Sales
田边直子　Naoko Tanabe (D&DEPARTMENT PROJECT)
芝生かおり　Kaori Shibo (D&DEPARTMENT PROJECT)
大道 刚　Go Oomichi (D&DEPARTMENT PROJECT)

支持 / Support
奈良县　Nara Prefecture

关于封面的只言片语

"横田福荣堂"的"鹿蛋糕"

"奈良号"的封面使用了鹿的图案，这是在平城宫旧址旁、奈良市二条的"横田福荣堂"里买来的当地经典特产"鹿蛋糕"的包装纸上所画的鹿。一条黄色的曲线缓缓流动，像河川又像是风，抑或是道路，在那能让人联想起吉野山樱花颜色的背景上，用翠绿色描绘着牡鹿的轮廓，它好像很舒服地向后仰着身子，仿佛正在小憩。这个形象同时也是传统工艺"奈良一刀雕"的主题，经常可以看到。

One Note on the Cover

Yokota Fukueido's "Deer Sablé"

The cover of this Nara issue features a deer illustration taken from the wrapping paper of the classic Nara souvenir "Deer Sablé," which I purchased at "Yokota Fukueido" in Nijo, Nara, very near the Heijokyu ruins. The background of the illustration comprises a slowly flowing yellow curvilinear form, which may represent a river or wind, set against a solid pink ground that evokes the cherry blossoms of Mount Yoshino. In the foreground, a bright green deer, shown in silhouette, rests with its head tilted back. It's a figure also frequently used as a motif in "itto-bori" dolls, a Nara traditional craft.

译者注

1 **目张寿司：**腌过的芥菜叶包裹的饭团。

2 **修二会：**每年3月1日至14日在东大寺二月堂所举办的宗教仪式，
自奈良时代开始一直传承至今。

3 **里山：**指由住家、聚落、耕地、池塘、溪流与山丘等合成的地貌。

4 **熟成：**干燥，熟成是传统的制面方法，在特殊的储藏环境下熟成的素面，
口感更为丰富。

5 **人形净琉璃：**一种日本独有的传统木偶戏，由三个人分工进行操作，
是日本四种古典舞台艺术形式之一。

6 **精进料理：**佛教的素食料理，最早起源于中国的斋饭。

7 **割烹料理：**作为会席料理、怀石料理、精进料理的总称，
泛指精致、正式的料理。

8 **铠掛松：**外形如披着铠甲的武士一般的松树。

9 **赤肤烧：**一种奈良的陶艺，用红色陶土烧制而成的陶器。

10 **大和三山：**橿原市内三座山的总称，包括香具山、亩傍山、耳成山。

11 **苏我入鹿：**日本飞鸟时代的政治家，当时掌政的权臣。他被刺杀后，皇室
得以重掌大权，颁布《改新之诏》，史称"大化改新"。

12 **山伏：**指在山中徒步、修行的"修验道"的行者，也称作"修验者"。

13 **草履：**日本传统的鞋履。

14 **鼻绪：**草履上的人字形系带。

15 **Kenko Misatokko：**直译过来就是"健康三乡子"。

16 **雪驮：**轻便的草履。

17 **吉野风格：**奈良吉野山周边依险峻的山坡而修建的一种传统建筑样式。

18 **芋版画：**在红薯或土豆的切面上雕刻图案的一种民间版画制作方式。

19 **枕词：**和歌修辞手法之一，用在特定词语之前表示修饰或调整音调。

20 **奈良晒：**奈良出产的高级麻织物。

21 **冰见冻冬：**富山县冰见市周边的乡土料理。

22 **虫笼窗：**日本传统建筑窗户样式的一种，为竖格的木窗。

23 **海鼠壁：**日本传统建筑墙壁样式的一种。

24 **拉姆萨尔公约：**以保护珍贵湿地为目的的国际公约。

25 **加藤清正：**安土桃山时代到明治时代的武将、大名。

26 **小构树：**桑科落叶灌木，树皮为和纸的制造原料。

27 **甲斐绢：**富士北麓地区的传统织造工艺。

策划
文化力研究所·雅信工作室

创意
令狐磊

特约编辑
刘小荻

图书策划
雅信工作室

中文版式设计
刘小凉

出版人
王艺超

策划编辑
李佼佼

责任编辑
李佼佼　窦娅楠

营销编辑
陈慧　杨思宇

特约美术
钱皙妮

扫 码 下 载
中信书院 APP

与世界同步 与大师同行

图书在版编目（CIP）数据

d 设计之旅 . 奈良 /（日）长冈贤明编著；张含笑，
毛叶枫译 . -- 北京：中信出版社，〔2020.2重印〕
书名原文：d design travel:NARA
ISBN 978-7-5086-9089-6

Ⅰ . ①d… Ⅱ . ①长… ②张… ③毛… Ⅲ . ①旅游指
南 - 奈良 Ⅳ . ① K931.39

中国版本图书馆 CIP 数据核字 (2018) 第 111778 号

d 设计之旅：奈良

编　　著：[日] 长冈贤明
译　　者：张含笑（早春游学） 毛叶枫
校　　译：刘大卫
出版发行：中信出版集团股份有限公司
　　　　　（北京市朝阳区惠新东街甲 4 号富盛大厦 2 座　邮编　100029）
承 印 者：鸿博昊天科技有限公司

开　　本：787mm×1092mm　1/16　　印　张：12　　字　数：170 千字
版　　次：2018 年 8 月第 1 版　　　　印　次：2020 年 2 月第 3 次印刷
京权图字：01-2018-0901　　　　　　　广告经营许可证：京朝工商广字第 8087 号
书　　号：ISBN 978-7-5086-9089-6
定　　价：58.00 元